F-VL
41⁰⁰

In Good Faith

In Good Faith

Kathleen Sharp

St. Martin's Press 🐾 New York

Design by Sara Stemen

LIBRARY OF CONGRESS CATALOGING-IN-PUBLICATION DATA

Sharp, Kathleen.
    In good faith : the inside story of Prudential-Bache's multibillion-dollar scandal that defrauded thousands of investors and fractured the Rock / Kathleen Sharp.
        p.   cm.
    "A Thomas Dunne book."
    ISBN 0-312-13093-7
    1. Securities fraud—United States—Case studies.
2. Prudential-Bache Securities, Inc.—Corrupt practicies.
I. Title.
HV6769.S53   1995
364.1'68—dc20   95-8791
                                                          CIP

First Edition: August 1995

10   9   8   7   6   5   4   3   2   1

To my father, J.R., my grandfather, J.T., and Our Father

Acknowledgments

THIS work is partly a collection of personal stories set against a corporate backdrop. To those people who so patiently and openly shared their stories, files, and insights, I am deeply grateful. This includes many unnamed sources who graciously answered questions and verified stories and details, no matter how many times I returned with "one last thing."

I would like to acknowledge that the executives, directors, and media relations professionals at Prudential Insurance Co. of America, as well as those at Prudential Securities, were contacted numerous times by telephone, mail, and fax. Their points of view were sought after, yet these people either declined to cooperate or, more often, simply didn't return requests for interviews.

Every reasonable effort was made to faithfully and accurately reconstruct dialogue that appears in these pages. The discussions detailed herein are the result of careful and painstaking interview and rewriting processes conducted with sources. In order to repeat only those words, gestures, and meanings that were actually spoken, seen, and understood, the conversations were often verified by more than one witness. Occasionally, the source of the dialogue rests with one participant. When humanly possible, other participants were at least contacted to give them the opportunity to confirm or deny the versions reported herein, or to offer their own viewpoints.

Except where noted either in the text or endnotes, quoted material is taken from my interviews with sources.

These pages are the result of many collaborative efforts, and I have been fortunate to count on many heads and hearts. My editor, Jeremy Katz, made this seem like fun, but my agent, Jane Dystel, made it real. My editorial assistant, Sylvia Luis, appeared at just the right time with her excellent skills. Noel Greenwood helped me shape the skeleton of this tale, while David Bradley inspired me to let it breathe. Although I owe these and others a great debt for their assistance and contributions, I alone am responsible for whatever flaws lie herein.

I am grateful to Deanna Garza Brown for her guidance, to Nicola Gordon for her good cheer, and to George Briare for his regular mailings. Thank you to Emily, for all the loving things she did that made work easier; to the other members of my family who provided news clippings and warm meals; and to Raymond, without whom I couldn't have started this project in the first place.

Contents

Cast of Characters

Prudential Insurance Co. of America,
Based in Newark, New Jersey

Robert A. ("Bob") Beck. Chairman of the board and CEO from 1978 until 1987 and man responsible for decision to purchase securities brokerage firm The Bache Group. Chairman emeritus from 1987 to 1991; temporary CEO of Prudential Securities for three months; director.

Robert C. ("Bob") Winters. Vice president until 1984 (along with three other men); vice chairman in charge of central corporate operations until 1987; became chairman of the board and CEO and served until 1994.

Garnett L. Keith. Executive vice president until 1984; supervised seven Prudential operations, including Prudential-Bache Securities (later Prudential Securities) and PruCapital, which became an investment and merchant banking arm; vice chairman.

Prudential-Bache Securities (later Prudential Securities):
Key Officers at New York Corporate Headquarters

George L. Ball. Chairman and CEO from 1982 to 1991; architect of the brokerage house's expansion into retail, direct investments, mutual funds, and investment banking. Former president of E. F. Hutton. He was censured by the New York Stock Exchange for a check-kiting scandal at E. F. Hutton. Charming, self-effacing, and driven. Head of Pru-Bache's executive committee and a member of the Pru's executive office.

H. Virgil Sherrill. Former vice chairman of Bache Group; titular director at Pru-Bache from 1983 to present.

Harry A. Jacobs, Jr. Former chairman of Bache Group; titular director of Pru-Bache from 1983 to present.

Loren Schechter. Chief counsel and executive vice president of Pru-Bache from 1983 to December 31, 1993. Followed Ball from E. F. Hutton, where he was a deputy counsel for fourteen years. At Pru-Bache, became Ball's close associate and the firm's chief lawyer during the time Pru-Bache illegally sold LPs and was found to be lax in its supervisory duties.

Robert J. Sherman. Employed from 1969 to 1988; in 1977 became executive vice president and in 1982 chief of the firm's retail brokerage division, which included as many as seven thousand brokers. Member of Pru-Bache's executive committee. After leaving Pru-Bache, he was accused of sexual harrassment.

The Direct Investment Group Officers and Managers

James J. Darr. Head of direct investments from 1979 to 1988 and driving force behind the successful $8 billion LP sales program. Initially reported directly to Sherman, who later became his archrival. Former executive vice president and member of executive committee.

William E. ("Bill") Pittman, Jr. Employed from 1973 to 1990. Became a due diligence officer in 1980 and a Darr loyalist.

Paul J. Proscia. Employed from 1974 to 1992. A marketing specialist who in 1988 replaced Darr as chief of the direct investment group. Former executive vice president and member of the executive committee.

Michael John Kudlik. Employed from 1983 to 1988. One of nine regional product coordinators who worked for DIG and oversaw the Pacific South region. Supervised LP sales of $2 billion and won numerous awards for his performance at the time he was fired. Spent five years looking for a similar position.

F. Paul Grattarola. Vice president of Graham Resources and veteran oil LP wholesaler. He oversaw the sales of Graham's oil and gas LPs from 1983 until 1986. Was fired in 1986 in part for questioning too many policies and practices. Unemployed for two years.

The Investment and Merchant Banking Side of New York's Headquarters

Theodore V. ("Ted") Fowler. Cohead of investment and merchant banking and chief builder of Project '89 from May 1986 to November 1989. Former cohead of investment banking at CS First Boston, where he helped build that firm's revenue base. Former executive vice president and a member of Pru-Bache's executive committee.

James F. ("Jim") Crowley. Cohead of investment and merchant banking and chief visionary of Project '89, 1984 to 1990. Hired Fowler to share the job of building investment and merchant banking. Former executive vice president and member of Pru-Bache's executive committee.

James T. ("Genghis") Gahan. Executive vice president who joined the firm in 1985 to head capital markets and in 1986 oversaw that division as well as the investment and merchant banking unit. Member of the executive committee.

Christian Wyser-Pratte. Employed from 1984 to 1990. A managing director for investment banking in Chicago who was later brought to New York to help build Project '89.

John E. ("Jack") Welsh III. Employed from 1983 to 1991. A managing director from the investment and merchant banking group. Helped Darr with his corporate finance homework.

Andrew K. Simpson. An investment banker who believed he had found his own Holy Grail when he joined Pru-Bache's Project '89 in 1987.

Frank E. ("Chip") Barnes. A member of the corporate finance department who tried to work with Darr but was fired in May 1985.

Guy P. Wyser-Pratte. Employed from 1970 to 1990. Chief of arbitrage at the firm, and well-respected arb king on Wall Street.

The Regional Directors in the Field

James ("Jim") Trice. Employed from 1963 to 1989. Texan who built up Pacific South to the biggest region in the retail system. He unwillingly left Pac South to oversee the Southeast region, where he cleaned up a regulatory and financial mess left by Jack Graner. Was fired by Sherman's successor, filed claim against the firm, and won.

John Patrick ("Jack") Graner. Employed from 1963 to 1991. The son of two deaf mutes, this glib salesman was close friends with Sherman. He was regional director of the Southeast from 1982 to 1985 but was transferred. Became regional sales manager for the Pacific North and Pacific South regions for a year until March 1986, when he became regional director of Pac South until 1991. Member of executive committee from 1989 to 1991. Died of drug overdose in 1994.

Carrington Clark, Jr. Employed from 1982 to 1992. Director of Pacific North and a friend to Sherman. Subject of an arbitration claim for sexual harassment by a former Pru-Bache female broker.

Regional directors oversaw individual retail branches, one of which was managed by

Joseph Kett. Employed from 1982 to 1987. Manager of San Diego branch, and later La Jolla branch. Worked for Graner and informed him of alleged drug money laundering in San Diego.

Branch managers oversaw brokers, or salespeople, such as:

Robert ("Rob") Hughes. Employed from 1982 to 1990. Salesman who started selling LPs in a phone booth in Santa Barbara. Sold a large number of LPs, then realized they were not a sound investment and looked for other products.

Gary Zahn. Employed from 1982 to 1990. A baby-faced, award-winning salesman in Long Island who eventually landed in jail and was financially ruined.

Kristi Mandt. Employed from 1982 to 1987. Former alcoholic female broker in Seattle claims she was pressured to meet Sherman and Clark on a trip. She was fired in 1987 and filed a claim against the firm for sexual harassment.

Susan Clayton. Employed from 1991 to 1992. Broker trainee who was invited out socially by regional director, Carrington Clark, which she reported to the firm's ethics hotline. In retaliation, she claims she was harassed. Filed a claim against Pru Securities which was settled.

1

Widows' and Orphans' Friendly Society

IT was midnight, January 27, 1994, barely ten days after a horrific earthquake had shaken Southern California. By now, the earth had settled, the rains ceased, and the fires that had raged for days had finally been brought under control. Nearly every hotel room in the greater Los Angeles area was full of refugees from a trio of natural disasters. In Room 214 of the Burbank Travelodge Motel, a former vice president of Prudential Securities lay sprawled on the floor, wearing his underwear and a three-day growth of stubble.

John Patrick Graner had been lucky to find even this modest $49-a-night room in the midst of such disaster; his cramped quarters overlooked a cement pool area guarded by a chain-link fence. Had Jack Graner still been working as senior vice president and regional director of Prudential Securities, he would have known that the Dow Jones Industrial Average that Thursday had climbed 18 points to close at 3926. Jack always knew his numbers.

But tonight as the full moon rose, the fifty-one-year-old man lay unconscious and unemployed, stoned out of his mind, on the drab carpeted floor. Earlier that evening, he had somehow ingested a lethal mixture of cocaine, heroin, and ethanol, commonly known as grain alcohol. (Exactly how this occurred would remain something of a mystery to many people who believed they knew him well.)

Jack was snoring so loudly he awoke his companion, a petite Asian woman in her twenties with a hard-won knowledge of the streets and a long, creative list of aliases. His companion turned to Jack, who by now had stopped breathing. She tried to wake him, but he didn't budge. She moved the 176-pound man onto the bed and hastily covered him with the bedspread. Then she ran out of the second-story room, down the stairs, and onto the busy boulevard, where she flagged down help.

At 1:45 A.M., the police arrived, but it was far too late. The former key senior executive of Prudential Securities was pronounced dead.

When he died, so too did all of his long-kept secrets, both carnal and corporate.

Graner's quiet graveside funeral attracted about fifty people, most of them men and women who had once worked with him. Some genuinely loved the man. A few harbored hate. "I went to his funeral just to make sure he was dead," said one former employee. Yet, in eulogy, Graner became better, brighter, and bigger in death than he had ever seemed in real life.

Graner's sales abilities were remarkable, said his friends, who claimed that he could sell umbrellas in the Gobi. With his dark wavy hair, blue eyes, and beguiling manner, he could dazzle strangers with his charm. "He was a father to the world," said his wife, Patricia Graner. "He could counsel anybody about anything, whether he knew what he was talking about or not."

As word of Graner's death passed along the Prudential grapevine, employees past and present speculated on what, under different circumstances, might be scoffed at as patently ridiculous. "Rumors were that Graner had been knocked off by Prudential," said one female colleague. Many people, including Graner's wife, couldn't fathom why the gregarious salesman would commit such a desperate act as suicide—it simply wasn't his nature. Nor, apparently, were hard drugs part of the executive's lifestyle, according to many friends. Said one coworker: "I wouldn't put it past Prudential to do something like this to silence Jack."

Within forty-eight hours after Graner's death, detectives from the Burbank Police Department ruled out the possibility of murder. At the scene of the death, detectives uncovered rocks of cocaine in a woman's cosmetic bag, and subsequently they arrested his companion. Inside the room, police found a discarded pizza box, drug paraphernalia, and $13,000 worth of Tiffany jewelry that Graner evidently had purchased days earlier on his charge account. Amid the clutter was a note scrawled on a paper napkin. The message was vague and unsigned, but the note clearly indicated that its writer was tired and unhappy.

Given the note, the drugs, and Graner's unemployed status at the time, the police had a choice. "It was a coin toss between suicide and an accidental drug overdose," said Detective Roger Mason of the Burbank Police Department. "Suicide" was listed on the police report as the cause of death.

Still, neither suicide nor accidental overdose rang true for those who knew Graner. Over the ensuing months, the vast network of people who worked or had worked for the Prudential Insurance Co. of America unit discussed and dissected Graner's mysterious death. Gradually, bits of information emerged. Graner had been talking with the Securities and Exchange Commission in its investigation of Prudential Securities and its top executives. Word was, Graner had known too much and possibly had been implicating individuals, perhaps even himself. Whatever the nature of his disclosures, they did not bode well for a number of high-ranking executives, said one former friend. "You have to remember," said Bill Davis, an attorney, "a lot of people's careers are at stake in this investigation."

Most ex-employees sneer at the idea of Pru Securities putting a "hit" on a former officer. Nevertheless, it is startling that so many longtime employees would even consider that a part of "the Rock"—one of the oldest and most venerated companies in America—might arrange the murder of one of its own. Such deep underlying distrust says much about a corporate culture that fostered mistakes, omissions, lies, and crimes for more than a decade.

In some ways, the fate of John Patrick Graner mirrors the history of Prudential-Bache Securities, just as it shadows the parent company's vain attempts to bury the seed that spawned both tragedies in the first place.

Graner's death was not mentioned in *The Wall Street Journal* the following day, although the struggles of his former employer, Prudential Securities (formerly known as Prudential-Bache Securities), were duly noted on page C6. For the past four years, Prudential Securities Inc. had been the subject of printed stories and rumored speculation that centered around allegations that for more than a decade—from 1980 to 1990—the securities brokerage unit of the giant Prudential Insurance Co. of America had sold $8 billion worth of limited partnerships to its customers, in many cases using fraud, deceit, and illegal means. Beginning in 1989, a handful of investors began to sue Prudential Securities to recover their lost funds; some filed arbitration claims against the brokerage firm. In 1991, the Securities and Exchange Commission and various state regulators began investigating the firm for shady practices stemming from the limited partnership sales. Still, for five years, the firm vigorously and loudly denied any systemic wrongdoing and defended all of its sales practices as sound and legal. The real culprits for the soured investments, it claimed, were down markets and pure bad luck.

But in October 1993, the company suddenly changed course and settled fraud allegations with the Securities and Exchange Commission in order to avoid a protracted court proceeding, which probably would have bankrupted the firm. As part of its covenant with the SEC, the nation's fourth-largest securities firm agreed to pay $41 million in fines—including an amount to every state in the nation—plus at least $331 million to individual customers in an open-ended fund specifically formed for that purpose. At the time, investors who had pumped $8 billion into the limited partnerships had received little more than $3 billion back in distributions—or about thirty-eight cents on their dollar. Any client who could prove that he or she was misled in some way, or that the investment was unsuitable, could potentially recover the money.

That settlement was unprecedented on many levels. It was the largest and longest-running securities scandal involving retail individuals, as opposed to corporate chieftains or professional traders. Also, it would prove over the following year to be the most expensive Wall Street debacle in history.

Significantly, the SEC settlement did not include Prudential's admission or denial of guilt in connection with selling limited partnerships. This crucial omission allowed the company to continue to fight investors in court and in arbitration hearings and permitted the firm to avoid any responsibility for deceiving its customers about the benefits—and pitfalls—of the risky commodity-type products it sold. Many Prudential Securities clients were middle-class investors who had invested their savings for retirement and were clearly ill-suited for the dicey instruments. A disproportionately large number of investors were senior citizens who lived on the funds they had entrusted to a piece of the Rock. The Pru, it turned out, had specifically targeted that vulnerable group.

But the SEC reckoning arrived too late for those people who had already faced Prudential in court or in arbitration hearings. Many investors prior to 1993 had already settled with Prudential for pennies on the dollar, or had lost their cases entirely. Still, even after the historic SEC settlement, Prudential continued to battle former clients privately, going so far as to blame any wrongdoing on the actions of a few "rogue brokers" rather than on corporate-wide practices.

Out of 701 limited partnership products the brokerage had sold to 600,000 investors, only a handful ever performed as promised. By 1991, the value of many of these holdings had dropped sharply, and only partly because of poor market conditions in the oil, gas, and real-estate sectors in which the bulk of the partnerships engaged. Other factors played a major role. Pru Securities and the firms that packaged the limited partnerships grabbed inordinately high partnership fees for themselves. False income projections, undisclosed and, therefore, illegal loans, and the personal deals some senior executives struck with sponsors also spoiled the integrity and performance of the investments.

Prudential Securities sold oil and gas partnerships riddled with deceptive accounting practices that made them seem more profitable than they actually were. Other limited partnerships, such as those packaged by a firm called Watson & Taylor, were tainted with unethical and unsavory arrangements that benefited a Pru-Bache insider and the general sponsor that formed the deals, but not investors. In many of these cases, Pru Securities knew about the deceptive and illegal practices—or certainly should have.

And then there are investors. In order to sell $8 billion worth of LPs, rogue executives fabricated dishonest sales pitches and phony claims, which they pushed brokers to recite to their customers. In some cases, Pru Securities' executives instructed its salespeople to target the investments to clients, though these risky, sophisticated deals were clearly inappropriate for them. This was against the cardinal rule of the industry, which is that brokers must know their customers well enough to recommend appropriate investments. All told, investors lost not only money but faith in what could have been the largest, most sterling broker-dealer house on the street, given its parentage.

Finally, after years of denial, the brokerage firm in October 1994 confessed to systemic, company-wide fraud in a unique arrangement with the Manhattan U.S. District Attorney. Pru Securities admitted wrongdoing in selling about 20 percent of the $8 billion in limited partnerships. Federal prosecutors filed a criminal complaint in court charging Prudential with fraud in the sale of $1.4 billion of oil and gas limited partnerships, sponsored by Graham Energy. The United States accused the Pru unit of lying to investors about the safety, returns, and tax benefits of the partnerships. Convinced it could prove its charges, the government stopped short of indicting the company. In a highly unusual procedure called a deferred prosecution agreement, Pru avoided a grand-jury indictment by agreeing to a three-year probation; the hiring of an independent ombudsman to review alleged misconduct by a Pru employee; and an independent law firm to monitor Prudential.

Importantly, Prudential Securities admitted for the first time since 1989 that it had indeed performed widespread criminal acts. For its crimes, it agreed to place another $330 million into the special restitution fund. Combined with the $330 million it had paid in its October 1993 SEC settlement, the $41 million in fines, the $490 million in settling arbitrations and lawsuits, and $185 million in expenses and legal fees, this brought costs of the scandal to $1.3 billion. The tally could easily climb.

That amount eclipses any price ever paid by a Wall Street firm for breaking the law—including the now-defunct Drexel Burnham, the former employer of the infamous Michael Milken. (In 1988, that firm pleaded guilty to fraud and paid $650 million in fines; two years later it collapsed as clients abandoned the onetime bond messiah.)

The government's unusual arrangement with Prudential was created precisely to avoid bankrupting the firm and thus throwing out of work some 18,000 people, including 5,600 brokers. Yet nearly fifteen years after the first LP sales, the government conceded it didn't have the resources to investigate *all* of the partnerships the firm sold. While the firm during the 1980s used deception as a sales tool, government prosecutors were busy chasing higher-profile prey, such as Milken and arbitrage king Ivan Boesky. Then, in the 1990s, government cutbacks have truncated white-collar criminal law enforcement agencies and, recently, legislators have threatened to emasculate the SEC further by whittling down its funds and slashing its already lean budget. One newspaper editorial noted: "With more money than ever pouring into stocks, bonds, mutual funds, and other investments, this is not the time to scale back on the watchdog agency assigned to oversee the securities business and look out for consumer interests." The government continues to investigate Pru executives for possible criminal indictment, penalties, or censures.

However, the roots of the scandal spread far beyond Wall Street and into the nation's heartland in the Midwest, where Prudential Insurance Co. of America for generations has cultivated its reputation for rock-solid reliability. "What is different about Prudential's situation, compared to E. F. Hutton, Drexel, or Salomon [firms also accused of criminal wrongdoing], is that this is about the little old lady from Des Moines, Iowa," said a criminal attorney defending a Pru Securities senior officer. Truly, this is the first time since America's securities laws were created in the 1930s that a major Wall Street power has robbed so many average individuals. For their part, investors relied upon the company's image rather than upon a careful scrutiny of the investment products themselves. In that sense, the crime stretches beyond the Hudson to other regions of the country, where live the bulk of Pru's investors and policyholders.

Wrongdoing flourished in states such as Florida, Arizona, and California, where trusting elderly investors were eager to obtain returns on their investments that seemed too good to be true. It thrived within the echelons of educated professionals who sought to shelter their wealth from taxes. Even Pru Securities employees, many of whom were financially astute, invested in the LPs. "The thing that surprised me in all this is that investors were too easily parting with their dollars," said Commissioner Gary S. Mendoza of the Department of Corporations in

California. How could so many people be so easily deceived? "We were all driven by greed, all of us," said one investor. What better place to cast one's lot than with one of the oldest, richest, and most respected institutions in America? That a corporate symbol—a big, bland boulder—could exude such magnetic power indicates what even sophisticated consumers will buy, based mainly on blind faith. And so this tale belongs more to Main Street than to Madison Avenue or Wall Street.

Consider, too, the thousands of loyal employees who worked for Prudential during the period in which the fraud occurred. Many managers, brokers, secretaries, and clerks processed the work attached to the creation and sales of the limited partnerships and gave personal assurances of safety. Some eventually questioned the firm's practices and products. A few who persisted were penalized or fired. Many lost their careers and marriages in the wake of the scandal. Some suffered nervous breakdowns or mental illnesses that required treatments and medication. A few people, such as Jack Graner, lost their lives.

Said one executive: "A lot of us feel betrayed, but by whom?" Employees, like investors, believed Pru's representations about its investment products and never questioned the company's oft-stated virtues. Yet at what point are workers culpable? When they have suspicions? Once suspicions mount, should managers jeopardize their careers or the paychecks that feed their families in order to do the right thing? What is the right thing, anyway? "A lot of us have debated this for years," said Joe Kett, former manager of the San Diego office of Prudential-Bache Securities. "I don't think you can use the Nuremberg defense and say, 'My superior told me to do it.' Yet that's what a lot of people did."

And then there is the Rock itself. Once the crisis emerged full-blown at the onset of the nineties, company executives and directors grossly mishandled the problem, which became as much an issue as the LP fiasco itself. For example, the company claimed that many of the men responsible for the LP problems had departed by 1991, even though a few key executives remained for years thereafter. To baptize the "new" persona behind the Pru unit, the firm changed its name in 1991 from Prudential-Bache Securities to Prudential Securities, as though a different name would erase ingrained habits. A fresh slate of managers was installed, including a new president, Hardwick Simmons, who a year into his post announced, "It's all behind us now."

But rather, the chicanery continued. In the 1990s the firm carefully orchestrated a legal and public relations strategy born of deceit and denial. Since 1989, as details of the LP scandal have gradually emerged, Pru Securities spokesmen have blamed the problems on a "vocal minority" of investors. Later, Simmons pointed to rogue brokers. In 1992, he used the "rotten apple" theory to explain the firm's LP woes; in 1993, the blame was laid at the door of one unsupervised department. But as late as September 1994, regulators fined the company for abuses wholly unrelated to LP problems. For example, Prudential was forced to buy back $70 million of mortgage bond derivatives it had inappropriately sold in 1994 to small retail investors. The SEC accused a former broker of stealing $3.2 million from clients over a four-year period, right under the nose of the new Pru Securities. Idaho's state regulators fined the firm $1 million for improperly selling options to clients during the 1990s.

"Under current management, the firm has had serious problems," said Wayne Klein, Idaho's securities chief. "They've run out of excuses." Perhaps the New Pru unit isn't so different after all.

Then there is the corporate parent. The Prudential Insurance Co. of America owns about 140 subsidiaries, only one of which is Prudential Securities. The Pru owns more real estate in the world than any other entity except for the federal government and the Catholic Church. It is the largest private insurer in the world and ranks among the world's leading pension fund managers. It is the second-largest residential lender in the United States, according to Moody's Investors Service. One out of four Americans owns some sort of Prudential insurance policy. With its $220 billion asset base, its financial size rivals the annual government expenditures of Germany, Greece, and Norway combined. Yet very little is known about Prudential except that it is a mutually held company owned by policyholders—not shareholders— and is not often held accountable. Even its core business, insurance, is not easily understood, nor is it regulated by any one federal agency. The potential for abuse is great.

The company's stodgy, conservative, Middle American image clashes sharply with its disingenuous, pugnacious stance in what has become its most visible operation. And now, the public denials of wrongdoing, the scapegoating, and the scorched-earth legal tactics have backfired on Prudential's once gentlemanly reputation. In 1994, sales of Prudential's individual life insurance policies fell 20 percent. Said Rosemary Shockman, an attorney representing investors: "If the Pru had settled people's problems in a fair and respectable way, they would have contained the problem. But I'm convinced this will become a classic textbook case of how *not* to handle a disaster."

Our position of justice and equity in all our dealings with policyholders is neither new nor novel, but traditional with the Prudential. . . . I am sustained by the judgment, goodwill, and good faith of those who, throughout these many years, in unison and without a dissenting voice, have administered with rare skills the affairs of the Prudential, in due appreciation of the great trust committed to their care.

—John Dryden, founder of Prudential Insurance,
   in an address to directors, 1910

Prudential Insurance Co. of America was born as the Widows' and Orphans' Friendly Society. Formed in 1873 by an ambitious and penniless man named John Dryden, the company was supposed to sell what was then considered a revolutionary insurance product: industrial insurance. For about a century, upper-class people in America and England had been able to buy life insurance benefits in multiples of $1,000. This "class" insurance guaranteed that if the owner of the policy should die, his family would still be able to afford to continue living relatively well after his death. The policyholder paid his installments quarterly.

However, the poor who worked in the factories had no such assurances. The laborer no longer lived in the village and could no longer depend on neighbors for support. Where once he could till the land for food and sustenance, the advent of the industrial age drew him away from the farm and into the city, where no work meant starvation. This growing class of urban poor lived hand-to-mouth and couldn't earn enough money to guarantee a box *and* a burial, let alone security for their families upon their death. Dryden, according to a company-sponsored book, was downright rabid about offering the working-class people similar protection in the form of "mass" insurance, or industrial insurance. For three cents a week, the workingman could buy a policy to give him money when he was too sick to work and a family allowance if he should die. Thus was born what has become a modern necessity, perversely called term "life" insurance, written for a specific term, or period. Once the term ended, so did the working stiff's benefits. (In the more expensive whole life policy, one can build up a cash value in addition to death benefits.)

Industrial insurance was first sold in England through the Prudential Assurance Co. of Great Britain, formed in 1848. Prudential's name was well known in the mid-1880s in both England and America. So when Dryden's Widows' and Orphans' Friendly Society didn't take hold as he had hoped, Dryden established a new organization, "borrowing" the respected British firm's name and rechristening his operation the Prudential Friendly Society. Embracing the new firm, the *Newark Register* wrote in 1875: "One of the most gratifying facts connected with this society is its strength and security." Prudential "may be said to be founded upon a rock."

By the end of 1875, Prudential had 284 policies in force, many of them purchased by the men and women who labored in factories owned by the men on Prudential's board. Between 1876 and 1905, the value of industrial insurance policies in America grew from $500,000 to $2.5 billion, an enormous amount at the time. Industrial insurance became particularly lucrative because two-thirds of the workers who took out Prudential policies were unable to keep up payments. When a policy-holder lapsed on his pennies-a-week payment, Prudential pocketed the money it had already collected, with no obligation to pay out a cent upon the holder's death.

In the following decades, the firm created more products, many of them innovative, popular, and profitable. Prudential grew so big that it could afford to behave benevolently, which it did, according to the company's own account. During the Great Depression, some $1.5 billion of the Pru's home and farm mortgages fell delinquent, and the company tried to avoid foreclosing on customers. According to William H. S. Carr in *From Three Cents a Week: The Story of Prudential Insurance Co. of America,* "In one—by no means rare—case a Columbus, Ohio, home was purchased in 1927 and Prudential made a home loan on it. Time after time the mortgage terms were eased or payments suspended to enable the couple who owned the house to get on their feet. It was not until 1937 that the family was able to resume regular payments."

Still, there were sound business reasons for Pru's altruistic actions. To handle the problem loans in the 1930s, it erected emergency head-quarters. Later, the crisis centers became Prudential real-estate invest-ment offices. In subsequent decades, the firm pioneered medical insurance, dental insurance, annuities, and pension and investment products, all of which Prudential salespeople sold profitably. By the 1990s, Prudential had grown to become America's biggest farmer, big-gest oil and gas investor, and biggest investor of cold cash. The con-glomerate begins its day foraging for safe places to invest $200 million of its own cash; that's how wide and deep its cash stream flows.

Financial weight is implicit in the Rock, a symbol that Prudential's founder stumbled on during the Gay Nineties. Dryden was by then a rich man, yet he had kept his vision of helping America's working class. He had searched hard for a corporate seal and, in prior ads, had called Prudential a "Tower of Strength," a slogan that never caught fire. In 1896, an advertising man tried his hand at devising a "service mark" for the company. Whether he spied a rock elevation rising out of the Jersey

Meadows en route to his New York job one morning or whether he came upon a picture of Gibraltar in a book is still debated. But ever since August 20, 1896, the Rock has been used as the insurer's insignia, and now, a century later, it is the most recognized corporate logo in the world.

The symbol carries meaning, especially for the elderly who remember the Rock's compassion in the troubled days of the Great Depression. It's easy to understand how the Pru earned its reputation for integrity, fairness, and straight dealing, for, as John Dryden once said, the Prudential was more than just a company. It was a mission, he told directors in 1910, or a cause, to run the company "for the best interests of the vast aggregate."

And so the company was run for a time. During World War II, many Pru executives and employees took leave from work to serve their country in the military. Also during the 1990s, the Pru aggressively jumped into the group insurance business, the purchase by companies of insurance policies for groups of workers. That decision, made by Carroll Shanks, proved pivotal to the insurer's future. Shanks became president of Prudential during an exciting time of rapid growth, from 1946 to 1961. Under him, the company's group business introduced new benefits, such as long-term disability, which paid the disabled holder 60 percent of his base earnings. Shanks promoted dental insurance, variable annuities, and creative investment alternatives. At this time, the company devised Property Investment Separate Account, or PRISA, which allowed pension plans to invest money in real estate that appreciated rapidly in high-interest-rate environments. Decades later, in an interview with the author, Margaret Shanks Moore explained her father's motives for introducing PRISA: "My father felt strongly that policyholders should be protected against inflation." Indeed, he promoted insurance policies that many of us now take for granted.

Unfortunately, Shanks's term as president ended in personal disgrace. At the time—1960—he earned $250,000 in salary, and he found it difficult to put aside enough money for his estate because he was in a high tax bracket. As head of Prudential Insurance, he sat on the board of the Georgia-Pacific timber company. The two companies had engaged in many business transactions over the course of the years, and Shanks had grown friendly with Owen Cheatham, the chairman of Georgia-Pacific and a director of Prudential.

Upon hearing about Shanks's tax problems, Cheatham suggested that he take part in a complicated third-party timber deal, to which Shanks agreed. He borrowed enough money to buy about $10 million worth of timberland and, thirty minutes later, sold it to a Georgia-Pacific unit.

The unit, in return, agreed to cut and sell the timber over five years, pacing the harvest so Shanks could pay off his loan comfortably. Under this cozy arrangement, Shanks saved $400,000 in income taxes and Georgia-Pacific acquired timber with no debt.

The sweetheart deal was reported by *The Wall Street Journal* on August 15, 1960. "Is it wrong for a corporation officer or director to profit personally from sideline transactions with the company he serves?" the article began. The story prompted the New Jersey Commissioner of Banking and Insurance to investigate the matter, but he found nothing illegal. Embarrassed, Shanks shed the investment and the Pru established a committee to look into his financial arrangement. By then, however, conflict-of-interest cases had become a hot national topic. In the wake of the scandal, the newspaper won a Pulitzer Prize and Shanks was forced to resign after an otherwise stellar career.

Determined never to attract such unwanted attention again, the board of Prudential Insurance passed a detailed set of conflict-of-interest rules. It was meant to govern directors as well as managers.

Thirty years later, Margaret Shanks Moore recalled the hard lesson her father and the Pru had learned. Although he had never been found guilty of any wrongdoing, the mere appearance of a conflict of interest had prompted Shanks to step down from the Pru's top post. She said: "He always told me that whenever I saw the Rock, I could count on integrity, safety, and prudence. That's what I was brought up to believe."

That's why, in 1984, Moore purchased about $70,000 in limited partnership units from Prudential-Bache Securities and Graham Energy. Her firsthand knowledge of the company's stringent ethical standards, as well as her father's advice, made her confident that the investment was a sound one. The retiree told her broker that she needed conservative income because her husband had recently fallen ill; the couple would soon be living off their savings.

After Moore's husband died, she discovered that her savings were gone and her LP investment was worthless. She contacted the company, assuming it would stand behind its assurances. However, she was told that the firm couldn't do anything, and she grew distraught. Said Moore: "The company was trading off its image of being rock-solid. That used to mean something."

2

The Bache Family's Jules

THE Bache name appeared in America in the 1870s after a number of German and Eastern European Jews had immigrated to New York. Some of these people had started in the new country as peddlers who traveled the countryside selling ribbons, soap, and sealing wax from rickety wagons. After saving enough money, the peddlers had moved into downtown Manhattan to become merchants with storefronts. What is now New York's financial district was, at that time, a pungent, noisy, rambunctious port of trade. Bales of hides arrived from the West, and cotton from the South, copper from the Great Lakes, other commodities from all over the country. Stocks and foreign currency were traded on street corners, right up the block from where men unloaded produce and goods from ships and wagons. New York was an indiscriminate trade center, and immigrants such as the Lehmans, Guggenheims, Kuhns, and Loebs built their banking houses from these modest vendor roots.

In time, the traders amassed enough money to invest in other ventures besides their own, such as gold mines, railroads, timber companies, and cotton firms, just to name a few. Before long, these men made the transition from peddlers to financiers, lending money or extending credit to a new class of immigrant merchants who always needed cash to finance their inventories. Former merchants such as Marcus Goldman started buying from waterfront merchants items such as promissory notes or "commercial paper," which was merely postdated checks sold at a discount. No longer merchants, the new wealthy financiers started referring to themselves by the grandiose term "merchant bankers," and they now covered their routes trading IOUs and mining stocks instead of wool and candles.

One such Old World immigrant was Leopold Cahn, who in 1879 formed a brokerage and investment banking company on Wall Street— Leopold Cahn & Co. The investment side of Cahn's firm offered advice to clients, who might ask for the best type of security, or financing, to issue for sale, given the current investment demand. The brokerage side of the firm would then sell the resulting securities, which gave the buyer an interest in the fledgling venture. Leopold Cahn & Co. was one of many such companies operating on Wall Street.

Cahn had married the sister of another immigrant, whose nephew, Jules S. Bache, joined the firm shortly after it was founded. Bache started as a cashier at nineteen years old, and over the years he worked his way up until he became managing partner of the firm in 1892. At that time, the company was reorganized into J. S. Bache & Co.

By the turn of the century, Wall Street finance was as wily and savage as the Wild West land boom had been some fifty years earlier. There were no rules and few ethics, and to be a financier or merchant banker in the wake of the Panic of 1873 was to possess some of the avarice and evil that the nation associated with "the wickedest street in the world," which is how Stephen Birmingham refers to it in *Our Crowd*. At this time, Eastern entrepreneurs, robber barons, and speculators were developing factories, rails, and oil companies—all of which required money to finance. The descendants of the onetime cart merchants now owned the investment firms of Lehman Brothers, Goldman Sachs & Co., and J. & W. Seligman & Co. By dispensing investment advice and financing the ventures of the entrepreneurs and speculators, the investment firms helped the new ventures eventually grow into national corporations.

J. S. Bache & Co. had a hand in this growth. Some of its better-known clients included the stingy John D. Rockefeller, founder of Standard Oil of New Jersey; the dour-looking Edward Harriman, who tried to corner the stock of the Northern Pacific Railroad; and Jay Gould, who was jailed for stock manipulation before he successfully conspired to inflate the gold market. (Indeed, avarice and greed were commonplace on Wall Street during the Gilded Age, which lasted until the landmark Securities Act of 1933—also called the Truth in Securities Act.)

Spotted frequently on Wall Street, Jules Bache was a handsome man with dark hair and a medium build who had a handlebar mustache and wore dapper suits. By the turn of the century, he had wedded the sister of another Bache partner, but matrimony did nothing to cramp his philandering style. He frequently traveled to Canada, where he acquired mistresses and founded Dome Mine Ltd. During the Depression, Jules amassed an art collection of sixty-three Old Masters, including such world treasures as Rembrandt's *The Standard-Bearer* and a Titian *Madonna and Child*. By the time he donated his collection in 1944 to the

Metropolitan Museum of Art, it was conservatively valued at about $15 million, although today, a few of the famous masterpieces would easily fetch that amount individually.

Wall Street firms have long followed an unwritten Salic law by which women are excluded from the line of succession. Jules was the father of four daughters, all of whom married well, according to the era's social register, but none of whom he could appoint as his successor. In the interest of posterity, Jules brought his nephew, Harold L. Bache, into the firm in 1914. However, the two men did not take to each other, as Jules was a dandy and Harold a plugger. Perhaps as a way to minimize family tension, Harold spent time in New Orleans, where he traded commodities and lost his heart. Corporate lore has it that he asked "a nice little peach" named Alice Kaye for her hand in marriage, but she refused in order to marry another. Some twenty-five years later, the sixty-two-year-old Harold again met the woman, who was newly widowed. This time, she accepted his proposal.

During the Roaring Twenties, J. S. Bache grew with the fortunes of the country, financing among other enterprises the building of the New York subway system. The firm, fearing a reversal, advised a conservative, measured approach to the market. Right before the Crash of 1929, it reduced the amount of credit it had extended to its customers and warned them of a potential crash. At the time of the crash, none of the firm's capital was invested in the market, and it had no investment trusts to protect, unlike so many of its neighbors.

However, two embarrassing and costly episodes undermined its prudent approach at the time. Right before the crash, a cashier was caught embezzling $625,000 from the firm's New York branch office—a huge amount of money in those days. Also around that time, the firm discovered that a number of phony accounts had been opened in another branch by the president of the State Bank of Binghamton. The president, who was the bank's largest stockholder, had used these accounts to trade on margin—which is borrowing from the brokerage firm to purchase stocks. In the wake of the crash, the president lost all his money, the bank collapsed, and the state's regulators sued Bache for negligence—and won. The suit produced an enormous bill against Bache and, more important, a new industry rule. The "know your customer rule" of the New York Stock Exchange (Rule 405) required all brokerage firms to obtain crucial facts from all of their customers who opened new accounts. From that point on, brokers were required to know their customers and their credit-worthiness. Half a century later, that industry canon would surface to haunt the Bache brokerage.

The post-Crash days were dark ones for the firm, and it was in danger of folding. "Bache was saved when Jules dug into his pockets to bail out the firm," says Edward I. du Moulin, former vice chairman of J. S. Bache, in a recent interview. Although the firm didn't emerge totally unscathed from the Crash, it was not destroyed, either, as were many other brokerages at the time. Rather, it provided fresh opportunities for Bache. In 1933, for example, Chrysler Corp. was trading at a ridiculously low price of $5 a share. Jules bought at least 100,000 more shares of Chrysler stock, and watched as, the following year, the stock paid a cash dividend of $14 a share and shot up to $120 a share. Old J. S. had received a 2,600 percent return on his money and a major stake in what would become a giant automobile manufacturer.

During the Great Depression that followed and into the war years, Bache continued to expand. Suddenly, in 1945, Jules died, leaving the firm in turmoil. "At the time, people at the firm thought that either [Jules's sons-in-law] Clifford Michel or Mr. Pershing would take control of the firm, but Harold surprised us all," said Mr. du Moulin, who worked at the firm from 1933 to 1981. The firm's solvency was threatened after one of Jules's daughters requested her inheritance, a substantial amount of which was locked into the company. In order to pay her, Bache & Co. would have to be either merged, liquidated, or recapitalized. Harold immediately took charge and quickly raised several million dollars through two sources. One savior was the Ryan brothers of Troy, New York, who were textile merchants as well as the firm's longest-running commodity traders. In return for investing cash in the firm, they became general partners in Bache, and so oversaw the daily operations and shared responsibility for its debts. The second savior was former Ambassador Joseph P. Kennedy, the patriarch of what was to become America's leading political family. For his money, he became a limited partner, who had no say in the firm's operations but also had no liability beyond his original investment.

This quick and easy solution elevated Harold to the top job, and there he flourished. Short, pudgy, with a florid complexion, Jules's nephew began to earn his own reputation as a tough businessman whose most frivolous trait, it seemed, was a love of bridge. Conservative and steady, Harold began to use the firm's cash to merge with and buy other "wire" houses, so called because they had private wires that linked their branch offices to one another and to the exchanges, over which they signaled orders. Bache, like other houses on the street at the time, was modeled after its British merchant banking cousins. In this system, the senior people, who had worked at the firm for years and had proved themselves worthy, became partners, sharing in the firm's profits and losses. Harold didn't like this system, as he saw how its clubby protective arrangement undermined overall efficiency. He fought to convert the partnership into a private corporation so that hard work and talent would be rewarded. In 1965, Bache finally became a private corporation in which men were promoted to senior positions based on their abilities, not tenure. "It was quite a struggle," recalled du Moulin. "I felt that even after the change, it was always a partnership in corporate clothing. It was hard to change the attitude of some people that this wasn't just a personal, private club."

That attitude would remain deeply ingrained in Bache's culture, regardless of how many times it would shed its leaders or change its name.

After Harold changed Bache's formal structure, he continued expanding at home and abroad, promoting vice presidents, not partners, to the new corporate masthead. During the sixties, the firm added a mélange of new offices, firms, and people. In 1967, in one of the last significant acquisitions, Harold welcomed into the fold a Parisian arbitrage firm called Wyser-Pratte & Co. Eugene Wyser-Pratte came aboard, along with his son, Guy. (Another son, Christian, would later join the firm.) In March of 1968, Harold died and the firm's leadership began to splinter.

By the end of the 1960s, America's stock market had boomed in the wake of a decade-long uninterrupted economic expansion. Business had bulged to the point where a firm needed an enormous capital base to handle the swelling volume of transactions, the cyclical swings in earnings, and a new voracious demand from institutional customers, who had reaped bull-market profits. The Securities and Exchange Commission set minimum capital requirements for broker-dealers; they had to have cash on hand equal to a certain percent of all their liabilities. But business had boomed so fast that many firms were in danger of breaking this rule. To accommodate its own growth and comply with the SEC's rule, Bache in 1971 raised $40 million by issuing 2.5 million shares, and so became a public corporation. It then rapidly merged with or bought up other companies. In 1973 it merged with Halsey Stuart & Co. of Chicago and in 1977 merged with Shields, Model & Roland of New York. By 1979, Bache Halsey Stuart & Shields had became one of the larger brokerage houses on the street—but one of the least well capitalized.

The seventies were a turbulent time for all securities houses because of consolidation and runaway inflation, which scared away customers. When interest rates are high, as they were in 1979, the stock and bond markets tend to suffer. It's difficult for a company to raise money when the public stock market is depressed; generally business slows down.

As business became tougher, Bache's internal life grew more turbulent, too. Instead of shoring up business, the firm's numerous acquisitions began to sap its vigor. In the past, the firm had often been caught up in political battles, but now the posturing intensified as new people climbed aboard from the raft of mergers, jockeying for position. Jack Graner, for example, had come to the firm with Halsey Stuart & Co., where he had been a senior officer. H. Virgil Sherrill, a top Bache executive, had come via Shields, Model & Roland. These and other men brought idiosyncrasies and different styles, especially as compared to longtime Bache men such as Robert Sherman, who had risen up through the retail ranks since 1960. Overseeing the motley group was Harry Jacobs, chairman of Bache Halsey Stuart & Shields, a balding, avuncular man who was fiercely proud of the firm's immigrant roots and could be a formidable street-fighter. Jacobs would have to be spunky to handle the challenges ahead, for by the time Bache was celebrating its hundredth anniversary, trouble was brewing on a few fronts.

By 1979, internal backstabbing and political intrigue had become so commonplace that insiders joked about Bache-ball. The game involves slugging (metaphorically) a colleague in the back to disable him and knock him out of the game, and the following tale exemplifies the perfect play.

In 1979, a small group of people worked in Bache's tax shelter department, which created limited partnerships as investments that could be sold to Bache clients. The department was small but collegial. "It was the only time on Wall Street that I felt I really had to exercise my mind and come well prepared, because people really knew their stuff," said one man who worked there at the time.

In November 1979, James J. Darr joined Bache to head the department. He had come from Josephthal & Co., where he had also headed the partnership division. Of medium height and built like a fullback, Darr had prematurely graying hair and a self-confident, some say arrogant, attitude. Shortly after joining Bache, Darr aroused suspicion and, perhaps, envy among the men who had been working there for many years. The mood in the office became tense.

By the summer of 1980, some employees had heard rumors that Darr had taken kickbacks while working at Josephthal. Specifically, Darr had received checks from two sponsors, or general partners, whose limited partnership deals were sold through Josephthal. One check, for $30,000, had been paid to Darr shortly before he bought his house in Stamford, Connecticut, and an attorney had told the employees that he had a copy of that check. He warned them to watch out for their new boss.

One evening, five Bache employees gathered at the Gold Street apartment of one of them, a few blocks from work. The "Futon Five," as they later called themselves, sat on futons and discussed the disturbing rumors into the evening. What should they do? After much discussion, they decided that one of them should report the allegations to Bache's security department immediately.

The next day, the firm launched an investigation, which continued for a few months. The rumors of Darr's accepting illicit payments from sponsors who, at the time, did business with his employer turned out to be true.

Many years later, Darr would contend that the payments were proper. One check was for consulting on a deal he had put together and he said was disclosed to the firm. The second was intended for Josephthal and mistakenly given to Darr. Four months later, he returned the money to Josephthal, which then gave him half—an unusually high split. Officers at Josephthal would say they hadn't known of Darr's payments, and no one at Bache had ever contacted them back in 1980.

Yet, at that time, the small, collegial department at Bache darkened with suspicion and mistrust. That summer, a newcomer joined the staff and immediately sensed the friction. He noted that in the morning Darr headed straight for his office, while others huddled in their particleboard cubicles. The newcomer kept his head down and worked, unaware of the rumors and ongoing investigation. But he couldn't ignore the static in the air.

Meanwhile, Bache continued scrutinizing Darr's history until, finally, it had completed its review. The word was that Darr was "dirty," said one Futon Five member. "That's a fact," he added. (An executive later confirmed that his review provided damaging evidence of payments.) Now speculation about Darr's imminent departure ran through the firm.

Darr, however, emerged unscathed. Bache formally cleared him of any wrongdoing. Around Halloween 1980, he assembled his staff in the reception area—the only place big enough to gather all thirty people. He alluded to an investigation, but many lower-level people didn't understand what he was talking about. The Futon Five knew. Some of them were lined up against the wall as before a firing squad and faced Darr as he addressed his troops. He slowly scrutinized their faces; the room fell silent. Darr spoke slowly, clearly, and with unmistakable authority:

"I want to tell you right now, if anybody ever jeopardizes me, my career, or my family again, I will kill you."

No one spoke. The newcomer turned and, from the corner of his mouth, whispered to the fellow next to him, "This is going to be an interesting job."

Darr remained at Bache for eight years, but within months, all of the members of the Futon Five—the very people who had brought to light the serious allegations—either were fired or resigned. In their naiveté, the men had made a fatal mistake. Said the newcomer: "They should have known that Darr played to win. When you charge after him, you have to shoot for the heart. Those guys didn't understand that."

That investigation—and others like it—would shadow Darr for years.

That incident set the tone for what would become the direct investment group (DIG). But in 1980, Darr and his troubles were nothing compared to the more pressing and immediate problems that faced Bache outside its doors.

One difficulty had to do with the firm itself. Between the in-house battles and outside market forces, Bache's condition had weakened considerably. Without interest income, Bache would have lost money for the last four years. It had acquired too many firms too rapidly and couldn't assimilate them easily during the increasingly competitive period. By 1979, Bache had grown so vulnerable that its chairman, Harry Jacobs, then fifty-eight, feared that Bache itself would be taken over. After spending thirty-three years at the firm and surviving bitter office scraps, Jacobs was not about to let that happen without a fight.

That summer, a volley was fired by Samuel, Hyman, and William Belzburg, three brothers who controlled a raffish Canadian real-estate and financial empire. They began to buy up Bache stock, saying it was an investment, but judging from Bache's earnings record at the time, it was a strange one. By the time the Belzburgs had acquired 10 percent of the stock, Jacobs started looking for ways to repel the brothers. "It was the German Jews fighting the non-German Jews," said Perrin Long, an analyst at First of Michigan. The disdain between the two immigrant groups had been a part of New York society for generations, but now it spilled across international borders.

Meanwhile, Bache's salvation appeared in the form of another set of brothers—Bunker and Herbert Hunt. The Street had always looked down upon Bache because it accepted business from anyone, including small-time investors and Eastern Europeans working in the garment industry. So when the two enormously rich men and their commodity business had been turned down for sound business reasons by other firms, such as Shearson, the Hunts turned to Bache.

For the past several years, the Hunts had been buying silver from various sources; they had hidden some of their interests in offshore firms, and others had been parked with their friends in Saudi Arabia, thus defying federal market rules. Meanwhile, the spot price, or today's price, of silver in the commodity market had climbed from about $5 to $30 an ounce. The silver mania had soared to such ludicrous heights that people were carting their family silver downtown to be weighed, melted, and sold to warehouses. The whole country was swept up in the speculative silver frenzy that the Hunts had created simply by demanding so much silver from the world market.

At Bache on Gold Street, the Hunts bought silver contracts on margin, which essentially meant that Bache lent the Hunts millions of dollars so the Texans could gamble in the market. According to *Beyond Greed* by Stephen Fey, Jacobs lent the Hunts even more money for their silver chase after the Hunts bought Bache shares. By March 1980, the Hunts owned about 7 percent of the shares, which was enough to stop any Belzburg attack. Bache, in return, lent the Hunts a quite generous sum of $233 million—far more than the shareholders' capital of $147 million—but the loans were backed by silver that was worth far more than that, based on current prices. Still, those loans were only a smidgen of the Hunts' total borrowings, which rose to $1.3 billion in February and March 1980. To state it more dramatically, for every $10 lent to businesses during those two months, $1.30 was borrowed by the Hunts. The greedy brothers were not only close to cornering the world silver market, they were the best customers of American bankers.

Then their silver strategy blew up. Market regulators had unraveled the Hunts' plans and had heard that the brothers intended to bid silver up to $85 an ounce. Meanwhile, the market had climbed to an all-time dangerous high of $50. The market regulators tightened the rules to discourage speculation, and within a week, the price of silver plummeted to $34 an ounce—and continued dropping. The brothers' expensive future contracts came due, and they had to pay the higher contract prices, although the current price of silver was lower. Because Bache had a financial stake in those contracts, it too had to pay more money than the current value of silver. Bache had met $135 million of those margin calls, but it couldn't keep paying the calls without collapsing.

On the last day of March 1980, a huge futures contract was due for nearly double the amount the contract was now worth. The Hunts couldn't borrow any more money, as Paul Volcker, the chairman of the Federal Reserve Board, had ordered all banks to stop financing speculators. Bache couldn't bail the Hunts out, since they simply didn't have the cash, and the holder of the enormous contract wanted cash only.

In the end, over tense negotiations involving Volcker, bankers, a silver mining firm, and the Hunts, a compromise was reached. The Hunts gave some of their rich oil holdings in the Beaufort Sea to the mining firm as payment in kind. But in the end, the brothers' attempt to corner the silver market nearly ruined several banks, firms, and clearing houses. The Hunts themselves would file the largest personal bankruptcy in American history.

The debacle certainly spelled the end for the century-old Bache. Debilitated and reeling, the once-proud brokerage house asked the investment banking firm First Boston to find a white knight to rescue it from collapse. The following year, in June 1981, Prudential Insurance Co. of America announced that it was buying Bache Halsey Stuart & Shields. The price was $345 million.

3

A Piece of the Schlock

BLURRY-EYED from working late the night before, Jim Trice walked into his new office and grabbed the ringing telephone.

"Jim, drop everything." It was his boss, Bob Sherman.

"Now what?"

"We've got to fly to New York this weekend. All of the Bache directors, senior officers, and regional directors are supposed to meet the Prudential people on Sunday."

"Hell, they just bought us," Trice mused to himself. He spoke into the receiver. "Fine, Bob."

"Listen." Sherman sounded nervous. "Why don't we just fly out together Saturday morning? We can talk then. TWA has a morning flight from San Francisco."

"I'll make a reservation."

"Make sure we sit together," Sherman added. "I know you like to fly coach or whatever the hell that cheap class is. But I fly first class, so get yourself a first-class ticket, too." Sherman hung up.

Since his promotion four months before, Jim Trice's life had taken a frenetic turn, quite unlike the steady pace of his last eighteen years at Bache. But this was different. He hoisted his pants snug against his belly, as though to gird himself for combat.

At six feet, Trice was bald, with a round pasty face. With his bushy eyebrows and protruding brown eyes, Trice can issue warnings quite effectively with just one unwavering glare. People joked that he resembled Kojak or J. Edgar Hoover, depending on whether you were on Trice's good, protective side or his dark, suspicious side. A man of deep-rooted loyalties and few public displays, he was well respected by those both above and below him in the Bache pecking system.

For the last fourteen years, the Texan had lived in the Spanish colonial town of San Antonio, Texas, where he had supervised a relatively small office for Bache Halsey Stuart & Shields. The city was located not far from Trice's birthplace in Victoria, Texas, and he and his wheel-chair-bound wife had built a nice home in San Antonio for themselves and their two children. Over the years, their lives had settled into a steady rhythm of home, work, and church. Then, on a winter day in 1981, Trice had told his office staff he was leaving. Many people cried, because, over the years, the thirty-three-person group had become more like family than office; not one broker, secretary, or professional support person had left in the entire twelve years Trice had managed the office. As people came up to hug Trice good-bye, the normally unflappable manager struggled to hold back tears.

Still, the occasion was cause for celebration; Bob Sherman had promoted Jim Trice to head the West Coast region. Sherman himself oversaw four of the firm's nine regions in a territory that ran from Ohio to California. (The Eastern, five-district region was run by Bob Errico.) The retail system was the source of Bache's profits. In "retail" brokerage offices, brokers earn commissions serving individual clients, who buy or sell stocks, bonds, or other securities. Brokers were often shoehorned into crowded cubicles, their ears soldered to telephone receivers, their brains wired to a sales pitch that they might repeat in numerous "cold calls"—a securities salesman calls on strangers "cold" without an introduction to warm the prospects' interest. Over time, the brokers or salesmen develop steady customers and form a "book" of accounts. Taken individually, the broker's task seems dismal and daunting, but, collectively, the daily calls and orders form the engine that propel most retail brokerage operations, including Bache's.

Trice's territory covered the area between San Diego and Seattle, stretching from Utah to Honolulu. Geographically, the territory was large, but from Bache's point of view, the region formed the dregs of its bush-league system. Despite the sprawling eight-state area, Bache had only sixteen retail branches in the West, and they were broken hubs of activity. Like the firm's 2,200 brokers in the other regions, the three hundred brokers under Trice's care were suffering from a malaise incurred during the wake of the Hunt scandal. Rumors of takeover threats had distressed employees, who worried about losing their jobs. But Bache's Western region had always been shunned for its low-quality managers and mediocre brokers. Many West-based managers felt ignored simply because of their distance from New York headquarters. Indeed, discontent was so high that on Trice's first day as regional director, the entire staff in the Woodland Hills, California, office quit.

Adding to the challenge of his new job, Trice had made some personal sacrifices. He had left his family behind in San Antonio to live temporarily in San Jose, California, where the region's headquarters were based. He had rented a Spartan apartment a few miles from the down-town office, where he usually arrived every morning at six and left most nights by five. In the evenings, he'd take home and read personnel files and legal documents. A few days a week, he traveled the length and width of his territory, meeting its managers and learning about the prob-lems and potential in the region.

Now, after eighteen sedate years at the firm, another curveball was headed his way. He was about to meet the new corporate parent.

After the airplane left the tarmac in San Francisco that Saturday morn-ing, Sherman ordered a glass of wine and Trice asked for a soda. The two men settled back to discuss the sequence of events that had oc-curred over the last few days. Bache had hired the investment banking firm First Boston to seek a white knight to rescue it from unsavory raiders. First Boston had taken Bache's dowry to Prudential Insurance Co. of America. Excited by what it saw, the board of Prudential called its first unscheduled meeting in its 108-year history and voted to acquire Bache. And so, only ten days after the matchmaker's first move, Pru-dential announced its latest acquisition. It would pay $385 million for the 102-year-old brokerage house. What would happen over the next few months was anybody's guess, but for now, the wedding was on.

Upon landing in New York, Trice hailed a cab. The two men checked into the sumptuous St. Regis Hotel, located on 55th Street and Fifth Avenue and built by John Jacob Astor IV. The turn-of-the-century build-ing was appropriate for the momentous meeting. After all, here was the first American outsider buying into Wall Street since the days of the Glass-Steagall Act of 1933, when commercial banks had been expelled from the Street and barriers had been erected to separate investment banking and securities brokerage firms from deposit-taking commercial banks. Now, half a century later, banks were challenging that law and those barriers were threatening to crumble. The St. Regis meeting sig-nified the union of two of the oldest, longest-running financial institu-tions in the country, an insurer and a securities broker. In time, this event would be recognized as a watershed mark in modern America's financial history. But that April day in 1981, none of the men who walked to the second-floor meeting room thought much about the day's historical significance. "We were all euphoric about the merger, which finally removed the threat of greenmail," said Stanley Klimczak, the Midwest regional director. In a room decorated in the fussy style of Louis XV, about twenty-five Bache managers and officers took their seats around the polished tables. Bache chairman Harry Jacobs stood and addressed the group.

Looking more rested than he had in months, Jacobs expressed his pride at the new alliance and relief that the firm's troubles had apparently abated. He then introduced two officers from Prudential Insurance Co. of America: David J. Sherwood, the then fifty-nine-year-old president, a tall strapping man with a wonderfully goofy grin, and the shorter, more somber-looking Garnett L. Keith, a forty-five-year-old senior vice president. Keith would become a central figure at Bache.

Sherwood spoke first. "Welcome to Prudential. We are delighted to have you in the fold. We don't know much about your business," he said, "and we recognize that you are experts. So, consider us silent investors. We want you to continue running your business as best you can."

Sherwood had been in the insurance industry for most of his career and had become the company's thirteenth president in 1977. He talked about Prudential's beginnings in industrial life policies, which had been sold for three cents a week to poverty-ridden workers who wanted a decent burial and an income for their widows. Although Prudential had stopped selling those inexpensive policies years ago, it continued serving those customers who regularly paid their three-penny premiums. "A few years ago," Sherwood said, "we decided to stop collecting on those policies because it was costing us more money to collect than those three pennies were earning." Prudential had told those customers that their policies had been paid in full.

The securities executives chuckled and exchanged glances. If they hadn't realized it before, they understood now that this was one enormous, benevolent patriarch. Clearly, the brokerage firm's penny-pinching days were over. "Everybody was looking forward to having enough dollars to do what we used to do with just nickels and dimes," said Klimczak.

Then Garnett L. Keith spoke. An industrial engineering graduate as well as an M.B.A., Keith was measured and methodical. He explained that Prudential had been looking for ways to expand into investment products and services for some time. In evaluating its future, Pru's directors had realized that it could either expand into the health services and products area, in which it was already strong, or it could develop its strength in financial services. Keith had headed a special task force formed to explore all the ramifications of Prudential's move into the financial field. Then, *voilà!* The Bache Group's tender offer had landed in its lap. Instead of continuing to shop for regional or boutique firms, the company jumped on Keith's recommendation, which was to buy the nation's eighth-largest brokerage house.

During the meeting's question-and-answer period, one man asked what some in the group considered to be a rather silly question. "Everybody knows about Prudential's great health insurance policies," the man asked. "Now we're part of the Pru, are we going to get medical coverage, too?"

Sherwood's answer was telling: "That's up to you. We expect you guys to continue running your own business. If you want health coverage, ask a Prudential agent for a quote. Get a quote from another company. Look at your costs and weigh the decision. If you can't afford to pay for coverage," he said, "cut your expenses."

The point was: Prudential's parentage of Bache did not spell corporate welfare, and Bache would be expected to run its own affairs in a thoroughly prudent, businesslike manner.

Sherwood made another significant comment. "We look at this as a long-term investment," he stressed. "We've had some subsidiaries that in the beginning didn't make money, but then a few years later became extremely profitable." Indeed, Sherwood himself had been president of at least two Prudential subsidiaries that had not immediately turned a profit. "We view the insurance business over the long range, and that's how we'll view this company.

"We're in this for the long haul. We'll make a formal, full-blown review of this merger in about fifteen years."

It was a magnanimous and laudable comment, but fifteen years would prove to be an awfully long time.

Prudential's marriage to Bache attracted much attention in the days that followed. At first, the reaction to the merger was incredulous; pundits joked about the Rock buying the Schlock. Then the unspoken consensus was clearly positive as a number of other conglomerates scrambled to imitate Prudential's move. Within weeks, Sears Roebuck & Co. acquired the brokerage firm of Dean Witter Reynolds, American Express purchased the brokerage firm Shearson Loeb Rhoades, and Phibro Corp. bought Salomon Brothers. The shopping spree would continue for a few more years as other entities snapped up securities houses: Travelers Insurance would buy Dillon Read & Co.; Equitable Life Assurance would purchase Donaldson, Lufkin & Jenrette (DLJ); John Hancock Mutual Life Insurance would snap up Tucker Anthony & R. L. Day; Aetna Life and Casualty would find Federated Investors; and General Electric would take over Kidder Peabody.

Every few years, the mention of a commercial development takes on evangelical tones, whether it's the rise of silver prices or the fall of independent brokerage houses. In the early 1980s, the popular buzz was "financial supermarkets," as though one could drive to an A&P and stroll the aisles for a home mortgage, a six-pack of securities, and a quart of bonds. At the time, however, it appeared that the financial walls that had once separated banks from brokerage houses were cracking in the face of what some said were outdated laws. Indeed, Congress considered bills that would blur those distinctions and potentially erase the traditional lines between insurance companies, thrifts, banks, and other financial clans. In no time at all, it seemed then, all financial firms would join in one unruly, fire-sale rush for the consumers' dollars.

Adding more pressure to the competition was the advent of inordinately high interest rates. With these running up to 22 percent, few people were foolish enough to lock their savings into traditional low-bearing savings accounts, which by law were capped around 3 percent. The dawn of the eighties produced shiny new wagons such as mutual funds, interest-bearing annuities, money market accounts, and other newfangled investments with high yields. These vehicles endeared themselves to inflation-weary investors, who lined up in nonbank lobbies to buy the new instruments and so earn more money on their savings.

All of these elements were crystallizing when Prudential made its move on Bache. Wisely, the Pru saw that more and more people were receiving insurance policies from their employers; Pru needed to diversify if it intended to move into the twenty-first century. In getting into the stock brokerage business, Prudential's idea was not only to diversify but to fortify its own franchise. The Pru could harness Bache's sales magic, which, although mediocre by Street standards, still outshone the insurance agent's style. Prudential could latch onto Bache's distribution network and so expand its own mighty web by "cross-selling" both types of products. In this scenario, brokers would sell their clients Pru annuities and Pru insurance agents would offer customers Bache mutual funds. Bache could access Prudential's "formidable investment management skills," as the 1982 annual report would later boast, and Pru could place its insurance agents in Bache branches—which is exactly what happened.

Yet, in all the hype about new frontiers and corporate couplings, no one stopped to scrutinize a potential flaw. An enormous chasm separated the mind of the insurance agent from that of the stockbroker, and this critical difference became a source of serious trouble in years to come. Without some gentle compromise and introspection, few of these supermarket alliances would easily survive their own culture clashes.

"An actuary is a person who doesn't have the personality to be an accountant," Robert C. Winters would frequently joke with securities executives. The remark showed Winters's self-deprecating sense of humor, for he started his career at Pru in 1953 as an actuary. At the time that Pru bought Bache, Winters had been promoted many times to become, by 1981, an executive vice president. He was tall, with thinning brown hair, modest sartorial tastes, and dark, lustrous eyes that drooped at the corners. Six years from that spring day, he would become chairman of the conglomerate.

Winters had been born in Hartford, Connecticut, home of many of America's insurance companies. He graduated from Yale in 1953 and subsequently joined Prudential. He took two years off to serve in the Army, but aside from that, spent all of his working life at the Pru.

As an actuary, Winters was a specialized mathematician who calculated insurance premiums, reserves, and dividends, using risk factors obtained from universal tables. These tables compile the age, sex, race, and other traits possessed by people who die from a given disease or accident. It is a somewhat morbid task, but a crucial one if a firm wants to calculate its odds accurately. The father of two daughters, Winters sat on numerous boards and served on various committees during his time with Pru. He belonged to the United Way, the Business Round-table, and the Trilateral Commission.

Winters's boss at the time, Robert A. Beck, had graduated from Syracuse University and had joined Pru as a salesman in 1951. He had risen in the sales ranks over a decade until he earned an executive position at the Newark headquarters in 1963. Renowned for his sales ability, Beck became chairman and chief executive of Pru in 1978. Short, rotund, and freckled, he often wore an easy smile. The soft-spoken man has been described by one former executive as the quint-essential career man "who makes genuine friends of everyone and rises to the top unopposed." The father of five children, he served on numerous boards while at Pru, including those of the Boeing Co., Campbell Soup, and Xerox.

The two Bobs—Beck and Winters—would leave indelible marks on Prudential, as would a third man, Garnett Keith. Garnett graduated from the Georgia Institute of Technology and, after serving time in the Navy Supply Corps, earned his M.B.A. from Harvard. His specialty was neither sales nor statistics, but investments. He had worked for other firms before joining Prudential in 1977 as vice president of the corporate finance department. His horn-rimmed glasses, thin upper lip, and square chin suggested an Ivy League rearing rather than his down-home Southern roots.

In 1981, Garnett and Winters shared the same title of executive vice president; both were vying for Beck's top position upon his retirement. All three men shared a unique corporate culture.

The insurance world centers around order. Prudential Insurance executives tend to work from nine to five, five days a week. After work, they drive home to the suburbs outside of Newark, New Jersey. As a rule, such men rarely divorce, don't do drugs, and are not prone to alcoholism. They are mild-mannered family men whose core business is to minimize risk. "Their idea of a good time is a tailgate party at a football game," said one former executive.

They insure against the odds of the unthinkable and unavoidable. They quantify death, disease, destruction, and loss of any kind. It's a business based on fear, and that fear is always fear of the future. Where will the next hurricane hit? What will the next incurable disease be? Thousands of people work every day at Prudential dealing in some way with losses that are often unspeakable to the rest of us when they inevitably occur.

The securities broker's life, however, is radically different. His or her day is long, and is motivated in no small degree by greed. A typical day for West Coast brokers, for example, might begin at six, when their East Coast peers begin work nearer the New York Stock Exchange. Their day may not end until nine, after dinner meetings with clients. In New York, many securities brokers live in the city during the week and travel to their country homes on weekends. Two and three divorces per person is common, and drugs and alcohol are just another way to combat the stress of fluctuating markets.

When a broker takes the time to look beyond the day's end, he or she sees the future filled with promise. Blue-chip stocks, greenmail plays, and gilt-edged bonds color the broker's world. The broker's vernacular is crass and primitive. It centers on bulls, stags, and tigers who collide as common stocks rise in a good market. On bad days, the bears, dogs, and skunks rule, but basically, the world is a rough but friendly place full of opportunity. Nothing in the industry but money is taken seriously, least of all the stuffy names of government bonds, which the broker flippantly calls Freddie Macs, Ginnie Maes, and Fannie Maes. The salesman's patois is rooted in a touchy-feely world not too far removed from Willy Loman's effusive optimism.

Driving that optimism is money. Unlike the insurer's lexicon of loss, a broker's script includes words like gain, hedge, volume, appreciation, yields, dividends, and price/earnings.

The insurer, however, sees life in radically different terms. The insurer's private, in-house language tiptoes around mortality tables, abandonment, malpractice, errors and omissions, casualty, and loss. Career men and women in this business grow cautious, knowing that the odds are stacked against them.

The paradox of insurance is that its painful language gets lost in translation. The client hears more palatable, easier-to-buy terms. Consider life insurance, which guarantees certain benefits upon the *death* of the policyholder, not the life of the holder. Indeed, the only thing that occurs during the life of the holder is premium bills, which must be paid to secure the benefits. Yet no one buys "death" insurance, even though that is precisely what it is. Likewise with "health" insurance policies, which insure a benefit to holders *only* if and when they fall prey to some disease; such insurance does not relate to health. So too with "home" insurance, which protects one only in the event that a fire, theft, or other catastrophe destroys or damages the home. Yet who calls a spade a shovel and asks for "homeless" insurance?

This sleight of tongue appears innocent, but it deliberately transposes reality into its cheery opposite. Although subtle, it is a form of delusion bred into the industry.

Given this cultural trait, it stands to reason that the executives of Prudential Insurance Co. of America might ignore danger signs, or call them by some other name until it is too late. In such a world, it makes sense that the conservative, risk-averse insurance executive would bridle at the style of the gambling, backslapping, risk-loving securities broker. Either way, by 1982, the stage was set for one of a few possible scenarios. Either the two cultures would clash until the friction threatened their very union, at which point the classic showdown might occur. Or perhaps one group would inadvertently ignore or misinterpret the signals emanating from the other, which could have a more damaging and long-lasting effect on the marriage.

4

Ball and the Blue Sky Years

SALESMAN Robert Hughes was so excited about his new job with Prudential-Bache Securities that he couldn't be bothered with details like desks and phones. On his first day of work, he had ventured downtown to Pru-Bache's rented headquarters in Santa Barbara, a newly built, two-story Mediterranean-style structure with a red-tiled roof, creamy stucco walls, and wrought-iron balconies. Upon walking into the office, however, Hughes found that workmen were still inside, unloading office furniture and pounding nails. He couldn't sell in all this racket, so he turned around, bounded downstairs, and walked across the street, where he found a pay telephone.

With a pocketful of change and his "book" of clients and prospects, the thirty-two-year-old spent his first day on the job dropping dimes in the pay phone. He made one sales call after another, determined to do as well for Pru-Bache as it was doing for him.

Of average height, Hughes had shining green eyes and curly black hair. His Welsh-born father and Jewish mother had created a comfortable home for their two sons, but it hadn't lasted long. His dad had been a prosperous wool broker until the advent of man-made fibers, which strangled the wool market. When that happened, the family lost its wealth, his parents filed for divorce, and Hughes and his brother went to live with their mother, who found a job. By the age of thirteen, Hughes had known prosperity and a genteel type of poverty; he had decided that he much preferred the former state. As he grew older, that decision spurred him to work hard and fanned his zeal to maintain his own family.

Hughes had been a securities broker for barely a year at another firm when, in the spring of 1983, he was recruited to move to Pru-Bache. He had done well for himself at the other brokerage firm after completing the broker trainee program. He had followed every lead and done everything by the book. In the evenings after a home-cooked dinner, he'd leave his wife and two toddling daughters to return to the office to make "cold calls." Like most new brokers, he'd try to sell new issues of a utility stock, because they tended to be safe enough for conservative investors. He had designed a sales strategy, written a script, and used the city's street directory to phone those people who lived in the affluent parts of town. Santa Barbara was chock full of rich folks, from the heirs of a baking soda fortune to the stars of mediocre films. Sometimes, when Hughes needed motivation, he would drive along the tree-shaded lanes that meandered through the foothills below town. He'd stop at a particularly beautiful mansion and think: "Whatever is going on in there, somebody did something of huge value for someone at one time." His belief was: "You give value out, and value comes back."

When other brokers in his office got discouraged after making twenty chilly cold calls, he'd pass along his motivational credo. By giving pep talks to his peers, Hughes kept himself pumped. Perhaps it was the fact that he had a young family; perhaps it was his background; but the Boston-born man went after business with a high level of dedication.

At the time that Pru-Bache was recruiting salespeople for its Santa Barbara office, Hughes hadn't known much about the firm. He had been contacted by the manager, met with him, and soon learned that the firm was offering generous signing bonuses and higher-than-average commissions.

At a time when most houses were paying brokers 35 to 45 percent commission on all revenue they brought to the house, Pru-Bache was paying 50 percent for the first year. Some brokers could negotiate a bonus worth 25 percent to 30 percent of their last twelve months' sales. Plus, Pru-Bache would occasionally offer other sweeteners: in Hughes's case, he could collect 75 percent of all commissions he produced after reaching $100,000. "It was a beautiful amount of money for a guy who was strapped and feeding a family," he said.

But, for Hughes, the clincher was not just the money. He may not have known much about Prudential-Bache, but he had heard plenty about its new chief executive officer, George Ball. Ball had been appointed head of the brokerage firm in July 1982, and nine months later, he had made a big impression on the sales force. Before making the decision to join the firm, Hughes had been encouraged to call Ball, which he did. To Hughes's surprise, Ball returned his call almost immediately and discussed the firm and its new direction. "He was a very professional, engaging, and personable man," Hughes remembered. "I was so impressed with the whole manner in which he had handled my call, I told him so." And he signed up.

Hughes had just learned why Ball was so revered by securities brokers. Any CEO who treated his troops with such respect was a leader who could easily gain the loyalty and affection of thousands. And Ball did.

Because Ball and Pru-Bache had wowed Hughes so profoundly, Hughes proceeded to wow Ball and Pru-Bache. After a few afternoons on the pay phone, he moved across the street to Pru-Bache's new headquarters. Stepping over workmen, Hughes found a desk and phone. Cupping his hand over the phone's receiver to mute the noise, he continued selling a phenomenal number of units in a limited partnership, a type of investment fund. Within a month, he had sold nearly $1.5 million worth of LP units, contributing tremendously to the firm's nationwide effort to crack the big syndication market. In 1983, many firms were selling $10 million to $15 million worth of these private LPs, but this was the first time Pru-Bache had raised as much as $50 million in this manner. Pru-Bache was making its debut in the big-league market, and Hughes had helped the firm.

In addition, he was paid well. Instead of a .5 percent commission for selling stock, or a 3 percent commission for selling a mutual fund, Hughes pulled down 7 percent for the firm, or almost $100,000. "That was the thrill of the victory," he said. His "payout," or take-home money, on the month's sale was $50,000, or half of the gross production he brought in. Plus, for every dollar that he brought into the firm from that point on, he could keep 75 percent as his payout.

On top of that, the man became a minor legend. In a conference call to all of his product managers from around the country, Jim Darr, the head of direct investments, used the example of Hughes to inspire his own sales force. "For crying out loud," he reportedly barked during a conference call, "we've got a new guy in Santa Barbara who just sold $1.5 million of these damn units from a fucking telephone booth. If a new broker can sell so much, what are you guys complaining about?"

Hughes was elated. He had been convinced that if he worked hard and gave people value, he'd get value back. Later, he received congratulatory letters from Jim Darr, Bob Sherman, and even George Ball. This new firm was a real delight, and for the first time in his career, Hughes felt he had finally found his niche.

Over the next twenty-one months, Hughes sold more units of VMS Realty limited partnerships than any other broker at Prudential-Bache Securities. He sold about $3.2 million in public and private funds during that period.

During the eighties, VMS raised about $2.6 billion from about 110,000 outside investors; about $1.3 billion was sold through Prudential-Bache Securities. The realty company became one of the two largest packagers of limited partnerships that were sold by Pru-Bache brokers (the other being Graham Energy).

VMS Realty was named after the initials of its three principals: Robert Van Kampen, Peter Morris, and Joel Stone. Initially, the Chicago-based firm had formed limited partnerships to purchase hotels, resorts, apartments, and other properties. Since its inception in 1979, the company had grown from an idea to $9 billion in assets, becoming one of the nation's largest real-estate syndicators.

The founders of VMS formed an unlikely alliance. Joel Stone was a dour-looking accountant and attorney who wore smoke-colored spectacles and a brittle smile. "He likes to think of himself as an ethical and good guy," said a former VMS employee, "but when push comes to shove . . . Joel takes care of Joel."

Peter Morris was a real-estate adviser and Harvard Law School graduate who was the happy-go-lucky sort. Later, while VMS investors fretted about their failing funds, Morris remodeled his mansion outside Chicago, installing marble floors, swimming pool, servants' quarters, and a twelve-thousand-bottle wine cellar.

The two ran the daily operations of the 280-employee company, which at its height had a monthly overhead bill of $5 million. "Someone once said they were two little kids who had never had a really good fight," said a former employee. "They had never learned to deal with things and so were little boys running around in men's bodies."

The "V" in the triumvirate was Robert Van Kampen, who had made a fortune in bonds before he cofounded the real-estate company. A devoutly religious man, he quoted Scripture and named his 125-acre estate Moriah, after the land where Abraham nearly sacrificed his son Isaac. Some considered Van Kampen a zealot: he pulled *Playboy* issues from his properties' magazine racks and wanted to ban liquor from all bars in VMS-owned hotels. He frowned on divorce and paid a man enough money "so his wife doesn't have to work," he once said. *Fortune* magazine in 1989 pronounced: "Robert Van Kampen is living proof that one need not be cynical or avaricious to accumulate a great fortune."

Maybe so, but you couldn't prove it based on what his company did to investors during the 1980s. Van Kampen preferred to distance himself from VMS, saying he had no control in the daily operations. But he clearly enjoyed the benefits he reaped from his 30 percent stake in it, and adopted as his own personal symbol the insignia of the firm's crown-jewel property—the Boca Raton Hotel and Club.

Its image graced Van Kampen's nouveau family "crest," which hung above the door of his Georgian manor in Illinois. Boca Raton was treated like the private country club of the three men, according to one ex-employee. Until the trio bought the illustrious property, however, VMS wasn't much of an entity. Said John Temple, who sold the Boca Raton Hotel to the trio: "The deal really put VMS on the map."

Boca Raton, Florida, sits on an inner lake about sixty miles up the coast from Miami. Discovered by Ponce de León in 1518, the site is inside a treacherous inlet whose jagged rocks were infamous for shredding the hulls of ships. The inlet was so hated by pirates and sailors they dubbed it Boca Raton—Spanish for "mouth of the rat."

Now a five-star hotel sat on the lake's shores. Built in 1926 by the architectural talent Addison Mizner, the 171-acre resort featured lush tropical grounds, a yacht harbor, tennis courts, and a 915-room hotel designed in the pink-stucco, red-tiled Moorish style. In the Roaring Twenties, the property hosted luminaries such as Irving Berlin, Elizabeth Arden, and George Whitney. At the time, it was the most expensive property built, at a cost of $1.25 million.

By 1983, the hotel was in financial trouble. On the books, it was valued at $55 million, but an appraiser figured a worth of $80 million. Its owner took a chance and asked for $100 million. "I was as surprised as anyone that I got the price I asked for," said Temple, who at the time headed Arvida Corp., which sold the hotel.

The buyer was VMS Realty. To purchase it, VMS organized an LP in 1983 and raised $50 million in a private offering. It then borrowed the rest of the money to finance the $100 million purchase price and told investors they could expect to receive a 10 percent cumulative return over the long term of about ten years.

That is, a $200,000 investment would at the end of ten years supposedly return $518,749 to the investor.

But a closer look at the 220-page private placement "memorandum" indicated that the proposal was not simple, and certainly no "deal" for investors. When VMS borrowed money to buy the hotel, it turned around and lent the bank's money to investors, charging a higher interest rate. As the first creditor paid by the LP, VMS pocketed an extra $1.1 million a year and passed the debt on to investors. So Pru-Bache clients who had handed over $50 million in cash now owned an asset burdened with $90 million in expensive first and second mortgages. The total cost now was $140 million.

Yet even if the hotel was worth $100 million (which was a high price in 1983), the $140 million bill was an onerous burden for investors. If the hotel did someday sell on the high side of $100 million, the money would first go to VMS to pay off its $90 million loan, and investors would receive the balance. That is, after investing $50 million, LP investors would get $10 million back, losing 80 percent of their original investment. Under this scenario, an investor who put in $200,000 would receive $40,000 back, which made the "deal" rather like a sinkhole. (In subsequent years, VMS would pile more debt upon the hotel.)

Where did the rest of the money go? To VMS, primarily—although Pru-Bache did get its share of the $7.5 million up-front fees and commissions the two general partners lopped off the top. In addition, VMS took another $3.2 million in loan fees, plus an $8 million markup fee VMS charged investors just for the trouble of buying the property. Add to that another $1.5 million in consulting and partnership monitoring fees taken by VMS over several years, plus the $1.1 million *a year* VMS collected by charging investors a higher interest rate on the two bank loans VMS borrowed, plus an estimated $20 million in supervisory fees over fifteen years, and VMS appeared, well, "avaricious." All told, the money collected by VMS and Pru-Bache totaled about $50 million, all of which investors paid through losses they suffered in addition to their initial cash outlay of $50 million.

Yet for all their profit, neither VMS nor Pru-Bache had put a nickel into the deal. Investors had initially bought units in the Boca LP because of the generous tax write-offs the government allowed at the time. Plus, unlike many VMS properties, the Boca Raton Hotel and Club was a genuinely valuable asset. Sold by a unit of what was arguably the most prestigious real-estate investor in the world—Prudential—the LP appeared to the average investor a savvy choice. Yet its outrageous fee structure could be unraveled only by the most diligent and patient of investors, who in 1983 tended to be wealthy LP clients who wanted a tax break. As one broker said later, "These guys knew what they were getting into." Fair enough.

But neither VMS investors nor Pru-Bache brokers who sold these LPs could have anticipated the outright chicanery and deceit that Pru-Bache and VMS would inflict upon limited partners by 1989. Indeed, bad as it was, the above-described Boca Raton investment was just a tooth in the rat's mouth.

In 1982, George Ball had a fabled reputation, perhaps more golden than that of any other retail brokerage firm leader at the time, with the possible exception of Sandy Weill, head of Shearson/American Express Co. Indeed, Ball and Weill were pictured on the cover of *Business Week* magazine that year, standing on the ledge of a skyscraper. But to the foot soldiers who worked in the securities branches around the country, George Lester Ball was the more charismatic of the two men. His ability to put people at ease and to establish a common link was extraordinary.

Unlike arrogant managers, Ball was accessible and never too busy to return a telephone call, although he wasn't one to waste time on chit-chat either. His focus was on the retail brokers—the sales force—and what they thought, wanted, and needed to sell better. His reputation was such that when he took over as head of Pru-Bache, he was deluged with calls from seasoned account executives who wanted to work for him. Some brokers went so far as to drive to his home and stuff their resumés into his mailbox.

Part of the reason why people held Ball in such high regard was his accomplishments at E. F. Hutton. He had worked his way up from the bottom, joining Hutton in 1962 as a broker trainee and advancing to branch manager in 1967. At that time, Ball distinguished himself in what would become a turning point in his career.

A broker and margin clerk in Hutton's Beaumont, Texas, office had siphoned off millions of hard-earned dollars from the accounts of teachers, ministers, and working-class people. The small investors had trusted Hutton, and Hutton had betrayed them by stealing their money. To calm them, the firm sent Ball to clean up the public relations disaster. "The reason they sent me is that, although I was thirty years old at the time, I looked like a seventeen-year-old choirboy," Ball said. "I don't look like the sinister type."

At five feet eight inches and with a bantam build, Ball has strawberry-blond hair, pale blue eyes, and freckles. His unassuming manner, self-deprecating wit, and quick smile can disarm the most suspicious. Some people confuse his mild demeanor with an angelic submission, but that's a mistake. Still, his common touch and friendly, sincere demeanor project a wholesome image that Hutton managers used to their advantage.

In Beaumont, Ball listened to angry customers' complaints and nodded compassionately when they detailed their losses. He spent long hours convincing the townspeople that their problems would be solved, using charm, elbow grease, and his ability to inspire confidence in others. Within nine months, he turned the office around, regained the customers' respect for Hutton, and returned to New York. In 1969, he was promoted to regional vice president. In 1972, he became national sales manager, overseeing the sales efforts of the entire retail brokerage staff.

As a leader of salesmen, Ball was wired into the broker's psyche. In the 1970s, brokers were akin to rug merchants who hawked stocks and bonds over the telephone. Despite their job title, "securities" brokers operate in an insecure environment. The market can swing dramatically up or down in one day. The broker is the first one a customer criticizes when a recommended stock falls and the last one a customer praises when a stock increases in value. He or she gets rejected daily in cold calls, and is pressured by the manager to sell. A broker has no base salary, no pension, and no paid vacations. Benefits are few beyond whatever he or she negotiates in a limited contract. A broker's paycheck depends on his or her own attitude and drive, and that drive is propelled to a great degree by greed and money. But Ball knew that money is rarely enough to satisfy a good salesperson.

Ball's real genius was in selling salesmen to themselves. He elicited stellar performances from brokers by treating them as professional "account executives." He wrote them eloquent thank-you notes and congratulated them whenever they made significant sales. He knew the names of their spouses and children; he knew what sports their kids played. Whenever Ball traveled to a branch office, he'd study a chart of all the brokers in that office and memorize names, pictures, and some biographical data on each person until he had the details memorized. By the time Ball arrived at, say, the Dayton, Ohio, branch office, he'd be able to meet each broker for the first time, yet talk to him or her as though they had known each other for years. "Hi, Robert," Ball would say. "How's Betty? Is Bob Junior still playing football?" That kind of small talk leaves a tremendous impression on the rank and file, said former Pru-Bache broker Dick Hechmann. "When the CEO of a company gives a shit about you, you'll follow him anywhere."

Ball used his photographic memory to motivate his people. If he gave a fifteen-minute speech to everyone in the firm, he'd mention a hundred people by name. "Now, as Karen can tell you," he'd say, or "As Eddie knows," using names to personalize a point. The subtext of such a speech was that the boss *knew* what you were doing in your office, which served to motivate further the far-flung troops.

As Hutton's sales manager, Ball effectively took control of the entire firm's retail side and hired smart brokers whom he trained in public speaking, effective writing, self-development tools, and even personal grooming habits. Ball elevated their self-image to the point where Hutton's fifteen hundred brokers formed one elite, efficient machine widely admired in the industry.

In 1977, Ball became president of E. F. Hutton, which meant only that his job title changed. "It was simply an affirmation of what I had already been doing for years at the firm," said Ball. His entrepreneurial style swelled morale, which in turn increased productivity. By 1980, Hutton's productivity per broker was $168,000 and was growing faster than that of any other company in the industry. Ball's personal credo worked well at Hutton: if you treated people well, they'd reward you. "I did, and still do, believe that people are going to do the right thing in a well-balanced environment," he said.

Still, Ball was growing restless at Hutton, primarily because of his boss's increasing dysfunction. When Robert Fomon first became chief executive officer in 1970, he led the firm by being a good listener and a quick decision-maker and by surrounding himself with capable men. Hutton alumni included Frederick Joseph, who became CEO of Drexel Burnham (which would later be charged with securities fraud); John Shad, who went on to head the SEC; and Loren Schechter, the firm's attorney, who would in time become chief counsel at Pru-Bache Securities.

Fomon had come to depend on Ball to run the retail side of Hutton, but by 1980, Fomon's alcoholism had progressively worsened until he was an embarrassment to the firm. Fomon verbally abused Ball and the other executives, often yelling obscenities and outrageous accusations. "Did he ridicule me, as he did others? Yes," Ball said. "Did it bother me? Not really. I could have taken the suggestion of a number of people at the time and moved to replace Bob.

"But," he added, "in all fairness to Bob, he had encouraged me, promoted me, and championed me." Ball would not mount a palace coup.

Instead, Prudential approached him with an enticing offer. Ball could become CEO of a third-rate retail brokerage firm and build it into a potentially first-class operation. "I could take some satisfaction from that," he thought at the time. But Ball did not accept the job solely because of the title or challenge. Rather, Pru offered him an opportunity to operate PruCapital Inc., a $3 billion Pru financing subsidiary that served a thousand midsized companies with loans, investments, and investment banking services. Formed in 1981, the new unit combined the conglomerate's regional corporate finance departments, but it wasn't very profitable. It lent primarily to safe and plodding utilities and industrial firms and pocketed the small difference between what its funds cost and what it collected in interest. It was a straight lender.

Ball saw that PruCap could be more profitable if it diversified. PruCap could be both an investment banking arm and a business bank, which was something no other firm on the Street could boast. Pru-Bache brokers could market the subsidiary's services to its corporate clients and so add value to the firm's lackluster investment banking unit.

When Ball joined Pru-Bache in July 1982—almost a year after Prudential had purchased Bache—brokers were elated. "The Pru was making the statement that they were serious about being in the big leagues," said one former director of Bache. Since the day when Pru acquired Bache in 1981, little had changed at the brokerage, and it had appeared to many that the acquisition had never occurred.

Initially, Pru let Bache leaders run their own shop. Chairman Harry Jacobs and president H. Virgil Sherrill were told to focus on strengthening management. Prudential's Garnett Keith told a reporter in 1982: "We were getting a management team that was conservative, that had some trouble digesting acquisitions, and that was spending a lot of time on things other than running the brokerage business. Our conclusion was that Harry and Virg . . . were men of integrity with whom we could work."

Jacobs was a man of his own convictions. An active Democrat and a former Air Force flight instructor, he had been the favorite of Harold Bache. "Harry [Jacobs] has a lot of wisdom and common sense," said a former director. He didn't follow fashion or imitate trends. He once wore red plaid golf pants to a company banquet, and later he ignored the tuxedo dress code at a Pru cocktail party. Instead, he wore a sensible suit and straight tie. He had spent most of his career at Bache headquarters and had a simple, perhaps naive, style of management. "If the market had two down days, Harry started putting twenty-five-watt bulbs in sixty-watt light sockets to save money," said a former executive.

Sherrill, on the other hand, is dapper, even something of a dandy. Born in California, he earned a law degree from Yale University. He and his wife, an interior designer who inherited wealth, belong to Manhattan's town-and-country set, and their names occasionally appear in social columns. Despite the different styles of these two men, they were best friends. After selling Bache, they worked closely to fulfill the new parent company's mandate, but within the year, Prudential executives grew disenchanted with their efforts. "Those two guys just couldn't manage change," said a former executive. To be fair, Keith was becoming more preoccupied with other matters at Pru headquarters. And besides, in 1982, Bache was just one of many multimillion-dollar investments the company had on its books. To manage the new subsidiary, Pru reached outside its own house to find the best man for the job. It picked Ball.

When Ball joined Pru, Hutton was devastated by its loss. Although Ball had told his Hutton colleagues that he was considering Prudential's offer, he hadn't told them that he had accepted it. Hutton learned of Ball's decision only after Prudential had announced his appointment as CEO of the Bache Group. Bache was ecstatic, but it would be another year or so before any major changes would be made.

———————

When regional director Jim Trice heard about Ball's arrival, he was impressed. "Any change is good, as we need new leadership," he had told himself at the time. Then, a few days later, his secretary said George Ball was on the line.

"Jim, this is George Ball. I'm just calling to introduce myself and say hi."

"Well, hey," Trice said, in his Texan twang. "Welcome to the firm. I'm delighted that Prudential has decided to bring in new senior management, and I wish you every success."

"Thank you, Jim," Ball said. "I just want to ask you one question."

"What's that, sir?"

"How did you get to work in such a great place as San Diego?"

Trice laughed. "That's where I told them I wanted to move the regional office. And that's where I moved it."

"Good move." Ball paused, then launched into business.

"I'm going to tell you what I've told the others," he began. "One of my perceptions is that Bache is a good firm that stagnated because it didn't try anything. You can't do much of anything right unless you try. You might make mistakes, but you'll never know unless you try."

Trice didn't say anything.

Ball continued: "If you're working on any project, assume you've got my approval. Don't stop. Just keep me informed. If you're building the region, go out and do it and make some mistakes if you have to. A year from now, we'll take a look at the successes and the misses and tally up the scorecard."

It was the best news Trice could have heard. He had wanted to build the West Coast, and now had the approval of the new chief.

Ball didn't direct the brokerage firm's expansion, other than to encourage and fund it. During this time, he was credited with single-handedly racheting up Wall Street salaries by launching a bidding war for talent. "He was the Father of Front Money," joked one executive.

But Ball didn't pay that much more than the going rate, he said, and his up-front money—the onetime signing bonus used to lure brokers inside—was at most 10 to 15 percent more than what other firms offered at the time. Indeed, many firms offer high up-front money at various stages in their history. In Pru's case, Ball deliberately let the market believe that he was paying top dollar. "We did nothing to discourage that perception, because that perception helped us attract new brokers."

Within two years, Ball more than quadrupled the retail force from 1,100 to 4,700 brokers. The number of branches grew 30 percent to 310.

Where once Bache had had a negligible presence in the West, it soon was a powerhouse. In 1981, the region had sixteen offices scattered across two time zones and eight states, which produced only $35 million in gross revenues. When Trice took over that year, he added seventeen more offices, and two years later the region had grown so large he had to split it with another manager. In March 1983, the West was divided into Pacific South, where Trice reigned as regional manager, and Pacific North, where new hire and Hutton alumnus Carrington Clark managed. Over the next three years, the two men would increase the region's sales to $136 million annually—four times higher than in 1981.

The two Western regional managers were as different as, say, Los Angeles and San Francisco. Trice eschewed alcohol and drank sodas and juices. His Texas drawl was slow and even, and he rarely got excited. He liked to play the role of the hayseed country boy, although he was brighter than that role allowed. He usually wore bland colors and polyester fibers and didn't own a hat.

Whereas Trice had a reputation as a family man married to an invalid, it was widely known that Clark was a ladies' man. Clark had a slight Boston brogue, talked fast, and often exclaimed "Perfect!" during conversations, thus earning the nickname "Mr. Perfect." He drank Cape Cods (vodka and cranberry juice) and kept his office refrigerator stocked with fine wines and imported beers. A natty dresser, he often appeared in unconventional outfits, as when he turned up at a regional sales meeting wearing emerald-green pants, an orange golf shirt, a paisley sport coat, Gucci loafers, no socks, and a shocking-pink ten-gallon Stetson hat. His regional sales seminars often allotted free afternoons for play and always scheduled a party in the evenings.

These two men built up the West Coast, calling each other almost daily for advice. They hired some of the company's best branch managers, who in turn oversaw many of the firm's most aggressive and productive salespeople. In time, the West became the biggest and fastest-growing franchise in Pru-Bache's empire.

At Bache headquarters on Gold Street, Ball's honeymoon ended in a frenzy of change. He cut Bache's two boards of directors to one, stripped Jacobs and Sherrill of their power, and fired five top executives and a layer of fifteen unproductive managers. He threw out the business-as-usual code, as well as the firm's old name.

"From the moment I met [Ball], I knew that one day I'd be working for Pru Securities," said Gary Zahn, a broker in metropolitan New York. "He denied it, but it was very clear we'd have our own identity." Ball polled brokers to give them a choice in the new name. "Almost every broker didn't want Bache to lose its identity," said Zahn. "We believed that Prudential was a Midwest name; Prudential didn't sell well in New York, and insurance had the reputation of being ultraconservative, waspy, and starched," he said. "If you went to the Midwest, everybody owned a Pru policy. But when you came out here to New York, we owned everything."

The brokers voted for "Bache-Prudential Securities"; Ball wanted "Prudential Securities"; the result was "Prudential-Bache Securities." The name change cost about $4 million in new stationery, forms, and signage costs and another $3 million in advertising. New plants were stuck in the firm's lobby and linen towels were hung in the men's lavatories.

Inside Bache, Ball put together his own cabinet of advisers culled from Bache and Hutton. Former Hutton attorney Loren Schechter joined Ball to serve as his right-hand man and Pru-Bache's top corporate counsel; another Hutton man became Pru-Bache's research chief. He, in turn, hired more Hutton analysts to build the research department, which was crucial to Pru-Bache's effort to become a top-notch broker-dealer.

Research analysts study industries, firms, and the market in order to recommend investment strategies for clients. At Pru-Bache, high-quality research reports began to attract big institutions, such as banks, insurance companies, labor unions, and other entities that trade big blocks of stock. Institutions brought business to Pru-Bache's corporate finance unit because its analysts' opinions were respected by investors, who followed the advice. Positive research opinions on a company can run up its stock price and so benefit the profiled firm, enrich the stock investor who follows that advice, and improve the brokerage firm, which earns commission. Also, institutions sometimes need to raise money, so when that time arrives, they would probably ask Pru-Bache to be their investment banker. All of this ancillary business stemmed from Ball's hiring a strong research director. In no time, the firm's institutional sales, as opposed to retail sales, jumped from nowhere to the sixth-biggest trader of stocks, or equity.

Ball also streamlined the brokerage firm into a few reporting units, and he kept many of the original Bache leaders. Robert Sherman remained head of retail (under him, James Darr would remain head of direct investments); Sherrill headed investment banking; Jacobs supervised the bond traders; Lee Paton oversaw equity traders; Al Hogan oversaw finance and administration; and Guy Wyser-Pratte continued to run arbitrage. George McGough, James Glynn, and Peter Barton wouldn't remain long, but most of these men remained with Ball until the late 1980s.

One other significant change took place. When Ball arrived, he found Bache's back office antiquated and desperately in need of a computerized system. The back office collects and stores accounting records, monitors compliance with government regulations, and transmits communications between branches and headquarters. It's crucial to a smooth-running network. In 1982, the securities firm installed a sophisticated new system in its branch offices and modernized its back office. One former accountant at Pru-Bache who worked at the firm at the time estimated that the installation cost about $500 million. That figure would be spread over a few years, but the enormous cost would add to the already-ballooning expenses of new hires and new offices. According to one investment banker with knowledge of Pru's investment, the total cost of all this expansion was nearly $1 billion.

When Prudential bought Bache it had saved the firm from death. Now Ball was rehabilitating the company, but at a steep price. To pay the enormous bill, Pru-Bache would have to generate enormous profits.

The question was, how?

5

Bull Markets and Phantom Expenses

In April 1983, Mike Kudlik had to find a new job. Kudlik had the smooth skin and flat, even features of his Ukrainian grandparents. He was stocky, with big hands and brown eyes. But on this afternoon, the man's features were clouded, as was his future.

For six years, he had worked at Dean Witter, making friends with the brokers in the Southern region, which was based in Atlanta. Kudlik had been responsible for helping all the brokers in that region sell as many tax shelters as possible. By 1983, after six years with the company, his success was unassailable; his region was number one in Dean Witter's entire territory.

The firm had recently been acquired by Sears Roebuck & Co., the Midwest-based retailer. Customers at the time had ribbed brokers about buying "stocks with their socks"; the image of the New York–based brokerage house had faded now that it was owned by a onetime farmers' catalog company. Employees like Kudlik were unsure of how well their jobs would fare under the new order.

But that was not the issue nagging Kudlik that April afternoon. Rather, he was upset that since he had been so successful in his job, the firm was about to cut his pay. His new boss had informed him that his compensation was too high, relative to that of other regional heads of tax shelters; never mind that his region outsold the others. To whittle his take-home pay, Dean Witter was about to shrink his region, which, to Kudlik's way of thinking, wasn't fair. So he had gone looking for another job.

Kudlik, of course, had heard about the Pru-Bache marriage and the appointment of George Ball as its new chief. "Wow!" he had thought at the time. "What a classy organization that will be." When he heard about the firm's aggressive expansion in the West, the Brooklyn man had to learn more. He had once worked in California and had been captivated by the La Jolla area, south of Los Angeles. He dreamed of living there.

He wasted little time arranging an interview with Jack Graner, who at the time was Pru-Bache's regional director of the Southeast in Atlanta. Kudlik knew that Graner could recommend him for the West Coast job; he resolved to impress this guy Graner. Kudlik at the time was a once-divorced, single guy with an ego inflated by his success. So when he dressed in his best suit for the interview and showed up promptly at the Pru-Bache regional office, he was confident he would get the job. He waited in the lobby, for fifteen minutes . . . for thirty minutes . . . reading magazines on the couch. Forty-five minutes after his scheduled appointment, he was ushered in to see Graner.

Graner looked haggard and overworked. He had sprained his wrist in a skiing accident and was wearing a cast. He chain-smoked unfiltered Camels, and although it was nearly four o'clock, he drank fresh coffee from a large mug. Graner coughed and leaned back in his chair.

"So, tell me a little something about yourself, Mike."

Kudlik sat ramrod-straight in his chair and recited his resumé. He listed his prior positions and his commission numbers. He detailed the tax shelters he had sold and described which ones he thought were best and why. Then he asked some questions.

"Mr. Graner, what type of products is Prudential-Bache packaging?"

"Oh, you know. A little of this, a little of that."

"Well, how are they structured?"

"Pretty much the same as everybody else's."

"What are your front-end fees like?"

"Like the front end of a doll."

Kudlik blinked. He thought to himself: "Maybe this guy has had a rough week." Kudlik tried asking a few more basic questions about limited partnerships, but Graner kept batting back evasive answers. It was clear to Kudlik that Graner didn't know the industry well. After five more minutes, Graner got up and shook Kudlik's hand warmly.

"Mike, thanks a lot for stopping by. We'll get back to you soon."

The entire interview had lasted fifteen minutes. Kudlik drove back to Dean Witter somewhat disillusioned. He wasn't going to get the job, he thought. His hope of returning to California was now just a dream.

But a few days later, Jim Darr, the head of the direct investment group, telephoned Kudlik and told him to fly to New York for an interview. Kudlik agreed. But after he hung up the phone, the palms of his hands turned damp and clammy. He'd see this Darr fellow and talk about his LP sales force. But he wasn't sure he wanted to join their club.

By the spring of 1983, stock fever was sweeping Wall Street, and the symptoms were everywhere. One could be spotted on the floor of the New York Stock Exchange, where an enormous bull was stirring, beginning a long, thrilling stampede up the market's chart. The bull run would be remembered for years to come. Just the previous summer, the Dow had stood at an anemic 700 points. Now the market was about to reach 1200, and its powerful climb caused a few market analysts to wax prosaic. "Not since the days of [bullfighters] Manolete, Ordóñez, and Escamillo had there been such a powerful brute. Straight and true it charged. Head down, powerful and regal," wrote one analyst at Legg Mason Wood Walker.

Outside the trading floor, life was equally giddy. On one spring afternoon that year, a five-piece jazz combo played tunes under the sculptured pediment of the Stock Exchange. Thousands of people milled around booths and tables as vendors barked out their wares: Maine lobsters, sausage sandwiches, Oriental rugs, psychedelic drugs.

The venerable Manhattan thoroughfare had been transformed into an Istanbul bazaar, which was appropriate, given all the exotic financial products that were flooding the market. Thanks to deregulation, tax laws, and savvy marketing, a slew of nontraditional products were booming on Wall Street. Brokerage firms were now selling Individual Retirement Accounts (IRAs), Keoghs, mutual funds, future funds, money market funds, real-estate partnerships—and limited partnerships.

Arguably, the riskiest and most complicated of these were limited partnerships. LPs had been around since the 1960s, when the federal government created them as a way to spur building and development. Basically, an LP allows an individual to invest in a piece of a hard asset such as a hotel, an oil well, or an airplane. It differs from a paper asset, such as stock in a publicly traded company, because one invests "directly" in a tangible asset—such as real estate, oil and gas, timber, equipment, cattle, or even films. Compared to stocks, LPs are exotic. "What better way to actually own a hotel or oil well?" said one salesman.

In the seventies, LPs enjoyed more tax benefits than other businesses. For example, a corporation's income was taxed twice: once on its profits, and again on any dividends it paid. However, companies configured as limited partnerships were not taxed as an entity, although their investors were taxed on their gains.

"It took a while to generate consumer interest in these investments, but by the late 1970s, Wall Street saw that LPs were something that they could really market and sell," said Keith Allaire, executive vice president of the *Robert A. Stanger & Co.,* which tracks LPs.

The brokerages began to act as middlemen between the sponsors—or general partners in the deals—and the limited partners, who funded them. Through a brokerage house's branch network, it tapped a pipeline of cash from customers—many of whom wanted LPs. As "placement agents," the brokerages assigned a group within the firm to do nothing but structure and market LPs, for a fee. Whether the department was called the tax-advantaged investment unit or a direct investment group (DIG)—as it was at Pru-Bache—nearly every big brokerage firm had such a division in the 1980s.

The beauty of the LP vehicle was that investors didn't worry about the day-to-day operations of the property. The general partner took care of that. In the case of Pru-Bache's products, the general partner (GP) was the person or company that supposedly was expert in the field. The GP managed the asset, made daily decisions, gathered money, invested it, kept the books, reported results, and distributed profits to limited partners. For its trouble, it collected fees and a percent of any income that flowed from the asset.

Although the GP had more control over the investment, it also had more liability. It was responsible for all the losses, debts, and obligations incurred by the asset. Limited partners, on the other hand, had no say in daily decisions, but they also had no liability. Thus they had "limited" exposure or risk in the venture; the most they could lose was their original investment.

Yet the risk of that was substantial. The underlying assets in an LP are more volatile than, say, the shares of Pacific Gas & Electric. LP assets are subject to fickle elements, including market cycles, economic trends, and politics. If real estate crashes, so will your real-estate-based LP. If the director runs off with the starlet before the film is wrapped, your movie LP may be worthless.

In return for taking such risks, limited partners could realize income and big capital gains. This was particularly true in the late 1970s and early 1980s, when inflation swelled, interest rates rose to 20 percent, and income tax brackets were as high as 70 percent.

Inflation pumped up the value of hard assets, such as oil wells and real estate. In 1980, the median price of a home in California climbed 18 percent. The double-digit rise in real estate continued unabated until 1988, when, for example, the average sales price of a Hawaiian home jumped 40 percent. "Nobody in the early 1980s believed that property values would ever fall," said one broker. "LPs in real estate were seen as fantastic investments."

But the real kicker to the LP deals was the generous tax benefits. Thanks to the Internal Revenue Service, a wealthy investor could not go wrong buying an LP in 1981 or 1982. Even after 1982, when the government lowered high-income tax brackets from 70 percent to 50 percent, an investor could still enjoy hefty tax savings.

The IRS allowed taxpayers to use depreciation, which was a "phantom expense." Although no cash was spent, taxpayers could declare depreciation to show they had lost, or spent, money on an asset; thus the "write-off." Depreciation didn't lower income, but it lowered taxable income through write-offs. The standard depreciation method spread write-offs over a fifteen-year period, but one could realize big write-offs during the first few years of buying a certain type of asset, such as real estate and oil properties. The rules varied.

Suppose a plastic surgeon who earns $1.2 million a year buys a $200,000 unit in a real-estate-based LP. He pays for his LP in four installments. The first year, he writes a check for $50,000 and is allowed to write off $200,000 from his taxable income. Now he is taxed on only $1 million at the 50 percent rate. That means the surgeon has just saved himself $100,000 in taxes—or 50 percent of the total allowable $200,000 write-off.

The second year, he makes a second $50,000 payment and takes a $125,000 write-off—and saves $62,500 in taxes. The third year, he makes another $50,000 payment for a $75,000 write-off. In year four, he pays his last $50,000 payment and takes only a $50,000 write-off.

The wealthy investor has now paid $200,000 for a sound investment and has received $450,000 in write-offs. In other words, he has received a $2.50 write-off for every dollar he invested. Since the plastic surgeon is in the 50 percent tax bracket, he saves himself $212,000 in taxes— or more than his initial $200,000 outlay.

"Buying an LP was like getting free money," said one broker. "You just couldn't lose."

The write-offs made the tax shelters so popular, people clamored for them. "We used to sell out in one hour," said a secretary who worked at Pru-Bache's DIG at the time. "In 1982, we could sell a $15 million deal just like that. It was amazing to watch how quickly they'd sell."

Nothing was inherently wrong with the LPs, so long as inflation kept aloft and the tax laws didn't change. But in 1982, the tax code did change, the IRS having realized the loophole it had created with loose depreciation rules. The Tax Equity and Fiscal Responsibility Act (TEFRA) prohibited overly "aggressive" or "abusive" write-offs, marking them as tax shelters. People who now owned tax shelters suddenly had their tax returns scrutinized; some were found to owe back taxes, interest, and penalties.

But in general, the types of LPs sold by Pru-Bache did not fall into this "abusive" category. LP holders could still enjoy legal write-offs, depending on the type of asset. You could write off $2 for every $1 invested in real-estate LPs and about $1 per $1 invested in oil.

For placement agents such as Pru-Bache, there were only three cardinal rules. Number one: Find a good, solid asset manager as your general partner. Number two: Make sure the general partner invests in sound underlying assets. Number three: Do your due diligence, or homework, before presenting the deals to customers.

Due diligence was key to the LP's success. If the firm didn't know exactly what it was selling—and with whom—it could be harshly reprimanded, and sued. Before offering an LP for sale, Pru-Bache's direct investment group had to make sure that, say, the proposed development was sound and that the GP was legitimate. What was the GP's background? Was the GP financially sound? If the GP was a former felon, the agent probably shouldn't do business with him. If the GP planned to develop a resort on a toxic dump, instead of the meadow he described over cocktails last night, the placement agent should walk away.

Federal regulators consider due diligence so crucial to the market's integrity that it's described in the Securities Act of 1933. Due diligence occurs on many levels. A sponsor such as Pru-Bache must complete economic and regulatory diligence to ensure that all claims are legal and correct. It must check the background of the GP and thoroughly study the properties in the offering. The broker-dealer must also determine that customers have a "reasonable chance" to profit from the deal.

But given the sterling reputation of Pru-Bache's parent, due diligence didn't appear to be a problem in 1983. Prudential Insurance Co. of America was not only the world's largest private owner of real estate, it managed billions of dollars of other people's money for pensions, unions, colleges, trusts, endowments, governments, and institutions. "Our consolidated portfolio of bonds, stocks, mortgages, real estate, and other investments exceeded $66 billion at the end of 1982, making us the largest investor in the insurance industry and one of the largest in the world," the Pru stated in its 1983 annual report.

The Pru went a step further and endorsed Pru-Bache's LP product. That year, three high-level Prudential officers joined the board and oversaw the limited partnerships sponsored by Graham Energy, a tiny Louisiana oil-drilling firm. The Pru thought so highly of this fund—the Pru-Bache Energy Income Fund—that it invested its own money in the public deal. Pru-Bache brokers boasted that its LPs were backed by the Rock, the world's biggest private money manager.

By the summer of 1983, Pru-Bache had an advantage that no other house on the Street could claim. Its parent was a world-class investor that backed its LP products. Buoyed by this affiliation, Pru-Bache barely squeaked into the top-ten list of all public LP fund-raisers that year. It sold its first significant number of public LPs—some $208 million worth—and ranked tenth, behind brokerage firms Merrill Lynch and E. F. Hutton.

LPs would help George Ball fund the growth at Pru-Bache, which was becoming expensive. The generous signing and other bonuses he gave brokers who joined the firm, the upgrading of the back office, and the other expensive talent Ball had brought to the firm began to add up. The direct investment group was one way for Ball to pay for the expansion.

LPs brought more money to the firm, as well as to the broker. Selling an LP was more lucrative than selling a stock, even in the bull market. For example, if a broker sold $100,000 worth of ABC stock, he would earn a commission of maybe 1 percent—$1,000—and pocket only $500. If he sold a $100,000 unit of a limited partnership, however, he could bring to the house as much as $8,000, $4,000 of which would end up in his pocket. With commissions of 7 and 8 percent, limited partnerships sales were seven or eight times more profitable to sell than common stock. Given the choice between the two, a broker would probably choose to sell LPs.

So too would Pru-Bache, as the firm received a bigger commission also; it earned $4,000 for every $100,000 LP unit. At the time, LPs seemed like an excellent way to fund the firm's aggressive growth.

Despite his experience in selling LPs, Mike Kudlik was not prepared for Pru-Bache's style in promoting its products. About a week into his new position as product coordinator of the Pacific South region, he flew to New York to join the rest of the regional coordinators. He met the DIG staff during its three-day quarterly meeting.

On a July afternoon, the DIG staff had assembled in the cramped lobby at 100 Gold Street. Darr reported on second-quarter sales and detailed how Pru-Bache was building its sales efforts. Sponsors discussed the status of their projects and talked about new projects they wanted Pru-Bache to sell for them. Darr introduced Mike Kudlik and Larry Forness, who was the new regional "product coordinator" in the Pacific North.

"We're glad to have these guys on board," Darr had told the group. "They're going to roll our products out in the West, and we will be the biggest force out there." He intended to head the biggest LP sales force on the Street, but Pru-Bache had a way to go. In 1982, Merrill Lynch was by far leading all brokerage firms, having sold $216 million worth of public LPs. E. F. Hutton was a close second with $169 million, and Pru-Bache didn't even have a comparable public LP sales figure. It was selling primarily small, private LPs, such as $10 million offerings, consisting of no more than thirty-five individual limited partners.

That afternoon, Darr had made it clear that he wanted to blow the other competitors out of the water. Pru-Bache was going to be the best, the biggest, the most powerful placement agent on the Street, and that was just fine with Kudlik.

What astounded him was the evening that followed. As was its practice after every quarterly meeting, the eighty-person staff met for dinner at Smith & Wollensky, located at 49th Street and Third Avenue. Squat, big, and red, the New York steak house had a private room upstairs. The restaurant had been open for only about seven years, but already it counted Pru-Bache's group among its regular customers.

That night, the group met upstairs in the long banquet room, lit by skylights and soft lamps. Darr and Sherman usually presided over the celebration. Amidst plates of Maine lobster and grilled Colorado steak, men and women reveled for hours, ordering so many shooters, chasers, and scotch-and-waters that inevitably someone would tumble down the stairs drunk with the evening's excess. Sometimes the sound of a man falling down the wooden steps couldn't be heard by those upstairs. Peals of laughter and bawdy singing muffled the outside noise.

No spouses were allowed at these soirées, but the evenings frequently turned amorous. Some senior male executives groped female secretaries, women hiccupped and slurred words, and couples grappled with one another silently in chairs and corners. Entire $150 plates of food sat untouched; $100 bottles of wine lay uncorked but full. Glasses were broken and smashed. Cigarettes burned through white tablecloths. People passed out on the floor. In the wee hours of the morning, many of the men slunk off to hotels with their girlfriends in tow.

Once a stripper was hired at a mixed-company event to celebrate the birthdays of two executives. Wearing a G-string and earrings, the entertainer eventually bared her breasts and shook them in the face of the celebrants. Many women left the room in disgust as their bosses hooted and howled.

Such occasions became routine for DIG during the mid-1980s. Kudlik and the others grew accustomed to the parties, and often left before midnight. But many of the sponsors who paid for the $40,000 blowouts objected. The president of Polaris was reportedly aghast at what he saw on his first visit; a Graham executive objected to ordering expensive dinners that went uneaten. "Everybody would get a hunk of prime rib that a pro football player couldn't eat, plus a three-pound lobster," said F. Paul Grattarola, a former president of Graham Securities, part of Graham Energy. "It was disgusting to see so much food go to waste."

The men who sponsored these dinners felt foolish when asked by Pru-Bache officers to stand up and entertain the mixed crowd with dirty jokes. "It was like a college fraternity hazing," said Grattarola. After a while, Grattarola's complaints about the bacchanalian affairs and their expense annoyed the DIG officers so much that they asked him to stay away from the dinners altogether. Instead, they said, just mail in your check to pay the bill, which the sponsors did.

And the bills for such parties would climb higher, along with the astonishing success of the direct investment group.

6

Marketeers and Buccaneers
on the Thirty-Third Floor

P U T some lipstick on," Darr yelled into a woman's office. He scowled, then walked away.

The woman sighed and reached wearily for her purse. She didn't feel pretty today, but appearances mattered to her boss, the chief of the direct investment group. He expected the women in his office to be attractive and outgoing. She uncapped her lipstick and did as she'd been told; she wasn't about to stand up to a boss whom others called God.

Born in the winter of 1945, James John Darr was a stocky man, the son of a shoe salesman. Darr said he had good, solid Midwestern parents who believed in the ethic of hard work. Educated by the Jesuits from the College of the Holy Cross in Worcester, Massachusetts, Darr graduated in 1968 with a degree in history and philosophy. He joined the ROTC during the last two years in college; in the fall of 1968, he signed up for active duty with the Air Force and moved to Hill Air Force Base in Ogden, Utah. While there, he enrolled as a graduate student at the University of Utah's Middle Eastern Studies Department. In the summer of 1970, he received a graduate certificate, not a degree, from the interdisciplinary program, which offered classes in Persian, or Farsi—Iran's spoken language.

"He was an incredible bullshitter who used to brag that he'd had so many jobs he should be seventy-five years old," said one man with whom Darr worked. Darr claimed he had worked at Rand Corp., a prestigious think tank in Santa Monica, California; he had said he was an Air Force pilot; he had fought in Vietnam; he had worked undercover for the Central Intelligence Agency. None of his stories could be verified, and some years later Darr denied ever making such claims. Indeed, in a 1991 deposition, Darr wouldn't list these jobs as part of his professional résumé. Still, he wove a mysterious macho image.

His real life was somewhat more plebeian. During his four years in the military, he worked in the matériels warehouse on base. He was promoted to captain in 1971 and earned two commendation medals, "which are pretty routine," said a spokesperson; Darr's other award— for small-arms marksmanship—"simply meant he could shoot a gun," the spokesman added. Darr remained with the Air Force Reserve until 1980.

In 1972, he worked for Management Recruits in Boston, and then another firm in the same field, he said. In 1975, Darr joined Merrill Lynch's stockbroker trainee program and became a licensed salesman. He rose to become a product manager who pitched Merrill's limited partnerships to brokers, who, in turn, sold them to customers. In 1977, he joined the small securities brokerage firm of Josephthal, where he became head of the LP division. While at Josephthal, Darr received at least two personal payments from company clients, including a $30,000 check in March 1978. Darr cashed a check shortly before he bought a home in Stamford, Connecticut, and right before his daughter was born. He later returned the money to his employer, but received half of it back again; $15,000, which was an unusually high fee for the type of services he had rendered. Payments of any kind from sponsors must be disclosed to investors; these were not. Years later, Darr claimed he had handled these matters appropriately, yet the chairman of Josephthal said he didn't know about the payments, and if he had, he wouldn't have permitted them.

By December 1979, Darr had left Josephthal to join Bache and run its nascent tax shelter division. Whispers of illegal payments followed him, and in 1980, Bache investigated Darr's alleged kickbacks from sponsors who did business with his former employer. Such personal payments are illegal when hidden from investors and certainly unethical when disclosed.

One senior Bache officer involved in the investigation remembered its outcome. "I know we did a thorough review, and that something came out of it," he said in an interview. But Bache officers gave Darr the benefit of the doubt, concluding that no wrongdoing had occurred, even though employees openly questioned the ethics of their new boss. "We asked Darr to take a polygraph test," said the officer. "We told him, 'Hey, just take the polygraph test. We'll give you a list of questions, you can study them, and then take the test. It won't take you but two hours. You can clear this stuff up and be done with it.' "

However, a Bache executive intervened on Darr's behalf. The officer said that Darr never took the test and kept his job. Darr said he was never asked to take a polygraph test and was told to fire the person spreading the allegations.

Now, some four years later, Darr was firmly ensconced as the chief of DIG. Mike Kudlik, product coordinator in the Pacific South, remembered his first meeting with Darr. Kudlik had traveled to New York for the job interview and arrived on time. He waited in the lobby, and after a while, William Pittman, one of Darr's lieutenants, came out to greet him. Pittman and another man ushered Kudlik into Darr's office. Darr didn't rise to shake Kudlik's hand; he remained seated behind his desk, reclining in his chair. "He was not warm, but aristocratic," said Kudlik. Darr motioned to an empty chair; Kudlik sat. One of the men stood behind Kudlik, who listened as Darr talked. Kudlik liked what he heard that day: "It was clear to me that this guy wanted to run the best, biggest tax shelter department on the Street."

Darr dressed well but conservatively, wearing the same style of navy suit nearly every day, along with a white shirt and subdued tie. His suits were tailored; Darr was not the kind of man who wore bow ties, suspenders, or pink shirts, although such garb was stylish on Wall Street in the 1980s. He strongly objected to having his picture taken. Darr said his goals at Pru-Bache were to do a good job and earn the respect of his superiors.

By 1984, Darr was a thirty-eight-year-old married man with gray hair. Members of his inner circle called him "the guy with the curly white hair." He looked ten years older than he really was, but, in his own territory, he often acted years younger.

Some women claimed he flirted blatantly with them in the office, using double entendres as his opening. "My, you look good today. Are you for lunch?" he'd say to a woman, with a wink. He teased one particular woman for months. She had dodged his invitations to meet for lunch, dinner, or drinks until one day she couldn't refuse any longer without overtly insulting him. Over lunch, he asked her seriously: "Aren't you getting tired of these word games? Ready to move on to something else?" She shook her head; sometime later, she quit.

Darr was cautious not to ask a woman out on a date in so many words. "He didn't want to get rejected," said one woman. Still, his not-so-subtle advances were notoriously well known and often were rebuffed. Said one: "He always wanted to get in my pants; he told me so many times. In fact, he told me during salary reviews that he would pay me more money and bigger bonuses if I would sleep with him." She never did. Darr later denied making any such propositions.

Such unprofessional behavior was par for the course for women. "Every time I hear about a sexual harassment case today, I just laugh," said one woman. "There was so much of that going on [at Pru-Bache] that if we stopped to file a claim for every time those guys hit on us, we'd have to stop working." Such treatment of women may have been common on Wall Street, but the sexual conduct at Pru-Bache was "absolutely aggressive and out of line," said a male veteran. "It was disgusting and often embarrassing. But it stemmed from top management, so how could you deal with it?"

Sexual innuendos and gender put-downs were viewed as jokes, and a "girl" had to take it or leave; a few well-qualified professional women finally left.

At times, the gender games turned ugly. Pittman, for example, verbally abused his secretary frequently, calling her "peon," "stupid," "paralyzed," and "bitch." Said one woman: "To this day, I think she believes that she is stupid." Locker-room language was common, although the talk frequently mortified the women who worked at DIG.

In his division, Darr prized loyalty above all else. He was kind and generous to the people who were loyal to him. After a longtime female employee had returned from a doctor's appointment, she was depressed upon learning she had a potentially life-threatening problem. She told her supervisor the bad news, and a few minutes later, Darr came into her office to commiserate. Unintentionally, he offended the woman by saying, basically, that here she was, an old maid about to die without a husband. "How bad can life get?" he asked the woman, who was younger than Darr.

Appalled at his insensitivity, she threw him out of her office. He returned a short time later, "his tail between his legs," a solution in hand. Through contacts, he had arranged for her to visit five doctors in the next two days at one of New York's most prestigious hospitals. Within a week, she underwent a successful operation. Darr called her at home while she was recuperating and told her to take the next week off to rest. Then he told her to pack for Switzerland and join some other DIG members who had qualified for an incentive trip.

"But he didn't want me to tell anybody about this," she said. He feared that others would discover his softhearted side and mistake it for weakness. That would destroy his carefully drawn dark and threatening image. "He managed by fear and intimidation."

By 1984, that style was working well. Darr had built the division into a prime revenue producer and was growing more powerful. Basically, DIG was responsible for creating the investment products that retail brokers sold to the public, and it performed two main functions. First, it located or originated solid, financially sound deals that passed the hurdles of "due diligence" tests and so qualified as good investments. Its second function was to market the product so that the brokers could easily and successfully sell the LP units to investors while remaining within the SEC's rules. A third task was to manage the LP assets.

The department's due diligence side employed young people who were expert in scrutinizing real-estate and oil deals. One man had recently graduated from the M.B.A. program at Harvard University, another from a similar program at Wharton. The two newcomers were initially thrilled to be working for Pru-Bache, although their enthusiasm would dim after a bizarre encounter with a senior officer.

One afternoon, the two were discussing a deal when Bill Pittman walked into the office. He interrupted to discuss an issue with the first man while the second waited.

Suddenly, Pittman turned on the second man and barked, "Don't give me that wiseass college look." Dumbfounded, the two men realized that Pittman was jealous of their educations.

Said the second man: "I was so scared, I was shaking in my boots. The last thing I wanted was to make a bad impression on the boss. And yet here I was getting in trouble for having some kind of 'look' on my face. I didn't know what he was talking about."

Before leaving, Pittman smiled and patted the frightened man's shoulder. "Don't worry," he said. "You'll get used to me."

As a boss, Pittman was unstable, said numerous people who worked with him. His volatile temper was so well known at the firm that others avoided him. However, Darr promoted him because of his unflagging loyalty. Darr paid him close to $1 million a year, but often ridiculed Pittman to his face and to others. "He was the butt of a lot of Darr's jokes," said one ex-staff member.

The two men's relationship was always rocky. Once, Pittman berated a woman who said she couldn't copy a stack of papers as rapidly as he had demanded. "He exploded," she said. "He called me a bitch and pounded his fist on the desk as he ranted and raved. I thought he was going to climb over and strangle me. I was crying and shaking."

From his office next door, Darr repeatedly yelled to Pittman to leave the woman alone, but Pittman was too deep in rage to obey. Finally, Darr ran into Pittman's office and told the sobbing woman to leave. He then dressed down Pittman for throwing such a fit. Darr later confirmed that from time to time, when he saw people being overly critical of their subordinates, he had strong discussions with them.

Darr then walked out of Pittman's office and took aside the weeping woman.

"What the hell did you do to the guy?" he asked.

"Him?" She bawled louder. "What about me?"

While the other side of DIG Marketing appeared saner on some levels, on many others it was wilder. Marketing's job was to make it easy for the product coordinators such as Mike Kudlik to convince brokers that the LPs were a good deal for customers. It designed brochures and sales tools, organized contests, and offered incentives and awards, such as trips, all in an effort to cajole, support, and reward the brokers.

The two departments, due diligence and marketing, ideally should work together yet independently. The integrity of a deal shouldn't be swayed by sales hype or advertising copy. A deal should have financial merit on its own. At DIG, however, the system was inherently flawed because both sides of the room reported to the same person—James Darr.

The incentive to do any deal, no matter how inferior, was overpowering at that time, according to some due diligence officers. From 1981 to 1984, Pru-Bache had recorded either paltry profits or steep losses. The firm thirsted for income, and consumers hungered for tax write-offs: DIG satisfied both appetites. Said Dick Hechmann, an ex-salesman, "LPs were like heroin at the time. Investors couldn't get enough of them." Money was pouring in from the public.

LPs would sell out within the hour; $15 million worth of units would be gone in no time. This delighted officers at DIG, whose bonuses were based on a percent of the volume of deals they sold; they were *not* paid based on how well those deals performed for investors. In addition, bonuses were paid quarterly, not annually, so DIG offered instant gratification. Darr allocated increasingly larger pools of money as bonuses. The pool was well known throughout the firm, but few understood its criteria. Secretaries earning $15,000 a year recall their bosses earning $1 million or more.

Darr had invited a few dozen associates to share in money that was pooled from fees charged to all LPs. F. Paul Grattarola of Graham Securities said: "I know that every quarter we sent humongous checks." Those lucky enough to be part of the pool were said to be wearing "golden handcuffs"; the payments were so generous that pool members would find it hard to ever leave the employ of Pru-Bache. Darr said that staff people recommended how the bonus pool should be divided and that he, too, had some say-so in the system.

Kudlik once asked Darr, Pittman, and a marketing officer, Paul Proscia, how he, too, could get into the pool. "I begged, I pleaded, and asked how I could achieve getting into that inner circle," he said. His bosses only told him "that when the time is right, and when we feel good about it, you'll get in."

But everyone in DIG wanted some of the bonus money that stemmed from doing deals. "The bigger the sales, the bigger everybody's bonuses," said one former due diligence officer. Any person who cut into the sales effort—even to stop a bad deal—was unpopular.

The Securities Act of 1933, which was created to protect individual investors, set the standard for due diligence. It required that directors, officers, accountants, appraisers, and others who packaged a deal use the same diligence "required of a prudent man in the management of his own property." An investor should know all about his partners, the project, and the use of their funds.

"There's a natural tension between marketing and due diligence," said one DIG staffer. "A good firm needs those checks and balances." But those balances didn't exist at DIG, and prudent standards were flagrantly ignored. By 1984, the conflict sharpened between expert due diligence people, whose job was to question deals, and the marketing people, whose job was to sell as many deals as possible.

By 1984, a number of due diligence officers were convinced that some deals were being sold by Pru-Bache that should not be sold. "A few of us were dead set against doing any business with Clifton Harrison," said one man. "A tremendous number of real-estate developers wanted to access our retail department at the time. We could raise money, and they knew it. There was no good reason to do business with a guy like him."

Harrison was a Dallas developer who in 1967 had been convicted of embezzling bank funds; he had spent time in prison. Upon his release, he sold real estate and limited partnerships, building his moderate successes until he wended his way into Dallas's social circles. There he obtained enough character references from prominent people to apply for—and receive—a Presidential pardon from Gerald Ford in 1974. That pardon, some within DIG argued, erased his felony status. (A New York attorney general at the time agreed.) Therefore, it wasn't necessary to disclose his financial crime to investors who gave him their money.

But few people in due diligence agreed. Said one investment banker who formerly worked at Pru, "I have a five-minute rule. Anytime a person spends five minutes telling me why we should *not* disclose a material fact, we disclose it." Added a former DIG employee: "We thought that Harrison's past conviction should be mentioned in the prospectus." By law, a prospectus must include all the relevant details surrounding a general partner and the deal. "If the deals did fine, no one would care if he was a former felon," said the former DIG employee. "But if the deals did poorly, and we didn't fully disclose his background, we'd all be in real trouble."

Some years later, that's exactly what happened. Between 1981 and

1985, Pru-Bache customers would buy nearly $100 million of Harrison's thirteen private placement LPs. (Unlike public offerings, private deals are not registered with the SEC.) Most of those deals would sour or need restructuring. Ironically, when the deals went bad, the fact that Pru-Bache had hid Harrison's criminal past from investors produced numerous lawsuits against the firm—just as the due diligence people had warned.

"At the time, it was a judgment call," said one officer. "Now it's a mess."

Bache had first embraced Harrison in 1981, the same month that Prudential Insurance had announced its purchase of Bache. At that time, marketing officer Paul Proscia had outlined how Harrison, with his European deals and experience in LPs, could bolster Bache's sales. Darr had agreed, although plenty of men and women at Pru-Bache would later scratch their heads over that decision.

A few years later, Pru-Bache investors in a Harrison deal would claim in a lawsuit that "officers and representatives of [Pru-Bache's] direct-investment group received a series of kickbacks, bribes, and other unlawful inducements and compensations from principals" associated with the deal. Harrison denied making any such payments and no DIG member was named, but other investors would repeat similiar claims in later lawsuits.

Likewise, allegations would appear inside Pru-Bache during a 1988 company investigation. Included were claims from an ex-employee that Darr had received $200,000 in "benefits" in connection with Harrison real-estate deals. In a written response, Darr would later deny this, pointing out that he and other Pru-Bache executives invested in several Harrison-sponsored deals in the 1980s.

And so they did. Vice chairman H. Virgil Sherrill, Darr, Sherman, Proscia, Pitman, Richard Sichenzio (who would later head retail), and Lee Paton (who was also Darr's boss and still works at the firm) were among those who invested in a deal with Harrison involving the Barbizon Hotel. The deal provided them with attractive tax write-offs. At the time, Harrison had so many debts that some executives assumed $1.3 million of his obligations in exchange for a majority stake in the Barbizon Hotel and a brownstone in New York. The private rescue saved the hotel deal, which was close to defaulting from cost overruns; it also relieved Harrison of his mounting burdens. But these pivotal facts were not disclosed to investors. A vague mention was buried deep inside a 1985 offering document of another Harrison project: Pru-Bache simply stated that several officers had participated with Harrison in one other real-estate venture.

Darr allegedly accepted other personal favors from sponsors at the time. Employees said that VMS Realty frequently provided a car and driver for Darr's use. The driver, Lenny, was a short, jovial Italian who frequently drank coffee with the secretaries upstairs or kept the car motor running outside while waiting on Darr. Darr later claimed he only used VMS's service from "time to time," and that he paid for its use.

Darr and others invested in horse-racing partnerships with another general partner, Almahurst Farms, which bred and raced thorough-breds. According to Darr, Proscia, Pittman, Joe DeFur (director of marketing), J. Barron Clancy (head of regional coordinators), and two coordinators who were close to Darr, Mark Harper and Jim Parker, invested in the racehorses. As a joke, the group named a horse Hanover Sherman in honor of the retail president, but the horse never ran well. When a wholesaler wanted to discuss business with DeFur, DeFur begged to postpone the talk so he could go to the racetrack.

"What the hell," the wholesaler told DeFur. "I'm here to talk business and you're too busy because you're going to a damn horse track?"

Years later, Darr claimed he lost $200,000 in the private racing venture. In a court deposition, he said that he had informed his boss, Sherman, of the investment and the losses "insofar as he avidly followed the career of his namesake." But LP investors weren't informed.

Over time, allegations of Darr's private deals and special favors circulated freely in the DIG office as well as in the field. There was much talk of rifles, foreign trips, and other favors. It seemed that many insiders knew about these exchanges between executives at Pru-Bache and its LP cosponsors—except for investors who funded the multibillion-dollar deals.

In 1984, Pru-Bache moved to new headquarters in what would become a watershed event. To many people, the address of 100 Gold Street sounded far more impressive than it actually was. As Bache's home, the building was simple and utilitarian, with dark windows and beige columns. It sat on a corner under the Brooklyn Bridge. On the east, the building faced a long graffiti-scarred wall that supported the bridge. Yellowed newspapers, shards of glass, and bits of Styrofoam stirred with passing traffic. Across the street to the north stood the New York Downtown Hospital, whose ambulance sirens regularly floated up Bache's walls and echoed in the offices. "Sometimes you couldn't hear yourself think," said one worker.

For years, Bache had rented its ninth floor to the New York City Housing Authority. It was common to see low-income renters wandering the halls looking for the offices of the city's housing projects. "Sometimes you'd ride the elevator with a transient person or bum," said an investment banker. Other unlikely guests frequently intruded. Once, George Ball sat in his office and listened as a corporate client outlined a deal: from the corner of his eye, Ball spied a "mama mouse and her babies" scuttle across the floor behind the client's chair. By the time Ball's operation was up and running, Bache had outgrown its cramped, airless, miserly quarters—and the image it conveyed.

By then, most of Manhattan's brokerage firms were located in midtown or closer to the New York Stock Exchange. "There's a Jewish word called *tummel,* which means to be in the center of everything, to be 'with it,' " said one broker. "Bache was never there." Rather, the company was a bottle's throw away from Woolworth's and Burger King, near stalls owned by immigrants who sold T-shirts and postcards.

When Pru-Bache moved out of its house on Gold Street, the change signified a bold new era. Situated just five blocks down the street from the old address, the thirty-five-floor skyscraper was tall and sleek, made of smoky blue glass and gray steel. The building had two addresses: 199 Water Street, which a taxi driver could find, and One Seaport Plaza, a designation unknown to most city dwellers. It sat on the edge of a renovated brick plaza that led to Pier 16, overlooking the East River.

On the top executive floors, enormous windows ran along the halls, showcasing an urban skyline that from such a height looked enchanting. The interior was hushed and spacious—the antithesis of Gold Street. Pale blue carpets muffled noise; plush green leather chairs invited guests; cherrywood desks gleamed with polish. Everything about the place announced efficiency, wealth, and better days ahead.

Yet not much had really changed. Back in the nineteenth century, the plaza had been the cradle of New York's fledgling trade, where buccaneer ships had disgorged ill-gotten wares and sellers had haggled with buyers. Sailors, bankers, laborers, merchants, longshoremen, carpenters, prostitutes, and ragpickers had plied their goods and services along these docks. Back then, a few people in the plaza grew rich, many got exploited, and most were not remembered.

Now, nearly two centuries later, the plaza was cleaner, more people were getting richer, and more people were getting exploited.

7

Laissez les Bons Temps Rouler

THE real genius of the direct investment group resided in its marketing side, which was responsible for generating and promoting sales. "The direct investment group was an amazing PR machine," said one broker. "They knew just what to do to get you to sell the product. They were better than any other area of the firm. They gave the perks that brokers wanted."

The perks included bonuses, high sales commissions, and rewards such as incentive trips—all of which were given to Pru's top-performing salespeople. One veteran salesman pointed out: "The toughest, most coveted product in the world is OPM—other people's money—and the competition for that product is intense. But," he added, "the problem occurs when you get morality, honesty, and a few others things involved."

In the LP business, sponsors or general partners such as Graham Energy, for example, hire their own salespeople to persuade decision-makers at retail brokerage houses, such as Pru-Bache, to sell a sponsor's product. The relationship between the LP wholesaler and the retail brokerage is not unlike that between a clothing manufacturer and a department store. The manufacturer's representatives sell to retailers, who in turn sell to the public. In the case of wholesaler Graham Energy, it formed an exclusive relationship with retailer Pru-Bache, which was unusual but certainly not wrong.

Graham's wholesalers dealt with Pru-Bache through the firm's direct investment group. The wholesalers made sure DIG's regional product coordinators not only were informed about Graham's LP products, but were excited about them as well. After all, DIG's product coordinators were touting to their brokers other LP products "manufactured" by other sponsors besides Graham.

Sometimes an LP wholesaler got carried away and tried to jam a product down the throats of the distributor. A wholesaler might lie about his product's value in order to convince the Pru-Bache DIG co-ordinator to sell a large amount of product in his region. Sometimes a wholesaler offered key people bribes such as cash, guns, or sex with tempting, if not beautiful, women.

But F. Paul Grattarola of Graham Energy didn't believe in jamming product. He had worked as a wholesaler in the securities industry long enough to understand that salesmen occasionally take illegal goods. As the son of two Romans, Grattarola had inherited a gourmand's tastes, an affinity for World War I history, and a gentleman's code of honor. A short, round, jovial man, Grattarola didn't tolerate bribes on his watch, not as president of Graham's wholesaling arm, Graham Securities. In that capacity, he oversaw the LP sales effort from Graham's side of the pipeline. He and his wife frequently traveled the world, because part of his responsibility was to design and organize incentive trips for the men and women who sold the most of Graham's LPs. The free exotic trips to reward the most productive salespeople were generally legitimate. To a point.

In 1982, Graham Energy was a small Louisiana company that had failed to find many oil and gas reserves. Headed by John Graham, whose father, Ford, had been a New Orleans oil executive, the firm was based in a drab commercial building outside New Orleans. Its record for finding oil was among the worst in the industry, and by 1982, John Graham was getting nowhere with his dream of becoming a big oil-patch player.

The company was run by the Big Four: Graham, a dark-haired man with a florid complexion and wire-rimmed spectacles; Anton Rice III, the firm's second-in-command, the chief financial officer; Mark Files, who was called the chief accounting officer; and Al Dempsey, a senior vice president.

The company had managed oil and gas properties for institutions such as Chase Manhattan Bank and St. Paul Cos., but it hadn't established much of a record at the time. With about a hundred employees and a net worth of $15 million, Graham desperately needed a new line of business. In an attempt to generate cash, Graham solicited Wall Street firms for opportunities. Surprisingly, the tiny oil company received a proposal from Prudential-Bache Securities: Pru would use its vast brokerage network to sell oil and gas limited partnerships if Graham would invest the millions of dollars that were bound to pour in.

The man responsible for helping seal the deal was Graham's Anton ("Tony") Rice. He was Jim Darr's Greenwich, Connecticut, neighbor and lived too far from Graham headquarters to oversee the firm's daily finances. Instead, Rice wooed Manhattan's investors as a consummate deal-maker and connoisseur of wines. "He was kind of a snob about being a ninety-eighth-generation American, like the rest of us were foreigners," said one man. During the mid-1970s, Rice had worked in corporate finance at Merrill Lynch, where Darr had been employed for a time. Initially, Rice had looked down upon Darr as being beneath his social station. Yet Rice's attitude toward Darr changed dramatically once Pru-Bache's army of brokers began to sell as much as $400 million a year in Graham LPs. Hundreds of millions poured into Graham's coffers for investment.

Over the course of the decade, cosponsors Graham and Pru-Bache would sell $1.4 billion of Graham's LPs to about 137,000 small public investors. The prodigious sales effort would make Graham the hottest-selling LP product in Pru-Bache's stable.

And Grattarola headed that effort, which at first was an uphill battle. Pru-Bache's key men in New York ignored him and his sales team's efforts, and one executive even told Grattarola to keep his wholesalers away from Pru-Bache's DIG coordinators. "I told [him] my guys won't jam the product," said Grattarola, but some Pru-Bache regional people refused to meet Graham people in the beginning.

In late 1983, Graham and Pru-Bache began offering Energy Income Limited Partnerships Funds. The idea was to buy already existing oil and gas reserves and sell them at a profit. It seemed like a smart idea, for in 1982 memories of gas lines in the wake of the Saudi Arabian oil embargo were still fresh in the public's mind, oil prices were about $33 a barrel, and respected economists were projecting more price hikes. Graham and Pru-Bache advertised that by buying proven reserves, investors could minimize their investment risks and enjoy big profits from expected price increases.

But the LP investments were not cheap, based on fees and commissions. Like many other LPs at the time, Graham Energy's limited partnerships charged about 8 percent for brokerage sales commission, which was split between Pru-Bache and its salesperson. The LPs charged another 4 percent for "offering and organization costs," which traditionally paid for printing and legal costs and did not have to be detailed; this charge would pay for incentive trips. Add to that a 3.5 percent "management fee," which was divided between the two general partners of Pru-Bache and Graham, and all told, investors immediately lost 15 percent of their money.

The 15 percent "up-front" fees were high compared to, say, the 8 percent fees frequently charged to the buyer when a house sale closes. It is also more than the 8 percent retail sales tax charged by some states, such as California. It meant an investor who paid $100,000 into the LP had only $85,000 to invest from the get-go.

But that figure dwindled even more after the other Graham fees. For example, on the oil wells it operated, Graham took an "operator overhead" charge against the LPs. The charge slapped on LPs varied over the years, but at one point it became the single largest contributor to Graham's profits.

Graham also charged investors "general and administrative" expenses every quarter, just for running the partnerships, and those charges were poorly documented and excessive. All tallied, investors in various Graham LPs would pay as much as 34 percent in fees, commissions, loan interest, and miscellaneous charges. Put another way, a $100,000 investment was actually only $66,000.

But Pru-Bache promised clients returns of anywhere between 12 and 19 percent a year on their investments. Some elderly clients naively believed that their $100,000 would be invested completely. Assuming a return of 15 percent a year over, say, ten years, the $100,000 would grow to $404,555—for a 304 percent cumulative return, which was fantastic. Indeed, such a return would match Pru-Bache's claim that investors could more than triple their money.

But again, because of the immediate 15 percent charge the general partners collected, one's $100,000 investment was actually only $85,000. Even then, however, assuming the same 15 percent return, investors had a fighting chance to enjoy a fine 243 percent return over ten years, or $343,872. This would still be a great 13 percent annual return—if Pru-Bache and Graham hadn't laden the LPs with other fees and charges.

"Wow, I thought," said one investor who fell for the scam. "What a great deal!" As advertised, it surely was.

But Graham and Pru-Bache nibbled away at the investor funds over the years, taking various charges every year to drastically change the picture. What really occurred in many of the energy LPs was quite different. A limited partner's $85,000 investment, after sundry fees and charges, was worth only about $66,000 at the end of ten years. This translates to an annual loss of 4 percent a year, or a cumulative loss of 34 percent, not including any appreciation. To return just the original investment, the LP would first have to increase by 34 percent.

"It was a scam from the very beginning," said one former broker. But it was a gold mine for Pru-Bache, which received the most attractive LP broker deal on the Street at the time, and earned a kingpin's reputation with LPs, plus an estimated $210 million in fees and commissions—without ever investing a nickel.

To entice investors into their deal, Pru-Bache claimed that the profits from the LPs would be "tax-sheltered" and "tax-free"; that wasn't true.

Still, given the forecasted jump in oil prices, the promised rates of return, and the advertised tax-free benefit, Graham's Energy LPs seemed to be an extremely attractive choice for anyone's investment portfolio at first. "It seemed like a good deal at the time, based on what they were telling us," said one salesman. Indeed, Graham itself was estimating an 8 percent rise in oil prices *a year.*

By the spring of 1984, oil had dropped to about $28 a barrel—or a 15 percent drop in just two years. Still, Pru-Bache's marketing material extolled "comparatively safe, predictable, and steady source of income from the production and sale of oil and gas for many years to come."

Despite the lucrative deal for Pru-Bache, none of its officers, including James Darr, fervently promoted Graham's LPs to their retail sales force. Not until the spring of 1984.

Under a breathtaking blue sky, a mariachi band struck up a tune just as Mr. and Mrs. James Darr alighted from their plane. In 1984, Cancún was a remote, hard-to-reach resort about three blocks long and relatively unsullied by gringo tourists. Located at the northeastern tip of the Yucatan Peninsula, Cancún sat on the Caribbean Sea. White-sand beaches, turquoise water, and balmy weather offered respite from the spectacular Mayan ruins that lay inland in the lush jungles. In the mid-1980s, archaeologists were still deciphering ancient glyphs and tourism was still young. "At the time, we were the largest single group of Americans that had ever visited Cancún," said John Corbin, former executive vice president of Graham Securities.

Cancún was the first incentive trip Graham had organized for Pru-Bache brokers. To qualify, a broker had to sell about $200,000 gross of LP units; those who qualified were allowed to bring a spouse or guest. Graham officials had invited Ball and Sherman, but both men had declined, which left Darr, who was just beginning to make his mark in the public limited partnership sector. By year end 1983, his division had sold only $208 million of public LPs and thus was barely a player on the Street. But here on the edge of the Central American jungle, Darr was treated like royalty.

As Darr walked on the tarmac, Cancún's mayor met him and warmly shook his hand. The official presented the American businessman with a plaque welcoming him to Cancún. Darr smiled, shook the man's hand, and breezed through customs without having to open a bag or pocket.

A chauffeur drove the Darrs to the most exclusive of the city's three hotels. There the Darrs were given El Presidente's Suite, which occupied two top floors and was reserved for the President of Mexico.

"Whenever the real President came to town, the occupant of the suite had to leave," said a woman who helped arranged the trip.

The suite's bathroom was as large as a lobby. Inside was an enormous hot tub that could accommodate a cabinetful of dignitaries. Darr was so impressed by the lush surroundings, the warm welcome, and the exotic locale that he immediately telephoned his boss and friend Bob Sherman. Darr told Sherman to get on the next plane; he'd have to see this place to believe it.

Later that day, Darr told trip organizers that Mr. Sherman would be arriving the next day. Panicked, the organizers scrambled to pull together the type of welcome and accommodations that Sherman would be expecting. They rehired the mariachi band; the mayor was busy, but sent his deputy instead; a plaque was purchased and affixed with Sherman's name; a hotel suite was found, although not of the caliber of El Presidente's Suite; the limousine was hundreds of miles away, but a Mercedes and driver were hired.

The next day, Sherman stepped off the plane—roaring drunk. At his side were two scantily dressed young women. Perplexed, the Mexican official stepped forward and warmly greeted Sherman; Sherman rudely dismissed him. Customs officials ushered Sherman through the line, as they had done yesterday with the other *norteamericano*. Only this man, he was different.

Robert Jules Sherman was a tall man with a paunch and a receding hairline. With brown eyes, graying hair, and what many describe as a competitive, arrogant manner, Sherman was head of the firm's retail system; he oversaw all the brokers who worked in the growing Pru-Bache branch network and some of the retail product divisions, including DIG.

The son of a doctor, Sherman became a broker and joined Bache in the sixties. In 1973, he was censured and fined by the New York Stock Exchange for engaging in unjust and inequitable (and undefined) trading practices; otherwise, his record was clean. He was admired within the system as an executive who could make quick decisions, and he didn't interfere with his regional directors. Said Jim Trice, regional director: "I never had a problem with Sherman. I'd tell him when I had a problem, what my options were, and what I wanted to do. He usually let me do what I thought was best."

Yet Sherman frequently bragged in meetings about how he had just fired men. Power appealed to him, and he was quick to demonstrate his power. "You have to have a big ego to be a salesman in this business," said one top broker. "Good sales managers are off-the-wall egomaniacs, and Sherman was an egomaniac."

Prior to Pru's takeover of Bache in 1981, Sherman had overseen the Western half of Bache's brokerage system from his San Francisco head-quarters. He had hoped to take over as head of the firm, even after Prudential bought Bache. Sherman reportedly was disappointed he wasn't named president of the firm, under chairman and CEO George Ball.

But here in Mexico, Sherman was treated like a deity; he demanded what he felt was his due. Paul Grattarola rode with Sherman for the twenty-minute car trip into town.

"What's my suite like?" Sherman asked, his words slurring.

"You're going to like it," said Grattarola.

"I want Darr's suite. I want El Presidente's room."

Grattarola cleared his throat. "Jim's in there with his wife."

"I don't care. Kick him out."

"I can't do that. I'm sure you're going to love your room. Wait until you see it."

"Do you know who I am?" Sherman turned ugly. "And who the hell do you think you are? I want the fucking best suite in town. I want it now. I also want you to send some more girls to my room tonight. Get the best."

"What?"

"You heard me." Sherman repeated himself: he wanted high-class hookers, and he wanted them now.

Grattarola was outraged. "Fine," he said, his face reddening. "You want me to do that? Write your request on your letterhead and I'll take care of it."

Sherman never did submit a formal request for the prostitutes, said Grattarola, although many eyewitnesses said that more unknown women showed up later that day. One reportedly was a model for a Mexican advertisement. By the time the two men arrived at the hotel, Sherman was angry. He cussed at the driver, at the attendants who took his bags, and at the people who checked him into the hotel. "Sherman was a real pig," said one observer.

That night, the top salespeople and their guests assembled for cock-tails. Sherman was still obviously drunk. His female companions were present, as was Darr. Another official presented Sherman with the keys to the city. According to six eyewitnesses, Sherman addressed the group and erupted in a stream of profane, abusive criticisms. "He basically told the brokers they were pieces of shit and they were lucky to be working for him," said Corbin. Sherman threatened to fire them all and insulted the Mexican official, who didn't understand English. "It was so foul and dis-gusting, I couldn't repeat his comments," said one man. Brokers were mortified; their wives were appalled; few could believe that this was a Prudential executive. The room was silent while Sherman rambled and cursed. Finally, Jim Darr approached Sherman and persuaded him to leave. "Let's talk about this another time, Bob," Darr said gently.

The ladies followed Sherman, who wasn't seen again for the rest of the night.

During the entire Cancún trip, alcohol consumption was so great that Grattarola had to place a limit on the amount of Dom Pérignon charged to the trip's account. Later, Grattarola was chewed out for imposing such limits. Except for the cross behavior of Sherman, most travelers fondly remembered the Cancún trip.

One evening, the group assembled outdoors on a patio overlooking a man-made lagoon. In honor of the *norteamericanos*, some Yucatecans had arranged a cockfight, but it was hastily canceled for fear of offending some people. Dinner was rice, beans, and fish, and a big mariachi band serenaded the guests, playing from boats that floated lazily on a lagoon. A guitarist lost his balance, causing a boatload of musicians to fall into the water. The diners burst into laughter as some brokers rushed to pull ashore the sopping wet musicians.

The Cancún trip had a dramatic effect on Graham's relationship with Pru-Bache. "I don't know what happened," said Grattarola. But from that time forward, the fate of Graham's venture with Pru-Bache took a dramatic turn for the better. "After Cancún there was a big, big, noticeable difference." Suddenly, Pru-Bache leaders supported the program wholeheartedly. Tony Rice, who had once considered Darr beneath him, grew friendly with Darr. He later sponsored Darr's membership into exclusive golf and shooting clubs and invited him on lavish hunting trips. According to Darr, these memberships had no influence on his business decisions.

Soon, Pru-Bache wielded enormous power in Graham's organization, which was highly unusual in conventional retail-wholesale arrangements. For example, up until that point, Grattarola said he had been the boss of Graham's sales force. He determined who was hired and fired. Yet after Cancún, Pru-Bache began to take a bigger role. One of Darr's close associates, Joe DeFur, called Grattarola one day to suggest that he interview a particular man for a Graham sales job. Grattarola did, but found him to be "too aggressive." Grattarola didn't hire the man. A short time later, DeFur telephoned Grattarola.

"I heard you turned that fellow down," he said.

"He was a nice guy," said Grattarola, "but he was a pusher. A jammer."

"Apparently, you don't understand," said DeFur. "I wasn't asking you to interview him. I was *telling* you to hire him. We want [him] in that area. Me and the guy with the curly white hair."

"Who's running this division? You or me?"

"Go talk to Tony [Rice]."

Grattarola approached Rice and recounted his conversation with DeFur. Rice told Grattarola, "I don't care what you think. Hire the guy or [else]."

Darr later denied that he played any role in Graham's personnel decisions. But at the time, Grattarola was incredulous. He considered his options and hired the man. "That kind of thing would not have happened before Cancún," said Grattarola. But now it became a frequent occurrence. That a retailer would exert so much control over a wholesaler was wrong, Grattarola knew. He was a stickler for going by the book and knew that the close relationship between Graham's top executives and Pru-Bache's officers was rare, if not unethical. Given the enormous LP fees both Graham and Pru-Bache could pocket, both firms and their key executives had much to gain by "jamming" product; quick, easy, hand-over-fist sales would in time deliver some $400 million to the sponsors.

Given Grattarola's penchant for rules and codes of honor, he would only get in the way of the flow.

Prior to Cancún, Graham and Grattarola had produced all its own marketing materials; after the trip, Pru-Bache began producing most of Graham's marketing materials—often without Grattarola's approval. "Once, Pru-Bache sent a memo to its brokers quoting me saying something I never even said," said Grattarola. Still, he struggled vainly to maintain some grip on his own operations.

Margaret Shanks Moore worried about her husband's failing health and her future. William Moore had been president and chairman of the Tejon Ranch, which is one of the largest and oldest tracts of undivided land in California. When she married in 1952, Margaret Shanks was a young bride and sudden corporate wife, but she had prepared for the role as a young girl. When she was twelve, her father headed the nation's largest insurance company, Prudential Insurance Co. of America; she had seen firsthand the sacrifices a corporate wife makes. She and her husband had shared a good, bountiful life: their five children were on their own and prospering; they were still together and now they had the time and money to enjoy their golden years.

Then William's health weakened. After years of supporting him, his career, and their family, Margaret assumed the burden of securing their future.

In late 1984, the Moores' stockbroker invited them to a seminar featuring Graham Energy. She listened intently as a broker addressed the crowd of mostly elderly people. The investment he described sounded wonderful. She could earn 12 to 14 percent a year on her money; in years to come, she could collect as much as 20 percent more as the price of oil increased. When her broker pointed to a picture of the Rock of Gibraltar—the symbol of Prudential—well, my gosh, a wave of confidence swept over her, and over many of the other elderly people. To them, the Rock was practically biblical.

She remembered what her father had told her scores of years ago: "When Prudential is behind you, that means safety is their primary object." Without hesitation, she entrusted her broker with $70,000 of her savings and told him she wanted safety and income from the LP.

The broker recited what he had been told by his superiors—the experts—in New York in DIG. Unwittingly, he repeated the lies: tax-free returns; low-risk and safe; 12 to 14 percent annual returns; and the promise that "before Pru-Bache ever got a dime, the limited partners would receive all of their initial investment."

Truth was, limited partnerships were anything but tame, as they have always been high-risk investments. The prospectus—the document detailing the LP offering—clearly warned that "these securities have a high degree of risk." Yet Pru-Bache regularly advertised the oil LPs as a "safe source of income," as "a means to profit . . . from a steady, safe source of income."

In many cases, the company dissuaded people, including brokers, from reading prospectuses, which are thick, dry materials written by attorneys. "Who reads those things, anyway?" as one broker said later. Turgid as they were, the documents included important warnings that DIG sales materials omitted altogether.

For example, the company's brochures claimed: "Approximately 33 to 55 percent of a partnership's cash flow you receive will be tax-free." The prospectus, however, said LPs were "not designed to provide substantial federal income tax deductions."

Another lie was buried in the returns Pru-Bache and Graham promised. The Moores believed that the Pru-Bache LPs' current yields were as advertised: that is, between 12 percent and 15 percent annually. But no broker explained to them that 15 percent of their money went first to the high one-time-only fees charged. Nor did they understand that the LPs had to appreciate by at least 27 percent just to recoup the 15 percent fees and to produce the minimum 12 percent promised as their return on investment.

Such a 30 percent return would have been astounding had it been true. But based on the "rock-solid" promises and personal guarantees that Pru-Bache brokers were told to give, investors handed over their cash with trust. They didn't question the bold advertised rates and certainly didn't doubt the Rock. "Oil in the ground is as good as money in the bank," the company crowed, ignoring a 50 percent drop in the price of oil.

In November 1984, the Pru invited Ball to Dave Sherwood's retirement party. Amid the speeches, Ball was singled out as the new holder of the Pru's white elephant. In 1971, Sherwood had been made president of PruPac—the property and casualty subsidiary—and that division lost money during its early years. As its first president, Sherwood at the time was given a statue of a mother suckling a child. The mother represented the Pru, and the infant symbolized the money-losing subsidiary.

Now, some thirteen years later, PruPac was profitable and Sherwood was retiring. In one of his last official acts, he passed the statue on to Ball, the head of money-losing Pru-Bache Securities. That night, Ball good-naturedly accepted the icon, although he sat down a few mornings later to write one of his infamous "Ball-grams." In his memo, he told all his employees: "I want to unload this statue as soon as possible. Accomplishing that quickly and loudly is one of our primary goals. Please do your utmost to produce the revenue and the net income to expedite the process." He closed with the sentence "Losses suck."

Later that year, Ball became a member of the Pru's Executive Office, a six-man board, and the Pru streamlined its decision-making process. The insurer created two vice chairman positions of equal importance: Garnett Keith was promoted to vice chairman in charge of investments and Robert Winters became vice chairman responsible for central corporate operations. In its 1984 annual report, the company noted Ball's promotion, the Pru's reorganization, and the new house affirmation:

> The Prudential is to be a leader in the financial services industry. We will be an aggressive, market-driven company providing quality insurance and other financial service products to individuals, businesses, and other institutions by using strengths in distribution, investment, and administration to achieve superior results for our customers and earn an appropriate rate of return.

The credo was telling for what it did not mention: honor, trust, and prudence. In the past, the company had with great success exploited those qualities in advertisements. Indeed, those were the very characteristics upon which investors like the Moores depended. Perhaps the Pru's reputation stood on its own; perhaps it was a new era. Whatever the reason for omitting the century-old company hallmarks, the Pru's dispatch to the world emphasized a new persona: big, first, and aggressive.

8

Going Global

WITH Pru-Bache now ensconced in its luxurious quarters, fortunes appeared to have turned. "Before Ball, if you got caught taking a taxicab instead of riding the subway, you'd get shot at sunrise," said one executive. But now, fleets of limousines lined the curbs at Seaport Plaza, ready to carry Pru-Bache executives, secretaries, and young female professionals across town or to the country on Friday afternoons. In one of the building's rooms, Ball had installed a $600,000 fireplace. To foster camaraderie, he initiated weekly cocktail hours on the thirty-fifth floor in which executives gathered over shrimp boats and Tanqueray to swap tales and gossip. Few expenses were spared for the new Pru-Bache.

The company's financials reflected a radically different tale. For the first time since Ball had joined the firm, it had reported an annual loss instead of a profit. On revenues of $965 million, Pru-Bache in 1984 had lost $90 million. Granted, none of Manhattan's brokerage firms had reported a good year in 1984, but few could rival Pru-Bache's explosive growth in costs.

In 1981, the firm's assets had been $4 billion. By 1985, they were approaching $12 billion. Expenses were also growing. In 1981, they had been about $67 million. By 1985, they were approximately $1 billion. "Ball was spending more, but he was also bringing in more," said one former accountant. Still, the pressure to produce profits squeezed everyone in the firm, and no one more than George Ball, who drove himself hard.

His habit was to rise at four-thirty at his New Jersey home. He exercised and ran for three miles. By six-fifteen, he was en route to work in his chauffeured car. After speed-reading at least two newspapers, he'd arrive by seven at the office, where he ate a light breakfast. Most mornings a woman arrived at six o'clock to slice fresh fruit for his meal, which he'd wash down with Diet Coke. Throughout the morning, Ball worked, taking telephone calls, attending meetings, keeping abreast of the details that kept the brokerage machine running. At lunch, he'd stop to eat a tuna fish sandwich and grapes. If necessary, he'd attend a sit-down lunch meeting, but invariably his secretary would interrupt to deliver a prearranged "urgent" message, which allowed Ball to excuse himself gracefully. He had no time to waste.

Even in his leisure hours, Ball worked. Evenings and weekends frequently found him playing squash, tennis, or racquetball, or bicycling or running. The diversions relaxed him and also gave him fresh solutions to old dilemmas. "I'm almost addictive about exercise, but I find it improves one's business stamina," he said. Working on fast tracks appealed to Ball, competition renewed him, and avid was the only game he played.

Still, the breakneck pace was taking its toll. By 1985, Ball was about to divorce his first wife, with whom he had raised a daughter. The past was returning to stalk him and shadow his once spotless track record. After suffering through four years of public accusations and investigations, Ball's nemesis, E. F. Hutton, dominated the news. In May 1985, the company pled guilty to two thousand counts of mail fraud stemming from a $10 billion check-kiting and overdrafting system that had occurred while Ball was president of Hutton. At the time, his close associate Loren Schechter was deputy general counsel.

The check-kiting crime worked like this: Hutton held $50 million in Bank Apple and $10 million in Bank Zebra. Hutton wrote a check on Bank Apple for $75 million—more than its balance—and deposited the check in Bank Zebra.

Now Bank Zebra's balance was $85 million ($10 million plus the $75 million). On this account, Hutton wrote an $85 million check and invested it in U.S. Treasury bills, thus earning interest. Hutton covered its $25 million overdraft at Apple with another check from Zebra. Essentially, it bounced another check at Bank Zebra to cover the bounced check from Bank Apple, and Hutton didn't borrow money but simply used the bank's money *for free*, often to earn more money for its own account.

Government prosecutors claimed Hutton did this regularly. By allowing the firm to overdraft its accounts, banks gave Hutton free use of its money, without charging penalties or interest, which in 1981 was 21 percent. As prosecutors pointed out, individuals who practiced the same ploy were routinely penalized for bouncing checks. Some banks overlooked this gambit, however, when it was practiced by a big corporate customer. The feds wouldn't stand for the double standard. Besides, the consequences of rampant, huge check-kiting schemes could devastate the nation's banking system. If enough people drew enough checks on bank funds they didn't have, sooner or later the entire banking system would collapse.

Hutton reaped enormous rewards from this illegal method for a few years. In fiscal year 1981 the firm's retail sales division earned about 70 percent of its total profits from interest alone, much of it by pushing the float game to its extreme. Given the numbers, the feds had to punish such flagrant acts—if for no other reason than to set an example.

But the truth of the matter was that Hutton's crime of check-kiting was not out of line with the money management practices of many other American companies at the time. Many firms "creatively" shifted funds from one bank to another before those funds cleared in order to create artificial balances—and tap those balances—before they were actually available.

In Hutton's defense, attorneys argued that the law was nebulous (which it was), that the banks condoned the practice (which many did), and that other firms were doing the same thing (which was true).

So why was Hutton singled out? Some observers believe that the firm's lawyers, including Loren Schechter, made a critical mistake. In the crucial early days of the government's investigation, the firm took an arrogant stance. It tried to bully low-paid government attorneys; it failed to return their phone calls; and when the Department of Justice decided to pursue Hutton, attorneys engaged in all-out legal warfare, firing off rounds of subterfuging motions to bury the government. The belligerent tactic backfired on Hutton by strengthening the government's resolve. This same "scorched-earth" strategy would backfire again when used by Schechter at Pru-Bache some ten years later.

Yet in 1985 neither Ball nor Schechter appeared to be scratched by Hutton's well-publicized battle (although the mess privately troubled Ball). While Hutton pled guilty two thousand times, the two Hutton alumni were rising stars at Prudential-Bache Securities.

Ball had left Hutton in July 1982—months after a federal grand jury investigation began and just before the scandal hit the national news. Ball had hired Schechter in 1983, as the Department of Justice's review intensified. Ball would later maintain that he had no knowledge of the check-kiting problems until Hutton chairman Robert Fomon told him in February 1982 what Fomon had just learned. "I had no knowledge of, nor responsibility for, the deficiencies in Hutton's . . . system," he later told Congress.

If there were links between Hutton's crimes, Ball's supervisory skills, and Schechter's handling of the affair, Prudential Insurance Co. wasn't connecting them. It didn't waver after a House subcommittee that summer released a four-year-old Hutton memo, dated June 1981, that indicated Ball *did* know of the firm's overdrafting practice. When Ball was told in 1981 that a branch earned $30,000 a month in interest "just from overdrafting of the bank account," Ball sent copies of the memo to hundreds, with a note saying it was "worth remembering." Perhaps Ball had forgotten the memo. He has always maintained that he advocated only "legitimate overdraft."

In any event, the Pru continued to support Ball, and indeed elevated him to two cardinal positions.

In the fall of 1985, Ball was named chairman of Pru-Bache Securities and became chairman of its parent company, Prudential Capital and Investment Services. Importantly, he was also allowed to build Pru-Bache's investment banking effort. To improve its global investment banking operation, Ball reorganized the company and streamlined bank functions. This was not the first time the brokerage firm had pledged to improve its corporate finance work. This time, however, the promise was backed by the sheer will of George Ball—and the checking account of Prudential.

Investment bankers are expensive intermediaries who match people or institutions *with money* to those people and companies who *need money*. The job title grew out of the Banking Act of 1933, also called the Glass-Steagall Act, which separated deposit-taking banks from the riskier deal-making banks. The idea was to save individual depositors from ruin when a bank delved into corporate finance and wrecked the bank, which is what had happened in the Great Depression.

Investment banking, or corporate finance, takes many forms but generally falls into a few matchmaking categories. Bankers help two companies merge into one, like Bache and Prudential. They launch or defend attempts of one company to take over another. They underwrite and sell a company's bonds, as well as other financial instruments— "securities"—that guarantee payment from the issuing company. Investment bankers bring private firms public in stock offerings, as happened with Bache Halsey; they take public firms private in "leveraged buyouts," in which a firm borrows funds to make the purchase. They structure limited partnerships. They advise state governments and countries such as Mexico and Russia on how to raise money, and when and where. They invest in fledgling ventures, as Bache did with railroads, in exchange for a piece of that venture; they swap currencies, loans, and other instruments held by clients in exchange for fees. Sometimes they speculate for their own company's accounts; regularly, they create a newfangled product to attract, in a new fashion, the same old OPM resource—other people's money.

Often a banker's deals help a firm expand and so add new jobs. Other times, a transaction helps trigger a firm's demise, and so eliminates jobs. No matter the business, no matter the outcome, a banker always takes his fee, which is relatively enormous.

Fees range from 1 to 9 percent of a deal, depending on the type of service rendered. If, for example, a banker helps Yucca Oil raise $100 million smoothly, Yucca's CEO doesn't mind paying the banker 3 percent, or $3 million, even though such work only engaged half a dozen people for two weeks.

"Securities can be a sick industry, as deals have fat front-end fees, regardless if you benefit the client with that deal," said Christian Wyser-Pratte, a former managing director at Pru-Bache. Sometimes a banker performs services for a relatively modest fee; sometimes he chases deals that never materialize. But in the mid-1980s, slow business was an anomaly at every firm—except Pru-Bache.

For years, the firm's investment banking unit had tried to polish its profile, with little success. In 1984, it was headed by Peter Bernard, a "nice guy" who once managed the syndicate department, in which the firm buys new issues of securities to resell to the public in an orderly manner. Having come from a routinely managed department, Bernard was not well versed in the rough-and-tumble world of deals, which is why, as one insider said, "the firm was dabbling around in investment banking, making a lot of amateur-hour attempts."

One such embarrassing episode occurred in 1983, right after Pru-Bache had midwifed a batch of initial public stock offerings to the public. The firm brashly announced that it intended to procure some of the corporate finance business of the Baby Bells, which were the AT&T spin-offs. But Pru-Bache was unceremoniously passed over by all seven Baby Bells in favor of more established investment banking firms. The unit lacked a strong leader who could bring in new business.

Christian Wsyer-Pratte joined Pru-Bache in 1984. At that time, his brother, Guy, headed Pru-Bache's respected arbitrage unit, in which he bought stock based on anticipated price increases, then sold the stock later, ideally for a gain. Guy Wyser-Pratte was well known in close-knit arbitrage circles. Sections of rival arb Ivan Boesky's ghostwritten book, *Merger Mania*, were based heavily on Wyser-Pratte's monograph *Risk Arbitrage II*. In return, Wyser-Pratte took to calling Boesky "Piggy."

While Pru-Bache's arb unit was in good hands, its IB unit in 1984 merely bumbled along, with a small group of talent and a short list of unimpressive clients. One was 1000 Trails, a company that sold time-shares in campsites. "I mean, really," sniffed Christian Wyser-Pratte. "If you can't afford to pay the fee for a campsite, maybe you shouldn't take a vacation." The unit may have hired talented people, but by 1984, it still had not built a list of fine clients.

Christian Wyser-Pratte is a portly man with olive skin, small eyes, and brown hair. A self-described intellectual snob, he is refreshingly blunt about people, including himself. "I'm a dinosaur. I have ethics and values." He doesn't suffer fools and punctuates his soliloquies with principles, such as "scrupulous," "fair," and "honest." Before joining Wall Street, Wyser-Pratte was a commissioned officer in the Navy, where discipline and accountability were anchors. Perhaps because of his rigid moral compass, Wyser-Pratte often is insufferable.

After the Navy, he joined A. G. Becker and Paribas, in its Chicago office. He remained there for twelve years, learning the craft of corporate finance. "We were experts a company relied on for financial advice. We had a deep knowledge of what they really needed," he said. "Every now and then, we'd throw a lot of free bread on the water, do some free services, in the hopes that it would pay off when the client needed a big deal." Back then, a banker told a client what he needed to know, rather than what he wanted to hear. In the Old World way of investment banking, the size of the fee was not nearly as important as the quality of the relationship. Although that truism once guided the business, it died with the advent of the mega-deal.

When Becker folded, Wyser-Pratte joined Pru-Bache, partly because it was the only firm that would hire his entire six-person department. Wsyer-Pratte brought to Pru-Bache his Chicago staff and some illustrious clients, such as Clark Equipment Credit Corp. He also brought some habits and procedures that he found lacking at Pru-Bache. Wyser-Pratte said, "I believe there were no lawyers on staff to deal with the Securities and Exchange Commission," regarding whether banking deals complied with SEC rules. He didn't find the elementary banker's tools, such as call reports, which detailed each visit a Pru-Bache banker made to a client; nor did he find many well-written proposals or company reports on file. Slowly, these elements were added to Pru-Bache's IB efforts.

That winter, Wyser-Pratte shepherded projects from Chicago. Three of his specialists had remained with him because they had been promised an opportunity to work with DIG, known for its ability to market and sell LPs. The Chicago trio planned to raise money for their client, a leasing company, by structuring an LP, which would be marketed by the formidable DIG and sold through the brokerage system. Importantly, the specialists believed the LP would be an excellent investment for Pru-Bache's customers.

They had sent their proposal to DIG in New York. Weeks went by and they heard no word. One day, Wyser-Pratte intervened and called the DIG people in New York.

"Look," he began. "We have some good guys who want to work for you."

The man on the other end knew about the deal but wasn't interested, he said. "Why would we want to sell that product for that company?" At the time, Pru-Bache was selling LPs in Polaris Aircraft Leasing Corp. "Why would we want to do another leasing deal and compete with what we already have?"

The same reason, Wyser-Pratte thought, a retailer sells more than one style of jeans. "For diversification," he answered. "You know, to give customers a choice."

The man in DIG dismissed the idea and rudely hung up.

After trying to work with DIG a few more times, the Chicago bankers realized it wasn't going to happen. Wyser-Pratte resolved to discuss the matter later with Ball. If nothing else, his CEO should know about the interdepartmental problem.

On February 14, 1985, Wyser-Pratte celebrated his birthday with his wife in Chicago. He caught the last flight to New York. The next morning, he attended a special meeting of IB's sixteen managing directors, who reported to Bernard, who reported to George Ball. Ball attended the meeting, in which the group discussed pending deals and strategies. Then Wyser-Pratte spoke.

"I have a problem with Jim Darr." He bluntly detailed the issue between DIG and the bankers, then summarized: "We just can't get access to the direct investment department as we were promised." He knew that without DIG's blessings, Pru-Bache's retail system wouldn't sell any LP deal initiated by the IB unit. "We can't get our deals packaged and done, and I think that's a big problem."

Ball turned and smiled at Wyser-Pratte. He said, "Darr is our Darth Vader."

Then Ball changed the subject. Stunned, Wyser-Pratte realized, "Holy shit. The emperor *knows* his underling is Darth Vader." From then on, his investment bankers in Chicago shunned the DIG people altogether.

By 1985, Darr's power extended beyond his DIG fiefdom. At one point, he met a promising newcomer in corporate finance, a friendly, eager fellow named Frank E. ("Chip") Barnes.

Six months after joining the firm, Barnes had worked on a $200 million junk bond deal for Turner Broadcasting Co., among others. A handsome, dark-haired man from North Carolina, Barnes is partial to suspenders, peanut butter, and Dr Pepper. "He's the kind of guy who, if you tell him you're working on a kangaroo deal in Australia, he'll say, 'You know, I was just down in Australia last week spending time with some kangaroos myself,' " said one colleague. Barnes could make even far-fetched connections with strangers.

In his first few weeks at the firm, Barnes had called on a cable television firm, First Carolina Communications, at a time when broadcast deals were jumping out of the water. Barnes and First Carolina's president and CEO, E. B. Chester, Jr., discussed ways to raise money so the firm could acquire other cable systems. Barnes tapped his Southern roots to befriend the executive. Before Barnes delved deeper into negotiations, he was told by his superiors to let Darr know what he was doing.

"Look," said Robert Barrett, then comanager of corporate finance. "Try to work with Jimmy Darr. It's the only way to get any limited partnerships done."

Barnes met Darr. He explained First Carolina's need for capital. The two discussed how Pru-Bache could underwrite and sell LPs for the firm. Encouraged, Barnes scheduled a meeting with E. B. Chester, Jr. Chester flew to New York, where Barnes introduced him to his superiors. At one point, one of Barnes's bosses suggested that Chester meet Darr. "It was all in the new spirit of 'Hey, let's work on deals together,' " Barnes said. He took the client for an elevator ride up to the thirty-third floor, where they met Darr and Bill Pittman, who was then head of due diligence.

The courtship proceeded. Chester invited the Pru-Bache group, including Barnes, to visit his firm's headquarters in North Carolina. As part of its due diligence, Pru-Bache had to ensure that First Carolina was a sound company with solid operations. A date was set.

Then, at the last minute, the men in DIG suggested that Barnes stay behind rather than travel to North Carolina.

"Well, now that doesn't seem right," Barnes objected.

Pittman explained. "We have to fully understand the cable system before we can decide its value" and raise money, he assured him. "You stay here. We'll take care of the legwork."

Reluctantly, Barnes agreed, and the DIG group left New York. A few days later, Barnes learned that what he thought had been a sure deal had fallen through. He was perplexed.

Indeed, First Carolina did not give Pru-Bache its investment banking business, although ten years later neither Chester nor Philips remembered why. Instead, they hired Morgan Stanley to underwrite and sell $45 million in subordinated debentures, or unsecured debt.

After that bitter experience, Barnes steered clear of DIG. For a time, he was successful. He worked on Pru-Bache IB deals involving British Telecom, Reader's Digest Association, 20th Century-Fox, and other large firms. Meanwhile, another broadcast customer had walked through the doors. This time, Barnes figured, he would suggest a master limited partnership deal, in which the LPs are traded publicly like stock, and so can be sold easily. The public deal allowed Barnes to bypass DIG.

In January 1985, Barnes had put together a proposal whereby Pru-Bache would underwrite $25 million for Sillerman-Magee Communications. All the necessary review boards had approved the deal, which Barnes kept secret from DIG. At one point, Barnes's boss told him it would be a nice goodwill gesture to introduce Darr to Sillerman. Reluctantly, Barnes arranged a lunch meeting in Pru-Bache's executive dining room on the thirty-fifth floor.

At lunch, the men discussed the deal. Darr proceeded to tell Sillerman that he should consider raising money privately through DIG rather than through a public master limited partnership. Darr enumerated some reasons, including that public deals required more SEC filings and so cost more money.

"My way will put more money in your pocket," Darr said.

During the rest of lunch, Sillerman asked Darr more questions. Realizing that Darr had just stolen another piece of his business, Barnes sank deeper in his chair.

DIG won control of the LP offering, although Barnes helped Darr's team structure it. On Super Bowl weekend, Barnes and Sillerman flew to Los Angeles and met briefly with Rob Hughes at the Bel Air Hotel. The Santa Barbara broker had been looking for wiser investments to sell than Pru-Bache's staples of real-estate and oil LPs. To his mind, those vehicles performed great in times of high inflation, but by 1985, inflation had cooled. In addition, the generous tax shelters attached to those LPs were about to disappear. However, broadcasting deals were bound to appreciate in value.

After Barnes outlined the deal, Hughes agreed to sell his clients the broadcast LP units. The offering arrived, but the LPs sold poorly in Pru-Bache's retail network. That was peculiar, since similar broadcast LPs sold out rapidly.

A few weeks later, Hughes was astounded to hear that DIG had put the kibosh on the Sillerman deal. Brokers were actually being steered *away from* selling the Sillerman LPs. Hughes and Barnes talked, and both concluded that Darr was sabotaging their deal behind their backs.

"After that, I got queasy," said Barnes. "I realized that Darr was punishing me for not telling him about the deal in the first place. I'd done an end run around him, and he didn't like it." A few months later, Pru-Bache's broker network had sold only $5 million of the Sillerman-McGee LPs—not the $25 million originally intended.

By now, Darr realized that Barnes could deliver big business. In the spring of 1985, Barnes was asked to move from investment banking to the direct investments group—an idea that repulsed Barnes.

"Direct investment is driving away my clients!" Barnes told his boss. "I don't want to move." Barnes staved off the transfer, but the issue didn't die.

One evening after work, Barnes needed a ride to an auto repair shop to pick up his red Volkswagen convertible. Darr generously offered to give him a lift. On the way out of the city, the two men shot the breeze from the backseat.

"You know, Chip," said Darr, stretching out his legs, "we make a lot of money in our area."

"Oh, yeah?" Barnes said lightly.

"Yeah. You tend to consider the clients too much. We structure deals the right way. We watch out for the 'buy' side of our deals," meaning the salesmen in DIG. Darr looked at Barnes for emphasis. "That's the way to do it. We make money."

"That's interesting, Jim." Barnes didn't want to offend Darr and jeopardize yet another deal. He didn't say anything. Just then, the car repair shop came into view, and Barnes asked the driver to pull the car over. Before he exited, Barnes thanked Darr.

Darr told him, "You come over to our side, Chip, and you'll make big money."

"Thanks, Jim."

Not long after that, Peter Bernard, the head of corporate finance, called Barnes into his office. "Chip, we'd like you to move into direct investment."

"I'd rather not."

Bernard sighed and leaned forward. "Listen. Darr is an ass to work with. He's unscrupulous, and for all we know he may be dishonest. But," he added, "we want you to make the move.

"That way," he said, "we can have our camel's nose under his tent so we can find out what he's up to."

"What about my contract?" Barnes said, referring to his employment contract.

"I can't protect you." Bernard explained that the contract with corporate finance could not be upheld in DIG.

"If I go, I want to report to you."

Bernard couldn't allow that, either.

Barnes realized he didn't have much room to negotiate, although it wasn't for lack of trying. Over the next few days, he talked to the people in DIG and grew more distressed. He told one potential boss he needed a support staff, but it became clear that DIG was not about to let Barnes dictate his terms.

At the end of a week, Barnes confided to his immediate supervisor, "I just can't take this job on."

"You don't understand, Chip. The firm wants you to do this. George Ball wants you to do this; Jim Darr wants this; I want this," said Barrett. "You don't have a choice."

Barnes was aghast and returned to his office. A short time later, his boss, Barrett, called him back in.

"I'm sorry," Barrett said. "I don't know what happened with you and the guys in direct investments. But they don't want you anymore."

Barnes was elated. "That's fine with me."

"Chip, you don't understand," he said. "That was the only job we had for you. I'm sorry. But you'll have to go elsewhere."

Barnes was fired. He could hardly believe it after all he had done for the company. In a last-ditch effort to save his job, Barnes wrote to Ball, listing his accomplishments and the money he had raised. He closed his memo with the question "Why am I being fired?"

Ball wrote back a consoling, handwritten note, saying no one was at fault in this regrettable situation. "It sounds like one of those unfortunate, inexplicable instances where everyone wanted things to work but where they didn't."

Barnes left Pru-Bache on the last day of May.

In 1985, Pru-Bache scored a record year in revenues and profits. The firm brought in $1.4 billion in revenue—or double the amount it had generated just four years earlier. Under Ball, the firm reported $42 million in profit in 1984, which was a remarkable rebound from the prior year's loss of $90 million. Ball could shed that mother-sucking statue, and its image, too.

In Newark, New Jersey, Ball was the Pru's golden boy. "Pru chairman Bob Beck thought that when the sun came up in the morning, it rose out of George Ball's head. He was enthralled with Ball," said one executive. Vice chairman Winters was less enthralled, but was still taken with him, clearly. Ball's star didn't dim even as he testified in November 1985 before a congressional subcommittee on white-collar crime—a panel prompted by E. F. Hutton's confession of fraud, which had occurred on Ball's watch.

At Pru-Bache, Ball now had DIG churning out product, and retail selling it. But somehow, success in investment banking eluded him. By year-end 1985, he was focused on building that unit so that it, too, could become a cash generator. He oversaw the hiring of more bankers; the investment banking unit built a fixed-income unit in Europe, Hong Kong, and Australia, which sold bonds to foreign institutions. It purchased an interest in a London brokerage house. It formed a unit to handle the fast-growing and important interest-rate-swap business. Yet none of these moves gave Pru-Bache the power to make a dent in the lucrative and prestigious investment banking business.

By now, Prudential Insurance was hit with what a former executive called "international-itis"; the Pru yearned to be a global entity. The symptoms of that virus crept into the firm's annual report that year, which stated: "The Prudential. It's strong. It's on the move. It's bigger than life."

Now if only the firm could get its corporate finance act together.

9

"Camouflage, to the Extent We Can . . ."

In mid-December, near-freezing temperatures chilled the air on Fifth Avenue, but the Pierre Hotel radiated warmth. The occasion was Pru-Bache's annual DIG Christmas party, and by 1985, the throng of par-tiers must have felt invincible. They were about to become the Street's leading sponsors of limited partnerships, directing a tidal wave of cash. Within twelve months, the firm's DIG unit would package and sell close to $1 billion worth of LPs in a phenomenal achievement that would defy both common sense and market logic.

But that Christmas, no one cared a whit for such concerns. Duty called, and the party began, as it always did, in the evening after work, in the middle of the week. Yet the curbside scene resembled a typical Saturday night during the holidays. Men in tuxedos and women in floor-length evening gowns stepped out of taxis and limousines. Spouses were expressly *not* invited to the company functions. "It might cramp the style of the guys who regularly paired off with the gals during the night," said one reveler. Sherman showed up with two female employees in tow, Darr arrived, and everyone headed for the banquet room.

Inside, the decorations prompted a chorus of "Aahhs." A dozen enor-mous, five-foot-tall stands of flowers filled DIG's reserved room with color and perfume. Each display flaunted a different theme expressed by the arrangement of flowers: calla lilies, roses, gardenias, chrysanthe-mums, lilacs, birds-of-paradise, hydrangeas, narcissi, poinsettias, tulips, and many more. By evening's end, a long-stemmed rose was plucked for every woman in the room. The flowers alone cost $50,000.

Coworkers nibbled at hors d'oeuvres of smoked salmon, caviar, and asparagus. Waiters proffered silver trays filled with flutes of Dom Pér-ignon. Four open bars served hard liquor, fine wine, and imported beers. Music from the thirteen-piece band stirred soles and passions so that before long people swayed on the dance floor.

On side tables, entrées simmered in stainless-steel hot dishes. White-aproned attendants served shrimp, mussels, lobster, lamb, veal, filet mignon, smoked turkey, pork roast, scalloped potatoes, wild rice, and a cornucopia of salads and vegetables. "I'd order everything because never in my life would I pay for it on my own," said one woman.

After a few hours of drinking and eating, the party combusted into civilized frenzy—as did many such parties. "Sherman'd be drunk, and Darr'd be gyrating on the dance floor suggestively air-humping a secretary or two," said one observer. Some executives would slink off to the men's room to partake of the "recreational drugs," according to many employees. After the Christmas party dinner, trays of liqueurs and boxes of cigars circulated, usually more than once. Toward midnight, one secretary distributed keys to a few dozen hotel suites, which had been reserved for members of Darr's inner circle in DIG as well as for the favored regional coordinators and directors. "By midnight, you could tell who these guys were going to share the room with," said the keeper of the keys.

The combination of drink, drugs, and desire sometimes erupted in volatile exchanges. At one Christmas party, a female DIG worker was confronted by her party-crashing abusive husband; he punched her as she stood at the corner bar. She, in turn, slugged him back. Two people who saw the domestic battle rushed to stop the couple from the other side of the room. Halfway across the dance floor, the rescuers got stuck in the middle of a thick, intoxicated crowd. Oblivious to the violence unfolding a few feet away from them, the dancers jokingly blocked the two. "I'll never forget that scene," said one woman. "Here was this couple battering each other with punches and screams, while the others were necking and laughing."

After a while, the parties grew too bizarre for even loyal employees. The bills swelled outrageously. Eventually, such a one-night soirée cost $250,000 and, to pay for the affair, DIG "passed the bucket" to the sponsors.

In 1986, DIG was on its way to becoming the chief moneymaking piston in Pru-Bache's expensive engine. Its list of LP sponsors was long and impressive: Graham, VMS Realty, Watson & Taylor, Polaris Aircraft Leasing, Spanos Realty (Alex Spanos owns the San Diego Chargers), Almahurst Bloodstock, the Fogelman Organization, Lorimar Films, the Related Cos., Clifton Harrison, and other sponsors.

By now, LPs were no longer just for the wealthy who wanted a tax write-off. The less expensive public LPs had grown popular also. The differences between private and public are numerous, but basically, they are as follows:

Private LPs pool a smaller number of investors who earn large annual incomes and hold considerable assets. In general, these people invest $100,000 to $200,000 for an LP unit. They cannot buy or sell their units easily, as no public market exists—which is a major drawback to the private offerings. Although the details of an LP must be outlined in a "memo," the offerings are not scrutinized thoroughly by the SEC, which doesn't require the sponsors to register private deals.

In comparison, public LPs are registered with the SEC, which supposedly reviews an LP's offering documents closely. Because of this review, public offerings typically take longer to complete; once they come to market, investors can easily trade them on a stock exchange. Generally, units cost about $1,000, although some were priced as low as $10 a unit. Therefore, middle-income people with average salaries and few assets qualified to join the larger, public pools of LPs.

In the early 1980s, private LPs had been a more popular investment vehicle than public LPs. They were used by the wealthy to legitimately shelter income. That's all. But 1984 proved to be the last great year for private LP sales; some $10.5 billion of them were sold that year.

"From then on, it was very clear which direction the Republicans were going in," said broker Gary Zahn. He knew that tax shelters were slated to die. Instead of offering tax benefits, LPs would have to package investments with strong underlying assets and offer real value in order to form an attractive investment.

Why? In a phrase, the Internal Revenue Service. Perhaps unwittingly, the tax man dealt a debilitating blow to LP investors that Pru-Bache and other Street sponsors did not foresee. Indeed, no single factor changed the fate of limited partnerships more dramatically than did tax laws. After years of allowing generous tax deductions to LP investors and spurring speculation, the federal government suddenly changed the rules.

The first change occurred in 1984, when the IRS lowered the tax brackets for high-income people from 70 percent to 50 percent. With lower tax brackets, the wealthy had less of an incentive to shelter income from taxes. In itself, the change didn't radically alter the sales of private LPs, but it foreshadowed more dramatic changes to come.

Still, wealthy clients continued to seek private LPs, even when the assets beneath the LPs were of dubious quality. Said Dick Hechmann: "There were multimillionaires out there who knew what they were getting into. The only reason they wanted these things was for the 50 percent write-offs" from their ordinary, taxable income.

On the other hand, middle-income people began to buy LPs because Pru-Bache brokers told them that the LPs' assets were valuable. Gary

Zahn, for one, recommended that his clients, who were firemen and teachers, invest $5,000 in real-estate and oil and gas LPs during this time. He believed in DIG.

Then came the Tax Act of 1986. Suddenly, accelerated depreciation disappeared. One could no longer "write off" or subtract from one's taxable income the nonexistent or phantom losses in a short amount of time. Instead, "passive losses" appeared: one could subtract actual losses from an investment only if losses didn't exceed the income gained from just that investment. No longer could the doctor earning $400,000 in salary save taxes by subtracting huge phony losses from LP investments. "Everybody knew we would lose some of these tax benefits, but no one expected the damage that actually occurred," said a former DIG employee.

Suddenly, many LPs were stripped of their value. Anyone who had ever bought a tax-sheltered LP now held an asset of dubious value. Devoid of any tax benefits, some LPs were barren of any value whatsoever.

In 1986, the government lowered income taxes again—this time to 32 percent from 50 percent. Aggravating the troubles of the tax shelter business was the *increased* tax on capital gains, which meant that any gains from investments were now taxed at 28 percent, not the 20 percent of yore. So, if you could sell your LP, you not only lost the write-offs that year, but had to pay a higher tax than you would had you sold it earlier. Together, these changes had far-reaching consequences.

"The law hurt a lot of big players," said one tax accountant. "But it also hurt a lot of middle-class people who had discovered a way to save sheltered money for their kids' education," only to lose it. Now some owed back taxes and penalties on these LPs.

The 1986 law, in fact, wreaked havoc in the economy. Businesses that had depended on tax write-offs, such as luxury-boat makers, starved in the ensuing years. Entire industries that had been fueled primarily by generous write-offs, such as real-estate development, began to shrink. Suddenly, there was no tax incentive to speculate and build, as there had been before, and the harsh realities of the marketplace took hold. Bad properties that had once been structured as good tax shelters suddenly became plain bad properties. LPs dropped in value; real-estate prices decreased as much as 30 percent; banks and thrifts that had lent money against real estate now found themselves in trouble. Now those loans were worth 10 percent to 30 percent *more* than the property that secured the loans. Foreclosures swelled.

"Banks called in the loans, not because the loans were in default, but because they were suddenly undercollateralized," said one former DIG member. Banks restructured the loans, and the real-estate industry began a long, steep, six-year slide. Said the tax accountant: "The law killed the real-estate market and was instrumental in causing the savings and loan crisis." The damage totaled billions of dollars and thousands of jobs.

Then the tax man dealt one last blow to limited partners. For the first time in history, a tax law was not grandfathered. "People who already held LPs, who had bought them in 1984 under the old rules, now had to pay taxes under the new rules," said Hechmann. Also, tax shelters that had been structured so holders could claim a percent of losses annually over four years could no longer be depreciated. The confusing result was an administrative nightmare for taxpayers and tax preparers everywhere.

But that didn't stop the party at One Seaport Plaza. The very year that the IRS rescinded tax benefits for American LPs was the one in which Pru-Bache's public LP sales ripped through the roof. Prior to the 1986 tax act, private LPs had been the rage primarily because of their attractive write-offs. In the first half of the decade, Pru-Bache sold about $3.6 billion worth of private LPs, which do not have to be registered with the SEC and thus are harder to tally. However, insiders claim that DIG's sales did not explode until 1984—and the bulk of that was in private LPs.

At that time, Pru-Bache was a bit player in the public LP market. For example, in 1984, it sold $280 million in public deals—or a measly 4 percent of the market's total. In 1985, sales of all private LPs dropped by 30 percent, while sales of public LPs zoomed 35 percent, to $11.5 billion. But even in the public market boom, Pru-Bache's sales were stagnant: again it sold only $280 million and barely squeaked onto the list of top ten public LP sponsors (Merrill Lynch headed that list).

But in 1986 Pru-Bache soared to number one by selling $828 million worth of public LPs—triple the amount it had ever sold previously. In the next two years, sales would climb even higher than that, propelled to a great degree by lies. The Pru's and Ball's unquestioning dictum to "produce or perish" worked wonders in DIG.

In the wake of tax changes, DIG now had to package prudent, well-advised LP deals in order for customers to receive a "reasonable" return. But given DIG's treatment of cavalier due diligence staff at the time, "reasonable" wasn't about to become the new standard. "There was a flood of questionable product going through" DIG's door prior to 1986, said one former due diligence officer. After that, the question became rhetorical: when would the dam of bad deals burst?

After 1986, DIG was selling so much product it was hard to turn off the spigot. That year, DIG contributed $40 million to the company's profits—more than any other division. In a curious twist to the tale, the Pru must have known how the tax law would wipe out the traditional investment benefits of LPs, for it stated in its annual report:

> In September, without even waiting for President Reagan to sign the tax bill into law, Prudential-Bache took the lead among Wall Street brokerage firms in holding seminars for clients on the implications of tax reform. By the end of the year, about 70,000 clients and prospects nationwide had already attended the ongoing seminars.

Yet Pru-Bache continued to stress "tax-free" investments and "tax-sheltered" LPs that after 1986 no longer existed. The phrases were repeated in marketing material and sales sheets for years later.

In hindsight, the tax law did indeed hurt limited partners, as many former DIG employees have pointed out. Said one broker: "The unfairness of what the government did was just mind-boggling." But the government's lone act doesn't approach the degree of injustice that the general partners inflicted on their investors.

Of all the LPs, Graham Energy's products were by far the biggest sales generator for Pru-Bache. This fact should have delighted Paul Grattarola: finally, it seemed, Darr, Sherman, and other DIG officers were firmly backing his company's product. But Grattarola was not satisfied, as his job had become a nightmare.

For him, life had become one long battle. Although he tried to control expenses, costs rose considerably. For example, Pru-Bache held regular seminars, or due diligence meetings, often at resorts in distant cities. Pru-Bache executives, managers, and top brokers frequently demanded that Graham pay for extra first-class tickets so their secretaries and female companions could accompany them. Usually, Grattarola checked with a DIG executive before acquiescing. "We kiddingly called ourselves Pimps Inc. because so many men were traveling with girl-friends," said Grattarola. But one day the executive made a similar request, and Grattarola stopped joking: he couldn't turn down a key man from Graham's main distributor. But he couldn't control his sales costs.

Other problems surfaced. Grattarola was never invited to the due diligence meetings, as he should have been. But now he was excluded from management meetings as well and wasn't even asked to attend basic information meetings. And whenever he requested data about a certain LP, he was ignored. "That's not your concern," John Graham would say, brushing him off. "Your job is to sell."

But Grattarola couldn't sleep at night. "I had intuitions and started asking innocent questions. Things like 'Where is the [LP] money going?' and 'Is that the money we are using for distributions [to investors]?'" He didn't suspect any one thing in particular, but he just knew something was wrong.

In the fall of 1985, he arranged a reward trip for the top Pru-Bache sellers of Graham LPs. The brokers began in Munich, traveled to Austria, visited the Alps, and returned to Germany in time for that country's Oktoberfest. Given his mounting troubles at Graham, Grattarola dearly wanted this trip to stand out. Rather than hire a travel agent, he and his wife personally arranged the details, a move that saved 50 percent on the trip's final bill.

Hosting the trip were Baron and Baroness von Frankenstein, the same Austrian family that had inspired Mary Shelley's classic tale. As friends of the Grattarolas, the baron and baroness shepherded the group to the Salzburg palace where Mozart played his first concert as a child. The Mozarteum, which is Austria's Academy of Music and Performing Arts, performed that concert in the same salon in which the young genius had performed more than two hundred years before. Afterward, the group retired to the castle's long formal dining room for a sumptuous meal by candlelight. The staff of the oldest restaurant in Salzburg served the Americans, using the palace's original china and silverware. (Since then, the palace has become a government building and is no longer available for private affairs.)

The baron and his wife introduced the group to the cathedral where Maria of *The Sound of Music* married Colonel Von Trapp (and where the host and hostess were married). Thanks to the Frankensteins' hospitality, the group was treated to unique experiences that today would be impossible. "It was a great trip," said Patricia Graner, widow of Jack.

At the time, Graner had just moved from Atlanta to become sales manager in the Pacific South region. It was a new position, created just for him. The Pac South region had sold more Graham products than any other division, and as the men responsible for this feat, Mike Kudlik and Jim Trice had been invited to Munich. Trice had declined, but he offered his spot to Graner, who for the first time met many of the regional people.

"We were so overwhelmed with all the money spent on that trip," said Pat. The Graners had a stretch Mercedes limousine at their disposal twenty-four hours a day. One morning, they asked the chauffeur to drive them to Italy, where they shopped for the day. The bill for the auto trip alone was $1,200. "The treatment blew us away," she said.

As the regional DIG representative, Kudlik spent time with the Graners on that trip. They joked and laughed, and during a long limousine drive, the two men discussed what Kudlik thought was a far-fetched idea.

"You know," Jack began, "I've got friends in high places."

"What do you mean?" Mike said.

"Wouldn't it be neat if we could work together? I like the way you interact with the guys, Mike. I think we would make a great team."

"Sure, it'd be nice, but it's never going to happen. Trice isn't leaving."

"You'd be surprised."

Kudlik turned to face Graner. "You mean, you've really got a shot at that?"

"I have a very close relationship with Bob Sherman. He knows that Pat wants to come back to Beverly Hills," Graner said, referring to his wife. "She hates Atlanta." Kudlik recalled meeting Graner in Atlanta two years before; Kudlik had interviewed for the very job Kudlik now held. Graner evidently hadn't remembered and continued: "I had already handed in my resignation a few months ago. I was going to move back to California to join another firm." He smiled. "Then they made me an offer."

Kudlik didn't say anything, although he was thinking. Graner may have been drinking, but he wasn't talking like a drunk. Kudlik looked confused, and Graner laughed.

"It's amazing how things work out, Mike. We could be working together sometime real soon."

Kudlik was floored by the audacious proposition. Later, the prophecy seemed like an off-the-wall comment made in a wistful, friendly moment. But in time, the prediction would come true to the detriment of Kudlik and his region.

But in Munich in 1985, the group members shared a memorable trip. In later trips, brokers and managers, along with their wives or girlfriends, shopped for personal items and charged them to the companies. "They became guilt trips," said Pat Graner; some people later realized that maybe this was wrong.

Boorish behavior was common. In Germany, some Pru-Bache managers insulted the young blond hostesses who had been hired to direct and guide the Americans. "The men would get a little too much champagne in them and then subject the young women to crude advances," said one observer. "Here these men were in a foreign country, repre-

senting the upper echelons of American business, and they were be-
having like pigs."

Jim Darr, however, "never had the courtesy to show up" on the Munich trip, said one observer. Although one planner said Darr had demanded from Graham a pair of tickets on the Concorde as well as a
particular room at the legendary George V Hotel in Paris, he never
showed. Darr said he doesn't recall planning that trip.

After Munich, Grattarola's sales were up but his worries mounted. He
sensed wrongdoing but couldn't confirm his suspicions. "I heard talk
about borrowing and I asked accounting why are we borrowing money,"
he said. He was ignored, and for good reason, as it turned out.

In 1985—as oil prices plummeted—Graham grappled with its own
financial woes. Its LPs were not bringing in the income investors had
been promised, oil prices were in a free fall, and competitors were folding. Meanwhile, Graham's expenses had escalated both in the oil field
and in the sales field, with trips, perks, and overhead. To compensate
for the resulting drop in income, Graham basically cooked up a deceptive arrangement, as outlined in a January 9, 1985, memo.

Graham accountant Mark Files wrote that chairman John Graham
had arranged for bank loans to fund certain partnerships and to "camouflage, to the extent we can, the purpose of the [loan] proceeds"—
which was to return to investors the promised 15 percent on their
money. "We should ask forgiveness rather than permission if Pru-Bache
sees through the borrowing plan"; the deception would lead investors
to believe that the funds were earning income. (It later helped establish
Graham's fabulous "track record" of 15 percent returns.)

Pittman, now head of due diligence, wrote a 1985 memo in which
he expressed concern that the borrowed money augmented returns that
"did not reflect the true returns but were inflated."

Yet Pru-Bache also borrowed $5.7 million for the partnerships during
1985 and 1986. Later Prudential would say the borrowing was appropriate because it was for capital expenses, but Chanin in a July 1985
memo approved loans that were clearly intended to sustain distributions. Between them, the cosponsors approved $18 million in borrow-
ings to the LPs through 1990 and never told investors.

Yet they paid for the loans, as well as for other undisclosed items. In
his 1985 memo, Files suggested that Darr not be invited to an upcoming
all-expenses-paid hunting trip. "Darr would not enjoy turkey hunting as
much since there is little shooting and a great deal of waiting. . . . We
already have a number of 'kings' to take care of there." The tab was
high.

Graham frequently treated Darr, and other executives, including Pru Insurance executive Matthew J. Chanin, to expensive "hunting trips" at a "camp" that cost as much as $11,000 a day. The free trips included travel, lodging, and meals for the Pru officers. Darr later said the trips were for "business and had a social component," explaining that they "establish a closer working relationship." SEC rules require that free gifts, including vacations, be disclosed to investors; NYSE rules at that time prohibited members from accepting gifts worth more than $100.

Still, Graham openly toasted Pru executives at the 3,200-acre Longleaf Plantation in Purvis, Mississippi. The expensive events were accounted for as "due diligence" meetings. "The only due diligence that was done was these guys would go out and hunt quails," said Grattarola.

The executives were flown first-class from New York to the South to rest for a few days in the plantation's main lodge. In the evenings, they ate rich meals and drank fine wine. During the day, men nursing hangovers joined the group outdoors, where fattened bobwhite quail awaited in cages. As soon as the "hunters" were ready, with their shotguns aimed and cocked, a "guide" lifted the cage door and kicked it so the quail would fly skyward. Gunshots cracked the air in clumsy rounds; the quail fell dead. "Pretty sportsmanlike, huh?" said Grattarola.

Graham and Pru-Bache later claimed that these costly trips were business-related, and so were legitimate. But when asked in a deposition about one such trip, Darr said he didn't recall whether any business talks were conducted on the trips: "I don't like to distract people who have a loaded gun in their hands," he explained.

Pru-Bache executives flew home with extra quail, cleaned and dressed, and pecan pie.

Since 1983, the Pru had invested in Graham Energy's LPs, but like Grattarola, the company by 1985 sensed trouble. Chanin, John Childs, and another Pru executive sat on the oversight board that directed Graham's funds. Based on Darr's strong recommendation, the Pru had invested its own money right alongside the public's; at various times, it contributed about 15 percent of total funds raised.

When the price of oil dropped steeply, the Pru worried about its own investment. In October 1985, Chanin told DIG officers he was willing to ask the Pru for more money to invest in the LPs, but first he wanted to come to an understanding with Graham about the company's high costs. "He feels that the distributions on these partnerships will have to be cut not only because of decreased revenues, but also because of expenses that are higher than expected," a DIG officer wrote.

Pru was unhappy with high fees, as well as its puny returns of 4 to

5 percent. By 1986, Chanin and the other Pru officers had cooled on Darr, who they believed was more concerned with the quantity of sales than with the quality. The Pru decided not to invest in more Graham funds.

But what to say to the public? After some discussion, Pru-Bache officers decided they had "an easier story to tell" if they told their sales force that the regulators had forced Mother Pru to stop investing in oil and gas. "The marketing feeling" was that explaining Pru's "exhaustive" insurance company regulations created a more "believable story" than did the truth, said one memo. The truth was, Graham was no longer good enough for the rock-solid, market-wise corporation. The Pru said nothing.

But before Pru pulled out, Chanin approved the loans that were later used to inflate payouts and to fool Pru-Bache investors.

Still, even Pru may have been duped alongside the public with other, more complicated layers of deceit. In allegations that surfaced years later in a massive Energy Income class action, some charged that Graham employed an accounting sleight of hand that, from 1986 on, increased the apparent cash flow to investors. It worked like this:

Graham purchased oil properties, which unlike other real estate, yielded oil and, therefore, income. Thus, the date of purchase marks the day that buyers begin to enjoy income stream from such land. For example, investors alleged that Graham closed such a sale around June 30, 1986, yet purposely backdated the sale to April 1. The backdating falsely showed that the sale date had been three months earlier, which in turn inflated the purchase price by three months' worth of oil revenue. While masking the actual, lower sales price, the technique allegedly enabled sponsors to return investors' money under the guise of distributions. Investors were led to believe that the funds were performing well. In reality, investors claimed, many LPs were simply returning to investors their original dollars, making it appear as though clients were receiving fantastic returns of 12 to 15 percent.

In court, Pru-Bache's expert witness said that the accounting practice was a common feature of the oil and gas business. A Pru-Bache executive elaborated: "We think what we did was fine and in accordance with standard accounting practices." He added that the same accounting was used even when oil properties lost money between the two dates, causing an increase—not a decrease—in the real price.

Although an astute investor could perhaps see through the misleading DIG claims by studying the prospectuses, this was not the case with the alleged backdating.

"Nobody could have figured this one out," said Jeff Dennis Ferentz, an attorney who represented plaintiffs in the case. "The killer to the whole fraud was that there was income to the partnership before a partnership had ever been created."

Ferentz and attorney Stuart Goldberg helped unravel the fraud and figured that the LPs lost $730 million through this clever trick.

The alleged falsehood could have been exposed at one of a few checkpoints. Arthur Anderson approved the prospectus and audited partnership books; the SEC approved the prospectus; the due diligence team at Pru-Bache as well as the experts at Pru Insurance gave their blessing on the deal. "Some of the brightest minds and most trusted institutions signed off on these," said Ferentz. Yet who knew?

Grattarola enraged his top salesmen. One man submitted monthly rent for an apartment he didn't even have; another salesman submitted phony travel expenses for hotels in which he never stayed. Grattarola refused to pay the bills and lectured the men sternly.

Meanwhile, Graham's officers hid the LP borrowings from Grattarola until tense exchanges flared almost daily between him and officers in New York and in Covington, Louisiana. He knew the oil business was sliding downward. He didn't understand where all the money to pay LPs was coming from. What about distributions? Where were they coming from? What money was being borrowed? What was being disclosed to investors?

Finally, in January 1986, the showdown occurred. Al Dempsey called Grattarola into his office.

"I've got some bad news to tell you, Paul, and this time you can't talk me out of it. You have to leave."

"What are you talking about?" said Grattarola, frowning.

"I don't want to do this, because you've done a lot for the company. But you're causing too many problems. The salesmen are upset with you."

"Damn right they are," Grattarola snapped. "I found them lying on their expenses."

"What do you care? That's not your job," said Dempsey. "Besides, you're not going to talk me out of this one. And you're not going to talk Tony and John out of it. You have to leave."

"What the hell, Al! Because I ask too many questions?" Grattarola could barely contain his rage. "That's my job!"

"I know, I know. And you've done a bang-up job. We really appreciate it. You've launched our sales and built up our staff. But now things just aren't going well. If you don't resign, we'll have to fire you."

Grattarola sat stunned.

Dempsey continued: "If you resign, we'll pay your expenses, which I know you're entitled to. You'll receive your bonuses and anything coming to you."

Grattarola yelled, "Why am I being fired? Tell me!"

Just then, president Anton H. ("Tony") Rice III entered and paced the office slowly; he proceeded to humiliate Grattarola.

"You are just not cooperating, Paul." His voice was smooth and unctuous. "You're a hotheaded Italian. You're stubborn and uncooperative. Frankly, I'm not sure you've done such a 'bang-up job.' I believe our best interests are served with someone other than you heading our sales team at this important juncture." Rice continued the personal attack for what seemed like an hour. Psychologically, Grattarola felt as if he were being held down and beaten with lower and lower blows.

He was fifty-six years old and devastated. He had a stellar sales record, an unblemished compliance record, and a reputation as a reasonable straight-shooter. Sure he had a temper. But how had he failed?

After Grattarola left Graham, the sales of LPs cosponsored by Pru-Bache and Graham went through the roof. As the man watched from home, his sanity began to crack. He racked his mind for some meaning but couldn't find any. It was bad enough to be fired, especially at his age. But to see sales suddenly skyrocket at what became the most popular oil and gas company in the nation? That was wrenching. "Jesus," he thought. "I could have been the sales manager for the hottest product in the country. What the hell's the matter with me?"

For the next three years, Grattarola futilely searched for another position. In his search for jobs, he believed he made a good first impression, but as soon as a potential employer called his former employer for references, Grattarola never heard from them again. "That was no coincidence," he now says.

Finally, Grattarola finally landed a top management position at a national energy company.

10

The Year of the Deal

Take a look at this." Ball's secretary handed him the latest issue of an industry magazine.

He smiled. There he was, pictured on the cover of an industry magazine. The story inside featured his latest, boldest plan yet: Project '89.

That was the code name for Pru-Bache's investment banking effort. Its mission: to break into the cloistered top-ten ranks of Wall Street's most lucrative, most prestigious market niche by the year 1989. Such a lofty goal was one that no broker-dealer had ever accomplished, certainly not in three short years. Still, if Pru-Bache could accomplish this, the effort would pay dividends for years to come by providing another source of income.

Investment bankers are the dealers in the broker-dealer business. As middlemen, they help corporate clients who *need* money access the dealer's brokerage clients, who entrust money to the broker-dealer. To raise money, these bankers create new securities so that firms such as Pru-Bache can distribute the product through their enormous retail networks. In the 1980s, the dealing end of that pipeline was extraordinarily lucrative. "At the time, they were minting money on the Street," said Chip Barnes, former Pru-Bache banker. By 1985, Street banking deals totaled $138 billion a year; in 1986—the "deal-maker's year"—investment banking transactions would more than double to $288 billion. By 1987, they would double *again* to $576 billion—more than half a trillion dollars. With that amount of money sloshing around town, Pru-Bache could not afford to just stand by and watch. It had to jump into the corporate finance business and grab its share of the booty.

Like many things on Wall Street, the hierarchy of deal-makers is strictly defined. "You don't just wake up one day and decide to be an investment banker," sniffed one wizened veteran. Reputations, relationships, and client bases are built over many years and can be destroyed in one emotional, distraught moment. "People behave poorly when there's a lot of money on the table," said Christian Wyser-Pratte.

By the middle of the 1980s, this tendency became more pronounced. The time-honored emphasis on relationships withered considerably; corporate clients became more concerned with the "right" price, or lowest fee, for the best deal than with relationships. Around the 1900s, for example, an industry chief would take his company's financing needs only to his cousin's investment banking house; that tradition continued for generations. However, by the dawn of the 1980s, those relationships no longer held as much sway. Although talented people and trustworthy relationships remained important, they were not the sole considerations.

"Corporate clients continually sought more efficient and less costly ways to obtain Wall Street services," according to Samuel L. Hayes III and Philip M. Hubbard in *Investment Banking: A Tale of Three Cities.* "In certain instances, they brought financing related activities in-house rather than rely on securities firm vendors." Plus, the SEC adopted Rule 415 in the early eighties. This allowed companies to practically bypass the investment banker by preparing their own offering documents. Now, instead of requiring a customized, painstaking offering ritual including an investment banking team, a company could simply fill out the standardized paperwork, put it on the shelf, and wait for the right time to bring its issue to market. This streamlined method saved a company time and money, at the expense of the diligent banker. Now the choice of which investment banking firm to hire became a function of price: who could do the deal cheapest.

"It was an earth-shattering change," said a banker. As a result of these and other changes, many old, stalwart bankers began to fall by the curbside: names such as Kuhn Loeb and Blyth disappeared in the price-slashing crusades of the 1970s and 1980s. And big money, in the form of Prudential, came to town. By 1986, Ball and Pru-Bache rightly figured that, armed with a knowledgeable staff, the blessing of its corporate parent, and a focused strategy, Pru-Bache too could joust for market turf alongside industry titans.

That list included the most formidable players. Of the ten leading investment bankers, the first five firms occupy what is called the "bulge bracket" simply because that's where most of the money bulges. In 1986, those elite firms were, in order of business transacted, Salomon Brothers, which was primarily a rough-and-tumble bond-trading powerhouse; CS First Boston, a prestigious house with Yankee roots and Swiss connections; Morgan Stanley, the blue-blooded offspring of the Glass-Steagall Act, which split deposit-taking banks from deal-making banks; the ill-fated Drexel Burnham Lambert, whose 1980s rise to power was fueled, and destroyed, by Mike Milken's good-idea-gone-mad; and Merrill Lynch, a huge retail house that in two decades had built a solid, yeomanlike bank.

As measured by the Street's most important yardstick—money—the bulk of the industry's $288 billion in annual revenues that year flooded into these top five slots. In 1986, those five had gathered to themselves 66 percent of all new issues sold domestically.

Trailing the bulge bracket was the "rest of the best," which included the following, in order of transaction volume: Goldman Sachs, which over decades had refined its insular German-Jewish mind-set into a well-regarded teamwork ethic; Lehman Brothers, formed in 1850 by three sons who sold cotton, and swallowed in 1984 by Shearson/American Express; Kidder Peabody, bred by a Baltimore merchant who in 1837 peddled bonds from the colonies to the English; PaineWebber, a Boston-born wire house that once catered to the carriage trade; and Bear Stearns, known as roughneck traders who parlayed Rule 415 into a torrent of cheap and easy business.

They occupied slots six, seven, eight, nine, and ten and completed the list of deal-makers; they were the "second-tier" investment banking firms because in print advertisements that announced done deals—"tombstones," as they were called—they were listed beneath the bulge-bracket firms, on the second level. Their revenues trailed those of the bigger firms by a significant dollar amount; in 1986, they had captured only 24 percent of transaction dollars. Nevertheless, second-tier firms were well regarded and avidly watched in the quarterly and annual rankings. Sometimes a player would slip a notch or two or break into the bulge bracket; sometimes a player would be gobbled up by a competitor; rarely would an upstart appear out of nowhere.

Then came Pru-Bache. Prior to 1986, its efforts to break onto the list had been embarrassing, to say the least. In 1985, Pru-Bache had ranked thirty-fifth in global underwritings; it had placed thirteenth in domestic issues; and it had captured less than 1 percent of the market. Its net pretax income that year had been about $1 million—which was equal to the take-home salary of a solid banker at any other house. "Whenever someone asked me which investment banking house I worked in, I'd cough into my jacket, mumble Prudential-Bache, and quickly change the subject," said a former Pru-Bache banker. Among dealers, the firm was a nonentity.

Besides money, other sirens lured Pru-Bache to these waters. At the time, the job title "investment banker" possessed a psychological cache that attracted socialites, museum directors, and charity ball invitations. It held a degree of prestige and status that far surpassed the required ability to figure yields and spreads. Suddenly, bankers were featured in the glossy pages of four-color popular magazines and were immortalized in movies. A Salomon Brothers investment banker named Lewie Ranieri, for example, was profiled in the December 1985 issue of *Esquire* magazine—the same issue that featured songwriter Bruce Springsteen and screen actor Sean Penn. The following year, *Fortune* devoted a whole issue to investment bankers, who, like the masses, worked long hours and worried about their future, but unlike the masses, collected high six-figure paychecks with bonuses. On its cover, the magazine had snapped the picture of a white, thirty-one-year-old male, holding a cigar and arching his brow.

Ball, at least, held no cigar for his portrait when photographed in a head shot for the cover of *Investment Dealer's Digest*. His head was turned but his eyes peered straight at the reader. His mouth curved in a slight smile, Ball looked as though he had just accepted a dare. Could he really pull off Project '89? "Watch me," his eyes seemed to say.

By this time, Ball had already performed a set of "miracles," underwritten by Pru's open checkbook. He had fashioned Pru-Bache into a formidable brokerage firm in a number of ways. He had expanded the old Bache franchise by one hundred offices to a total of 320 branches. He had upgraded the quality of branch managers and had helped attract ambitious professional brokers. His cadre of well-paid salesmen numbered 5,500 strong, or about double what it had been in 1982. Educated, well trained, and devoted to their leader, these men and women displayed an esprit de corps that in the beginning had been forged by public doubts and later had been tempered in the celebration of victory and rewards. By now, the Pru's brokerage firm had arrived. It was an awesome network that sprawled from one national coast to the other and from Mexico to Canada, and extended to locations around the world. In four short years, Pru-Bache's retail system had climbed from the bottom of the heap in terms of productivity to become, in the Pru's own words, the most productive among the "big" firms.

Yet this operation needed product on which to feed. Generous payouts, sales commissions, and an expensive infrastructure cost money. The only significant "in-house" specials at the time were the LPs packaged by the direct investment group; the tax laws had nipped their allure. The firm also had about twenty-two mutual funds, but the commissions earned from those were lean compared to those from LPs. Still, Ball had formed a decent mutual fund company, whose assets would grow by more than 50 percent during the 1980s. But aside from these two main offerings, Pru-Bache had nothing exclusive with which to attract the most coveted prize of all—OPM, other people's money.

By now, the firm had spent an all-time high of $1.3 billion to improve and maintain itself. A strong banking unit could help offset those expenses. It could package and sell initial public offerings, corporate debt, and junk bonds. It could offer collateralized mortgage obligations (CMOs), which were pooled mortgages divided into long-term, short-term, and medium-term holdings, and private placements, such as limited partnerships. It could create myriad products and services. Like his clients, Ball had to diversify.

And that, basically, was the message written between the lines of the October 1986 cover story.

In his office at One Seaport Plaza, Jim Crowley swiveled his chair slightly and glanced at the magazine upon his desk. His boss, George Ball, graced the cover announcing Project '89, but Crowley knew he was one of its driving forces. The hulking, dark-haired man exhaled and swiveled back to face the panoramic view outside his window.

So much had happened in the past twelve months, since Crowley had been promoted to cohead investment banking. Almost a year ago, he had hired a consulting firm to determine the best way to build Pru-Bache into a formidable investment banking power. At the time, he alone headed the fledgling unit, which desperately needed leadership and direction. The consultant's study had determined that those investment banking firms that had focused on client relationships—the mainstay of the business for the past century—had withered in the new money culture. However, those firms that had become "expert" in certain product areas had grown exponentially. Junk bonds, for example, were now the purview of Drexel Burnham; commercial paper was practically owned by Goldman Sachs; mergers and acquisitions added a sheen to First Boston's once dull reputation.

So, too, Pru-Bache had to find its special corner from which to launch itself—and fast. Crowley knew he couldn't do the job alone, as he was skilled primarily in funding mortgage and financial institutions. In order to build a full-service investment banking unit, he'd need the help of people experienced in international finance, in mergers and acquisitions, and in other specialities. Whereas other men would not have admitted their weaknesses and, instead, would have lurched ahead blindly into dark waters armed only with the secret hope that providence and dumb luck would lend them success, Crowley was different. Unpretentious and relatively secure in himself, he knew he couldn't do this Herculean job alone. So he took matters into his own hands, as he had done so many times before.

At six feet three inches, Crowley is a big-boned man with olive skin and straight black hair. He fishes, sails, and hunts upland game such as quail. Born of Irish Catholic stock, Crowley was the eldest of five children. His middle-class family was comfortable until his hard-drinking father lost his job.

When Crowley was sixteen, the family suddenly had to scramble just to pay the heating bills. His parents grew unhappy. The family's humbling fall from a once leisurely life terrified the teenager, who now found himself worried about how to survive the winter. Later, this dark period would help him easily weather any "downturn" that Wall Street could ever offer.

With the aide of scholarships, he attended Villanova University, working seasonal jobs to help support himself. He dropped out twice but finally graduated. After traveling the world for a year, he returned to the East Coast and landed a job in real estate. Then opportunity knocked. He was asked to address a class at Wharton about how *not* to do a real-estate deal. After the speech, the dean invited Crowley to attend Wharton's graduate business school. Crowley said he didn't have the money, but the dean told him to take the admission tests anyway. He passed and was admitted, and called on enough financial donors listed in the Foundation Directory to pay for tuition. That, plus a teaching fellowship, helped him graduate in 1976.

Then he signed on with the investment banking firm of Smith Barney Harris Upham—a genteel, white-shoe house that counseled corporate clients in their financial hour of need much as a parish priest hears confessions. There, Crowley learned the business the old-fashioned way, from the bottom up, beginning in trading and bond sales. He was promoted several times, and rose into higher positions until he and a woman named Carol Curley helped pioneer mortgage financing—that is, the pooling of home mortgages for resale to institutions. The business boomed in the eighties into a multibillion-dollar arena.

Then, in 1984, Curley left to join Pru-Bache's nascent investment banking effort. Pru-Bache also tried to lure Crowley, telling him the unit had an army of bankers to pitch deals, computers to structure them, and traders to sell the product. Meanwhile, Smith Barney offered Crowley a partnership position, an offer whose benefits Crowley debated with himself late at night. After some soul-searching, he left Smith Barney to join what he believed was a spanking-new first-class banking operation at Pru-Bache.

However, that was not the case. On Crowley's first day on the job, Curley greeted him and presented a framed memento that read "Toto, I have a feeling we're not in Kansas anymore." Crowley learned that rather than a state-of-the-art banking operation, Pru-Bache had a skeletal banking staff, one trader, and no computers. Under Bernard, the entire corporate finance unit (which included investment banking) would hire more professionals, but still, the unit sputtered.

Over the next two years, Crowley and Curley turned their efforts to building the firm's financial institutions group, which packaged and sold mortgage bonds. They succeeded. They also helped the firm earn profits in the new but rather pedestrian area of interest-rate swaps, wherein clients exchange debts—say, a fixed-rate bond for a floating-rate bond—to suit their needs. The banker earned a fee, and sometimes was a party to the swap. By 1986, Pru-Bache's forty-person team did more than four hundred swaps valued at $13 billion. Later, these two areas would fuel the buildup of the stuff that makes *real* investment bankers: the mergers and acquisitions, buyouts, and takeover business.

By late 1985, Ball was displeased with Bernard and moved him to another position. Crowley was asked to act "temporarily" as head of investment banking. Crowley, basically, said forget it; he wasn't going to act as temporary anything while essentially performing the job with all of its responsibilities. In November 1985, Crowley became head of investment banking. Then he hired the consultants, who told him that, over the short haul, the unit would have to develop a market niche, as it had in mortgage finance and swaps. The long term was less certain, except for one thing: Crowley knew that he could not build a full-fledged investment banking house alone. Especially at the time, in the spring of 1986, when every other investment banking house on the Street was up and running with cash-rich deals.

Ball had interviewed some "star" names to help Crowley, but no one whom he respected as a well-rounded leader. Then, as if from the gods, Crowley had found his man buried inside a newspaper story.

The March 1986 article heralded the rising economic clout of Los Angeles from the point of view of an "itinerant New Yorker." It gushed about the city's diverse economy, its great population, and the advent of New York financial powers, which were opening new offices. The story continued:

> "Los Angeles is clearly going to be the biggest economic and people zone in the United States," said Theodore V. Fowler, a managing director of First Boston Corp. . . . When he arrived seven weeks ago, he became his New York–based company's first managing director to be posted in Los Angeles.

As most investment bankers will confess, L.A. is Siberia when it comes to the world of deals. Most of the investment banking action happens in offices located within the hollows of Manhattan, so something is wrong when a Wall Street banker is suddenly stationed three thousand miles away from the crush. Crowley studied the photo of Fowler for some clues. He noted the cigarette dangling from Fowler's mouth, his riotous wavy blond hair, his arms akimbo. Crowley wondered why an energetic guy like Fowler had been banished to the financial hinterland.

To find out, Crowley had picked up the telephone and dialed Fowler's number. Half a dozen unreturned calls later, the two men finally connected:

"You don't know me, but I'm Jim Crowley, head of investment banking at Prudential-Bache Securities." Silence hung on the other end. "I've got a plan to build up the banking division here."

Fowler snorted. "You've got to be kidding."

"I'd like you to take a look at our plan. Maybe consider joining us."

"There is no way I'd consider Pru-Bache as a serious contender in banking. Besides," he added, "I'm talking to some other people now."

Crowley's suspicions were confirmed; Fowler wasn't happy in L.A. "Look," he said quickly. "Just give me a half hour. If you don't like what you see, fine. We'll forget we ever met."

Fowler didn't answer.

Crowley pressed: "I'll buy you a first-class, round-trip ticket to New York and breakfast if you just tell me what you think."

"Fuck your ticket," said Fowler softly. "I'll be in New York in a few days anyway. But you can buy breakfast."

Fowler walked into the Plaza Hotel on Fifty-ninth Street overlooking Central Park South. At seven-thirty this April morning, a large breakfast crowd had already gathered in the five-star hotel's breakfast room. A waiter led Fowler to Crowley's table, and Crowley stood to shake Fowler's hand. In that second, the two men sized each other up. In many respects, they couldn't be more different.

An affable man, Crowley could usually detect knaves, yet his political skills allow him to deal with such people, to a point.

Fowler, on the other hand, couldn't "see a curveball coming if it were right on top of him," said his friend. He could not care less for small talk, and in business he can be impatient and rude. A tad over six feet, Fowler is fair-skinned and blue-eyed and appears patrician, but actually hails from a comfortable, middle-class two-kid family and was raised in Toledo. Soft-spoken and no-nonsense, Fowler has a truck driver's mouth and a quick, some say brilliant mind. He strikes many people as crude, even arrogant; he hides his softer spots.

Fowler was one of the last children in the United States to be struck with polio before the advent of the vaccine, having contracted the virus when he was four years old. Fortunately, all that remains is a slight limp when he walks, and a fierce ambition when he works, which is most of the time.

While Crowley is warm and garrulous, Fowler can be gruff and peevish. While Crowley is expansive and visionary, Fowler is direct and detail-oriented; he can fashion deals that custom-fit others' dreams or dilemmas. Yet, as different as the men were on that April morning, they warmed to each other immediately. It helped that Crowley got right to the point.

"I want you to look at this," he said, handing over a report.

"What is it?" Fowler flipped through it.

"It's our plan to build Prudential-Bache's investment banking unit into something relevant."

The fifty-page report compiled mission statements, bar graphs, and strategic goals. The "manifesto" also included annual projections of revenue, profit, and market share over the next three years. Fowler flipped through the first few pages, stopping to double-check the figures and to read the headings in big sans serif type. The presentation was audacious.

"This looks great," said Fowler, glancing up at Crowley. "You know, it will only work if your management is really committed. I mean *really* on board."

"I assure you they are committed," said Crowley, relieved at his guest's interest. "They've agreed to invest $92.5 million."

"What do you mean by that number?"

"That's what Prudential's board said it would take."

"You mean they're willing to fucking lose that?"

"Well, not exactly," Crowley explained. The Pru would allow the fledgling investment banking unit to reinvest $93 million of its *own* profits—after certain expenses. Under normal circumstances, the unit's pretax profits would have been handed over to the firm. But during the buildup of Project '89, the Pru would allow the unit to fund itself by essentially allowing it to reinvest up to $93 million.

"Well, let's look at that number," Fowler said, lighting up another cigarette. "How much can a start-up cost you, really? You've already got the building. You've got the desks and the equipment, right?"

Crowley looked sheepish. "Well, we have the building and desks." But the department needed more than that.

For the next four hours, the two men huddled over the table and penciled in the possibilities. After the first hour, most of the restaurant's patrons had left their tables to start the workday. But Crowley and Fowler continued talking, even as the bushoys quietly cleared the tables around them. An hour became two; a waiter occasionally appeared to refill Fowler's coffee cup, and to replace an overflowing ashtray with a clean one. The men continued to figure through the entire morning, swapping histories in between projections.

Fowler had built a similar unit before at First Boston. After graduating from Amherst College and later Columbia's Graduate School of Business, Fowler had worked at a special-bracket investment firm, which after mergers became Blyth Eastman Dillon. Then he worked for a joint-venture operation of Union Bank of Switzerland and Deutsche, for which he executed deals for European clients. In 1976, he joined First Boston, where he helped steer the firm's project finance department toward international business; he soon directed project finance and built it into the top contender in its field. Fueled by his success, he cowrote a three-year business plan for investment banking at year-end 1980, as requested by the firm's CEO. In 1981, Fowler was promoted to cohead of investment banking at a time when the noted duo of Bruce Wasserstein and Joseph Perella coheaded the firm's merger and acquisition business. Within four years, First Boston's revenues grew fivefold, from $150 million to $700 million; the firm jumped from sixth place in worldwide lead-managed underwritings (underwritings in which the investment banker performs the lion's share of work) to the top spot. By spring of 1986, First Boston had become a bulge-bracket house, spurred by the firm's top talent, which included Fowler.

Yet office infighting had made Fowler's job hell. Some of the friction can be laid on the desk of Hans-Joerg Rudloff, a short, balding German who had been raised in Switzerland and was fluent in Schweizerdeutsch, a dialect spoken in Zurich's banking circles. In 1978, the cash-strapped First Boston had formed a joint venture with Crédit Suisse, the oldest of the major Swiss banks, and so had inherited Rudloff. By linking hands, the two firms, now called Crédit Suisse First Boston, intended to grow strong in both international and U.S. markets. But the alliance produced culture clash and a number of well-publicized defections, some of them triggered by Rudloff himself, otherwise known as "the Red Baron." Still, the baron was key to CSFB's success; in 1986 he became deputy chairman.

Fowler, who is decidedly unskilled in the art of political intrigue, had battled with Rudloff and had lost. Hence, Fowler's exile to L.A., where he was building an eight-person new business development unit.

At the time of Crowley's telephone call, Fowler was preparing to leave First Boston. He had already been offered several jobs and was about to take one opportunity that would bring him back to New York. Now this.

"Prudential?" Fowler asked Crowley again. "I mean, you guys aren't even in the race, for Chrissakes. Why would I want to join you at this point in my career?"

"Because you have a chance to build something yourself," Crowley said evenly. "You have an opportunity to start it from the ground up. Look what you have. The Prudential—the Rock—a high-profile name both in the U.S. and abroad. A strong commitment from management." Crowley used his fingers to tick off his points. "You have the Prudential's financial muscle to weather the tough times, when they come. You have a hell of a distribution system through which to sell product. Plus, we have an all-star team of research analysts."

Crowley explained how Ball had already hired a respected pool of analysts, who wrote opinions on Fortune 500 companies, exciting new firms, and other investment opportunities. These pieces were read and respected by pension fund managers, corporate leaders, and institutional investors; a "buy" recommendation could influence the fate, for example, of Auto Maker Inc.'s new stock offering; it could also bring to Pru-Bache Auto Maker Inc.'s investment banking business, which is why research is crucial to a broker-dealer.

Fowler listened intently. By now, the waiters were setting tables for lunch. The two men would have to leave.

"Look," said Crowley. "Why don't you at least come and talk to some of our people. Meet George Ball. See what he has to say."

"Sure, what the hell." Fowler rose from his chair, cigarette in mouth, and gathered up his papers.

"I'll call you," Crowley said.

Three goals of Project '89 would be key in judging its success. The first: Prudential-Bache wanted to become the "best of the rest" by overtaking the number-eight spot on the top-ten investment banking charts by 1989. The second: its "five-year-goal [was] to double P-B's share of the leading investment banking firms' revenues." That is, by 1991, Pru-Bache intended to double its share from 1.2 percent to 2.4 percent of the pie. The third goal: "Longer-term, our goal is to become one of the top five global investment banking firms," according to the report submitted to Pru-Bache's executive committee. Yet these three statements would be overlooked later.

In the fall of 1986, Project '89 was greeted enthusiastically inside the firm, and skeptically outside. In time, the skepticism would grow so loud as to drown out the facts.

With the inauguration of Project '89 came other changes as Ball installed new players on his executive committee. One new hire was James Gahan, a former Hutton man who had worked closely with Ball in the early 1980s. "Genghis" Gahan was known as the type of man you wanted inside your camp, rather than outside as an enemy. "I've got tire tracks all over my back from him," one senior executive said at the time. A mauling, shirt-sleeved, nicotine-and-Tab-addicted character, Gahan had grown up on the crass trading side of the business. He had joined the firm in May 1985 as head of trading; in May of 1986, he was elevated to head Pru-Bache's capital finance unit, which included all of its institutional securities investment, underwriting, trading, and investment banking activities.

Crowley reported to Gahan, and both became members of Ball's executive committee. Gahan began to publicly debase those who questioned Ball's decisions. Said one director: "If you disagreed with Gahan, he'd call you a 'low-life sleazy sack of shit.'" Such comments didn't foster open discussions, and by 1986, three frank-speaking men either left the board or were dismissed. "They tended to say things that George didn't like," said one director. Peter Bernard, James Glynn, and George McGough were removed from the inner circle, and eventually left the firm.

Said one committee member: "Ball began to surround himself with cronies. Soon, he had hired and promoted people who were loyal to him and told him only what he wanted to hear." Sadly, the message wasn't always what George Ball needed to hear.

11

The Rattlesnake Theory

Dammit," Trice bellowed. "I want an answer and I want it now."

Sweat beaded on his bald head, his eyes blazed, and his stare bore through the arrogant manager who sat on the other side of the desk.

"Do you know who you're talking to?" the manager asked insolently. Next to him cowered the nice, bow-tied broker—the man who had landed the firm's Richmond, Virginia, office in so much trouble.

The manager's self-important question hung in the air.

Angry now, Trice slammed his meaty forearm down hard on the desk. He yelled, "I want direct, complete answers, and I don't want to take three days to get them."

At this, the broker bolted from his chair. "I don't like violence," he screamed.

"Sit down," Trice said calmly. "I'm not threatening you. But I want the truth." The broker obeyed.

"Now," Trice began again, "tell me what the hell is going on with this account."

Finally, the story of the Tauber account emerged in painful detail. Clearly, the problem could cost the firm millions of dollars. As Trice listened, he thought to himself, "How did I get myself into this mess?" He considered the strange events of the last two years that had brought him to this point, to Atlanta, as head of the Southeast region. He'd known he'd find problems, but he had never expected to be waist-high in the swampy morass of ethical conflicts and legal violations.

Trice had had no desire to come to Atlanta in the first place. He hadn't wanted this job as regional director of the Southeast, but the firm had insisted. Back in late 1984, Bob Sherman, his boss, had told Trice bluntly that Jack Graner had wanted Trice's job as regional director of Pac South. Why? Graner's wife had wanted to return to Beverly Hills, Sherman had told him. At first, Trice had considered the suggestion ridiculous. After all, what billion-dollar firm would let a wife make its management decisions? As it turned out, Sherman had been dead serious.

"Jim, I want you to write a letter and say that for personal reasons you want to leave the West Coast," Sherman had told him.

"But I don't want to leave," said Trice. "All I want is to be left alone here in Pac South." He had built up the business, he told Sherman.

"In fact, this is the worst time for me to leave California," he confided. "My wife and I have amicably separated for a while, and I need to be close by to help with the kids. I can't go now. Besides," he added, "it doesn't make good business sense."

"Just think about it," Sherman had told him.

In April 1985, with two weeks' notice and no discussion, Sherman moved Graner out of the Southeast and into California. Neither Carrington Clark, the Pacific North director, nor Trice, the Pacific South director, had ever hired a "sales manager" in their regions, even though other regions had such a staff member. Both West Coast directors thought the job was an unnecessary post. Now Sherman was anointing Graner as the new regional sales manager for *both* regions. "Sherman told me he had to keep Jack and his wife happy," Trice said later.

Meanwhile, down in Atlanta, a notorious manager named Rick Saccullo had been promoted to replace Graner as the Southeast regional director. Saccullo had already been reprimanded once by the SEC in 1983 for manipulating the stock of Conner Homes Corp. He had also been penalized for "free-riding," or buying newly issued securities and selling them before they had been paid for. Those violations occurred shortly after Graner had promoted Saccullo to head the Atlanta office. After the SEC's 1983 order, Saccullo had been suspended from his managerial position for thirty days.

Now, two years later, Saccullo was again being investigated by the SEC. Senior officers at Pru-Bache knew of this, but they didn't realize how serious the second review would become. Indeed, the Atlanta office's wrongdoings would loom large many years later in yet another SEC investigation.

The situation started out as a good deal among two buddies who brokered in Atlanta. The deal centered on a publicly held company called Captain Crab, which was a seafood restaurant in Miami owned by the father of one of the two Pru-Bache brokers involved. As their supervisor, branch manager Saccullo knew of the father-son business relationship, which unfolded like so:

In the summer of 1983, the son/broker told Pru-Bache customers that Captain Crab's stock would soon jump in price. Because he was related to the company's president, the broker said, he had inside information that, once publicly announced, would kick up the stock's price. The broker promoted the stock in this fashion, even after one of the restaurant's two locations had closed and the remaining location had announced its imminent closure. While the broker misrepresented facts to his customers, the stock fell from $10 to $3.50 a share, and later to $1. Still, the two brokers sold shares to their trusting clients.

At Pru-Bache's headquarters in New York, compliance officers knew of the incestuous relationship and "the possible appearance of insider trading." They monitored the sales of Captain Crab in the Atlanta office. They told Saccullo that except in isolated instances, he should not sell Captain Crab shares. Thereafter, Saccullo's staff sold 97,000 shares to the public. "None of these transactions were cleared in advance by the compliance department," which sent several wires to Saccullo prohibiting him from approving the sales, the SEC later noted.

A few weeks later, Saccullo wired back that he did not understand the restriction. The compliance people—attorneys—repeated their instructions. In June, Saccullo's staff sold more Crab shares, despite a fourth, fifth, and sixth wire from New York prohibiting such sales. The lawyers in New York also prohibited the brokers from contacting the company's principals, a ban violated in June 1983 with Saccullo's knowledge. Saccullo then allowed the brokers to solicit more sales, which the compliance department again forbade. When confronted, Saccullo begged New York to let the sales go through or the firm "would 'lose face' with its customers and take their orders elsewhere." The compliance people backed down.

During this time, the compliance attorneys talked with "Saccullo's immediate supervisor," Graner, on many occasions. When Captain Crab issued a secondary offering, the brokers under Saccullo sold those shares, despite two more directives from Pru-Bache to cease and desist. All told, the two brokers moved 350,000 shares of Captain Crab stock.

Trice recalled Graner's concern about these trades: "Jack told me one night that he was concerned about being censured by the SEC, since he had been included in some of the compliance department's discussions and he had been Saccullo's boss." But, fortunately, Graner did not receive a formal regulatory reprimand; he was simply transferred to the West.

In the wake of Graner's departure, Pru-Bache promoted Saccullo to fill the position of regional director of the Southeast. He ran the region from April to December 1985—during the course of the SEC's inquiry. However, after reviewing his poor supervisory abilities in the infamous Captain Crab affair, the SEC demanded that Saccullo relinquish his management post, and scolded Pru-Bache harshly, chastising both the regional director, Graner, and the firm's compliance department for their lax supervision: "Under no circumstances should a firm continue to tolerate a supervisor [Saccullo] who persistently ignores legitimate Compliance Department recommendations or directives." The SEC demanded Pru-Bache improve its supervision of managers.

To settle the matter, Pru accepted a censure, agreed to hire an outside consultant and follow his recommendations, and vowed to improve its compliance procedures. In the SEC's December 31, 1985, order, Saccullo was censured again. This time, he was suspended from work for forty-five days and was prohibited from holding any supervisory position for a year and a half—until July 1987. This penalty was much harsher than that imposed in Saccullo's first SEC order. In 1993, regulators would decry the fact that its Captain Crab action against the firm "was the fifth time since June 1982 that the SEC found Prudential and its predecessor firm to have failed in their supervisory responsibilities."

At the time, it was the worst compliance problem in the history of the firm. Eager to make amends, Pru-Bache assured the SEC that the firm's counsel, Loren Schechter, was now responsible for all of the firm's compliance matters. He, in turn, assured the SEC that the firm had gotten rid of the incompetent people who had been involved in the matter. The truth of the matter was that they had simply transferred the two culpable managers out of the area to similar posts out West.

Weeks after the SEC's December 1985 order, Graner became head of the Pacific South region. By March, he had promoted Rich Saccullo, who now bore the new title "regional sales coordinator." That post had been Graner's prior management position. Despite its new name, the job entailed supervising people, according to many managers and brokers who worked under Saccullo from 1986 until July 1987, the exact period during which the SEC barred him from any management position.

"When Jack told me that Saccullo was going to be the new regional sales manager out here, I was amazed," said Joe Kett, former manager of the San Diego office. "I asked him how that could be, given Saccullo's suspension. He just winked at me and said he was going to change the job title, that's how." Within weeks after the SEC's order, Pru-Bache had already defied that order.

Meanwhile, Pru-Bache officers in New York were aware of troubles festering in the Southeast region. They knew they had to clean it up. In the middle of January, Ball and Sherman asked Trice to fly to New York. Trice met Sherman for lunch in the private dining room at One Seaport Plaza and listened to Sherman, who said, "You have a great background, a clean record, and no compliance problems whatsoever. We need your help."

"Do this for the Gipper," Sherman had begged Trice. "The firm will make it up to you."

After lunch, Trice took a limousine across the Hudson River to Newark, New Jersey, where he met Ball. Ball took time away from a Pru Insurance meeting and spent nearly two hours persuading Trice to move. Trice reiterated his position:

"I know the firm's got some problems, George. But I don't think my moving is the way to solve it. I think it's a bad decision for the company. We've been doing very well out there on the West Coast. I know better than anyone else what is happening out in the West." He told Ball that he had quadrupled sales in that region to $136 million; his managers were some of the best in the firm; he didn't want to leave.

"Jim," George said, "you're absolutely right. You've done tremendous things for us in the West. You've built up a solid, profitable region that is by far one of our best." By the firm's own account, Trice's region was first in productivity and revenue and was the second-biggest seller of DIG's LP products. Ball continued: "But we never anticipated that the Southeast would become such a huge problem. It has the weakest group of managers. We need you to clean up the region and get it running at optimum speed again." Trice agreed to consider the move, then left.

In the first few days of February, Trice telephoned Sherman.

"I've been with the firm for more than twenty years," Trice began. "The firm's been good to me. I still think this is a bad move. But if it means that much to you, I'll do it."

Sherman was relieved; he promised to make it up to Trice. In March 1986, Trice moved to Atlanta and Graner took Trice's position in the Pacific South region.

Now Trice had to untangle a knot of problems, far more than just Captain Crab. Some of the violations would soon be known to both the firm and the SEC; others the firm knew about, but the SEC would take years to discover; still others the SEC would never unearth, and the firm would learn only through Trice.

"The Southeast was a disaster," he said. In Fort Sumter, Virginia, Trice learned that a broker had "churned" the account of a client, or bought and sold shares in quick succession to inflate the broker's commission. The client complained, and Pru-Bache restored the customer's account to its original position; that cost the firm more than $10,000. Later, the broker was fired.

Then there was the problem in Richmond. The manager there had bragged to Trice that he ran an office that sold $13 million a year, an unusually large figure. "I later told him that he ran a $5 million office, with an oddball account of $8 million," said Trice. That "oddball" account belonged to Dr. Laszlo Tauber, a neurosurgeon who traded futures in Swiss currencies, an esoteric, complicated game. Dr. Tauber formed the strategies himself and traded them through his Pru-Bache broker, who clearly didn't understand the trades. Tauber had many different strategies. For example, playing the put/call or option market, he would bet that by a specific future date, the Swiss franc would not rise or fall in value. If he was right, which was often, he would earn money; if he was wrong, he would lose money.

When the Richmond broker saw how this tactic yielded so much profit for Tauber, the broker decided to duplicate it for his other clients, as well as for some of his friends, who were brokers in Augusta and Lynchburg. After all, for a time at least, Tauber's account was so successful it earned the firm millions of dollars in sales commissions.

But Trice began to suspect that although many people understood different facets of the complicated account, no one understood it completely.

The first problem occurred when a clerk, who tried to erase December 1985 option contracts, mistakenly erased all December options for both 1985 and 1986. "All the records were screwed up," said Trice.

Then the broker put his clients and friends into this risky business—even though they didn't understand options. "Some of the customers thought they were buying certificates of deposits of Swiss francs," said Trice. Placing clients in investments they didn't understand was a clear violation of the "suitability" rule—which was a corollary of the "Know your customer" rule that Bache had spawned after one of its clients nearly bankrupted the firm in 1929. The Tauber problem wasn't all that much different. "One guy thought he had invested $100,000 and a week later he now owed us $1.5 million," said Trice. The trades were unsuitable for the customers because they didn't understand what they were doing. At the time, not even the managers in the firm understood the full extent of these trades.

Then, in July 1986, the franc dropped in London. "We had a potential $40 million loss," Trice recalled. Sherman and Ball had to tell the Pru officers about the firm's enormous exposure; the Pru directed that Tauber cover his potential losses and wire more money to his account as collateral, which he did.

Meanwhile, allegedly unknown to other managers, the Richmond broker allowed an associate to place orders for his "special" customers while the broker was on a reward trip in Hong Kong.

The firm unwittingly had allowed many customers to take positions whose losses could far exceed their ability to pay; the clients' credit covered but a fraction of their losses. That exposed the firm to enormous losses, because Pru-Bache would have to make good on the losses somehow if the clients couldn't. The folly of such credit practices is clear once you realize that even Las Vegas casinos frown on them; before you lay your chips down at the craps table, the casino already has your money in its vault. Payment in advance is a time-honored policy at most gambling houses.

By January 1987, Pru-Bache's house of cards had collapsed. The Swiss franc soared in value, which placed the clients' numerous future contracts in loss positions. The loss was $100,000 on a Wednesday; by Friday it had climbed to $1 million and growing. Trice arranged to meet the Richmond broker and his manager on Super Bowl weekend. During the time, losses were heading toward $10 million, and neither broker nor manager understood the extent of what they had done.

The broker greeted Trice on Sunday, wearing his bow tie and a smile. "Why are you smiling?" Trice demanded. "Don't you realize you just lost at least $5 million in deferred compensation? You're basically bankrupt."

The broker didn't believe Trice; the manager turned surly. During the first hour of discussions, Trice couldn't get a straight answer out of either man.

Finally, Trice blew up. "Dammit," he said, slamming his forearm down on the table hard. "I want an answer and I want it now."

That's when the broker bolted out of the chair. From then on, Trice learned that fifteen other customers had played the options game, some of whom didn't understand the risks. Some trades had been made without customers' knowledge; it would take weeks for the firm to figure exact losses. To cover his individual losses, Tauber agreed to take out a mortgage on a $165 million building he had owned; the mortgage was used as collateral for his pending losses. Trice helped settle the other customer accounts, including those in Augusta and Lynchburg. All told, customers lost about $30 million. To its credit, Pru-Bache repaid those clients for whom the trades had been unsuitable.

But more storms were to come. In Charlotte, a broker had been overpaid by $100,000. In Atlanta, a new broker was found to be selling newly issued securities improperly. The compliance people in New York wanted to fire that broker's new administrative manager "to show the SEC a body" and prove that the firm punished errant managers. But Trice refused to fire the new guy; he hadn't done anything wrong. Even so, Trice lost that battle and Pru-Bache got its body.

In another branch office, Trice learned that two brokers had a client—a savings and loan—that had bought $10 million in bonds with the promise, allegedly given by the firm, that if the bonds dropped in value, Pru-Bache would buy them back.

When the bonds dropped, Pru-Bache naturally didn't buy them back. But the client was furious. The two brokers then formed their own trading company while still employed at Pru-Bache—supposedly with Graner's knowledge. That was a clear conflict of interest. Then their new trading company borrowed $10 million from the thrift and used the loan's proceeds to buy back the bonds.

Now the brokers were in debt $10 million through their secret side business. When Trice found out, he wanted to fire the two. But this time, the compliance people objected: "You know we don't want to terminate them. We need these guys as friendly witnesses later on."

"Fine," said Trice. "You don't want to terminate them? You write me a letter telling me you will assume full responsibility for this—not the local manager and not me, the regional director."

"You know we can't do that," the attorney said.

"Well, then, I'll fire them."

"No, no, no," the attorney said. "Look, we'll take care of them. Just wait."

A week later, one broker resigned but the other remained. The practice of keeping "rogues" employed at the firm, instead of firing them, became common, say many employees. It was one way to ensure that if clients later filed a claim against Pru-Bache, the "rogues" would testify on behalf of the firm. Said Trice: "It's like holding a rattlesnake. You don't want to let him go because he might bite you."

In other offices, Trice simply found incompetence, waste, and mismanagement, which he would weed out over the course of the following three years. Slowly, both profits and morale would rise again in the region, although, because of corporate forces, Trice would not be able to sweep the region entirely clean.

Meanwhile, in California, the Graners were "ecstatic" to be back in paradise. When Jack and his wife, Pat, first moved to Los Angeles, it was April 1981 and Sherman had just promoted Graner to manage the Beverly Hills office. "We were both struck by the sweet smell that hung in the air in L.A.," said Pat Graner. "We couldn't believe it. We figured that the city scented the place to make it smell so nice." Later, they learned that the night-blooming jasmine perfumed the air naturally. "We were like the Beverly Hillbillies driving into town for the first time."

Now, the second time around, the couple knew precisely what to expect. Graner moved the Pac South regional headquarters out of San

Diego and into Los Angeles. He worked out of the ninth floor of the Pru-Bache on Figueroa Street, which was in the heart of the financial district downtown.

Many employees in the Pac South region were shocked to hear of Trice's departure, but others initially welcomed Graner's arrival. "His charm could be dazzling," said Pat. He frequently joked and was considered the life of any party he attended.

As the only son of two deaf-mutes, Graner was fluent in sign language, and was generous with most words, except one. Said a peer: "He couldn't say no to people, and this would get him in trouble."

Still, Graner was finally ensconced in the area that he and his wife loved so much. But by 1986, a slew of problems had begun to surface. Pru-Bache was about to face a company-wide crisis in confidence, centering on the products emanating from New York.

In the beginning, the signs were obscure. Many brokers had simply grown disgruntled with the poor quality of LPs flowing out of the East. Some began to openly question the wisdom of selling the products given the changing economics of the time: inflation had cooled, speculation was rampant, and LP income no longer was sheltered from taxes. The post-1986 products had to package value in order for brokers to feel good about selling them. The more sophisticated brokers didn't see the value in them.

For example, Pru-Bache in 1985 was selling a closed-end, mutual fund of properties owned by Prudential Insurance. To Joe Kett, the manager of the San Diego office, the product seemed self-serving. "It didn't look right to me that a subsidiary of a firm was selling that firm's real estate," he said.

"First of all, you don't sell good real estate—you keep it. Yet here was Pru, the largest real-estate investor in the world: why are they unloading this stuff on our clients?" Kett didn't encourage his brokers to sell the funds.

But in a conference call to managers in the region, Sherman barked at them to push the funds. *Now.* "If you can't get this stuff sold, we'll get new managers in the region who can," he ordered. The pressure to sell even questionable product was building throughout the firm.

Another controversial offering at the time was a private $30 million LP for the U.S. Grant Hotel, a hotel project in downtown San Diego. At the time, the downtown area was known for its winos, shipyard workers, and nocturnal dangers. Hotels in the surrounding area charged $75 a night. Yet for the Grant to turn a profit, it would have to charge $300 a night, which Kett termed ridiculous. "I kept saying, 'How can this be a good deal for clients?' We didn't believe it."

In Santa Barbara, Rob Hughes didn't understand either. How could he sell such an expensive, dubious project that had no tax advantage to his clients, many of whom were now friends? "I remember calling [DIG] people in New York and asking, 'How can you possibly encourage people to invest in this deal? It will never work.' "

In response, he got "sales dribble." "They told me to 'adjust it for tax savings.' I thought they knew better than me." But, like many of his peers, Hughes wasn't convinced; he started to turn away completely from DIG and searched elsewhere on the Pru-Bache menu for sound investments to sell. By now, many of his clients were wealthy decision-makers who owned sizable companies. He sometimes learned that such customers' firms had investment banking needs, so he began to link his clients' firms with Pru-Bache's investment banking department in return for a legitimate "finder's fee." That market niche would serve him well.

Unfortunately, other brokers and managers didn't have the opportunity to break away completely from DIG and its products. By 1986, brokers and managers were under increasing pressure to either shut up and sell, or quit. The pressure could turn humiliating. At one awards banquet, Joe Kett was mockingly given a "booby" prize for selling the least amount of LPs of any manager in the firm. His prize was a bathrobe from the U.S. Grant Hotel. By 1988, however, investors would receive their own prize, bankruptcy notices from the hotel.

"Congratulations, Jack," said Kudlik. "That's neat you're the new director."

"Thanks, Mike. I told you we'd be working together."

Kudlik didn't say anything; Graner noticed.

He continued: "I'm moving regional headquarters to Los Angeles. I want you to move your operation up here, too."

Kudlik thought to himself, "Oh no." Slowly and carefully, he said aloud: "Jack, you know I have a home down here. I also have a secretary and two other women working for me. They have families and homes, too. I don't want to uproot them."

Kudlik explained that he paid for the two extra staff members out of his own pocket. He made enough money to afford the staff, and they helped him sell more product in the region. Besides, Kudlik added, he traveled so often, it shouldn't matter where he was physically headquartered, except to his employees.

"Listen, Mike," said Graner. "You have a lot of visibility in the region.

A lot of guys respect you. I want your support up here." He added: "I'll make it worth your while."

"I don't understand what that means," said Kudlik.

"It means if you base yourself up here, I'll pay for your [extra] staff out of the regional budget."

"Fine, I'll consider it."

After verifying his agreement with Graner, Kudlik agreed to move. He didn't have a choice.

A month later, Kudlik had packed his office, moved his secretary, and let go his two other assistants. He moved into the Los Angeles office near Graner. Then he waited for Graner to make good on his promise. A month went by; Kudlik reminded Graner. "I need those two additions to my staff, Jack. We are swamped."

Graner slapped his forehead as though he just realized he had forgotten something. "Gee. Right, Mike. I'm going to check with Bob Sherman and see where it stands. I'll get right back to you."

Two more weeks passed; Kudlik was desperate for help. "Jack, where do we stand?"

"What do you mean?" Graner looked harried.

"The additions to my staff," Kudlik said. "You promised to pay for the replacement of the two assistants I had in San Diego. We need them now."

For a second, Graner stared hard at Kudlik. "I don't remember that conversation," he said, and walked away.

12

The Men Behind the Corporate Veil

NEW Jersey sits just a mile or two from One Seaport Plaza, across the Hudson River. It contributes to the life of Manhattan thousands of commuters, and scads of corporate denizens. First settled by Puritans in 1666, Newark grew to sustain some of the nation's largest corporations: Sears, AT&T, Johnson & Johnson, Mobil Oil, and Prudential Insurance. Traditionally, business has fared well.

During the late 1800s, New Jersey was home to most of the nation's trusts, or industrial monopolies, which were illegal in many other states. New Jersey also attracted many holding companies, which controlled the stock and policies of other firms. By 1900, hundreds of corporations had obtained charters under New Jersey law, precisely because of its lenient business codes. Some of these corporations were not adverse to bending the rules on occasion, which helped trigger a special New Jersey Senate Committee's investigation of insurers in 1906.

Under Prudential's original 1873 charter, for example, its affairs were to be directed by a board of fifteen directors who were elected annually by voting shareholders. "In fact, none of the then approximately 40,000 policyholders had ever voted for directors nor had they ever been notified or invited to do so," stated the committee's 1907 report.

In 1943, the Pru became a mutual company owned by its customers, or policyholders, who received dividends as part of their share of company profits; that practice continues to this day. The state's chief justice, however, continued to appoint directors to Pru's board to "defend the interests of the policyholders and the public." The intent, said a government spokesman, was to include among Pru's directors people who reflected the customers' interests. Thus, its twenty-four directors include sixteen who are elected by policyholders, a few company officers, and six named by the state's chief justice.

Customarily, directors don't involve themselves in a firm's daily operations. Rather, they oversee senior management and set long-term corporate goals and policies. They help guide the ship during storms. In 1986, Pru's securities subsidiary was just part of the conglomerate's "bigger-than-life" growth strategy. Investment problems had not yet bubbled to the surface. Over the ensuing seven years, however, troubles would multiply until they burgeoned into one of the costliest corporate scandals ever.

Who sat on Pru's board during the crucial seven-year stint? From 1986 through 1993, directors included some illustrious business chiefs:

James G. Affleck, former chairman of the board of American Cyanamid Co.; James E. Burke, of the New Jersey–based Johnson & Johnson, who in 1982 distinguished himself for his swift and candid handling of the cyanide-laced Tylenol capsules; William W. Boeschenstein, chairman, president, and CEO of Owens-Corning Fiberglas Corp.; John R. Opel, chairman of IBM; Donald E. Procknow, former vice chairman of AT&T Technologies, New York; Robert M. Schaeberle, chairman emeritus of Nabisco Brands, East Hanover, New Jersey (who was called a "pushover" in the well-publicized 1988 takeover of RJR Nabisco); and Richard M. Thomson, chairman and CEO of Toronto Dominion Bank and director of seven other firms.

Others were expert in accounting and management: Robert J. Boutillier, former vice chairman of Peat Marwick Mitchell; and Burton G. Malkiel, then professor of management studies at Yale and a board member of six other companies.

Also aboard were four attorneys: the former New Jersey governor Brendan T. Bryne; United Way executive Lisle C. Carter, Jr.; Adrian M. Foley, Jr. (who left in 1993); and James C. Kellogg.

Although the state's chief justice regularly appointed six Pru directors—in order to "defend" the public's interest—the above list hardly represented the average policyholder. And there was uncommonly little turnover on the board. Directors have held their seats for years, regardless of whether their actions—or inactions—boded well for customers. "Those who do not die in office or have their service cut off by legislative change averaged almost nineteen years in the position," according to a recent government report.

From 1986 through 1993 the board also included three key insiders: Chairman Robert A. Beck, Vice Chairman Garnett L. Keith, Jr., and Vice Chairman Robert C. Winters. In that group, one small but enormously important change was about to occur, which would drastically alter the fate of Pru-Bache Securities.

In September 1986, Bob Beck surprised his colleagues by announcing he would resign the next year. Beck, who had once said that he wanted all of the nation's financial supermarket business, was retiring while he was still relatively young—sixty-one years old rather than the mandatory retirement age of sixty-five. Beck would be succeeded by Robert Winters, the vice chairman, who had bested Keith in the joust for the chairman's post.

The 1986 annual report featured only Beck and Winters in a prominent photo, instead of the six-man executive office as the Pru had done in the past. The unusual picture showed these two men suspended above Newark's skyline, high above the Pru's building. The portrait seemed sad; neither man was smiling, both looked pained, and as they floated above the streets of Jersey, one sensed an eerie isolation.

That year's report marked another break from the past. The book was bigger and printed on heavier, embossed paper with end sheets that were transparent, marbleized—and harder to read. No more was actually said, although it must have cost more to say it. Significantly, this customer epistle would be the last to disclose the salaries of the conglomerate's top officers.

After serving as CEO and chairman for eight years, Beck could look back proudly on what he had achieved. The Pru's assets had more than doubled to $134 billion in the last five years, making the Pru the largest nonbank corporation in the world. The company's income had also doubled, to $28 billion. (Although Beck's own salary had tripled during that time, to $1.5 million, it would not touch the salaries of about fifty other men who worked at the securities subsidiary across the river—including that of Darr.)

February 1987 was a fine time for Beck to bow out. Nearly all of the Pru's insurance subsidiaries were healthy. The stock market was high, and conflict was low. Beck's strengths were his open-mindedness, especially to change, and his ability to grasp the big picture, according to those who worked with him. His weakness had been that he was "vulnerable to a good pitch from a colleague" whom he might trust too much. His biggest fear was that he would fail "to retire before his numerous diversification strategies" hit a snag, according to one colleague.

Beck did not answer requests for an interview, but his timing in retiring was impeccable. By 1986, *Forbes* and other wags were questioning the wisdom of "one-stop money shops," or financial supermarkets such as those that had produced Pru-Bache. In one well-reasoned piece, the problem with these mergers was said to stem from executives who "are susceptible to 'fancy polished presentations' by consultants extolling the merits of proposed acquisitions as well as by their own staff personnel who stand to gain in power if the deals go through." A second fundamental mistake in approving mergers was that acquiring chiefs pay "too damn much money" for the asset. By now, some officers at the Pru certainly must have realized that it had paid "too damn much" for Pru-Bache, although one doubts that the board ever questioned that decision.

At some point, however, the Pru would demand a return on its investment. In 1981, it had pledged to be patient, and so far it had been. However, in the four years since then, Pru-Bache had lost a cumulative total of $40 million (even though Pru-Bache in 1985 posted a $42 million gain). By 1986, its parent, the Pru, had invested about $1.3 billion in it.

Now, the task of generating profit fell to Winters. He had been a vice chairman who, by personality, was less emotional and more focused on figures than Beck had been. He had little inclination for vision and strategy and was not a natural ally of George Ball, who had dazzled Beck for four years. By year-end 1986, Winters was ready to press Ball for some answers.

By the end of 1986, the fledgling investment banking unit had earned the Pru's most coveted possession—the Rock logo. In an advertisement placed in a trade magazine, the Newark-based company trumpeted its newest global operation: Prudential-Bache Capital Funding (PBCF). Read the ad: "It's a major commitment from The Prudential."

That commitment is exactly why Ted Fowler had joined the firm, he reminded himself. He tried to keep cool. He searched his brain for a clue in that pivotal meeting with Garnett L. Keith, Jr., vice chairman of the Pru.

About six months ago, he had crossed the Hudson to visit Keith, the man who supervised Pru-Bache, and to whom Fowler would have to answer. Before agreeing to help Jim Crowley build the investment banking unit, Fowler had to be sure that the Pru was committed to the massive undertaking.

He had considered the imposing building that was Pru's headquarters, whose lobby was dominated by a mosaic of the Rock of Gibraltar. It glittered that spring day in the afternoon sun. Fowler had met Keith, a short, buttoned-up man, and, over lunch, the two men had discussed the plan. As was his nature, Fowler had cut to the chase:

"Look. It's important for me to hear you articulate why the Pru is committed to an investment banking house."

Keith ticked off the points. At the time, the Pru was generating $100 million a day in cash—through insurance premiums, interest, dividends, and distributions from the sales and maturity of its investments. With a daily purse bigger than the annual income of a small industrialized country, Pru was desperate to find prudent ways to invest its cash. By the mid-1980s, a safe permanent investment harbor was hard to find.

The Pru, Keith explained, was a major institutional investor that relied on Wall Street to bring it deals and investment ideas. But by the 1980s, securities houses were taking the best deals for themselves. Clients like the Pru had been dropped from the dealer's inner circle. The Pru no longer had a competitive advantage, because money was flooding from all points to the street. The Pru's dollars had been reduced to a commodity.

"The Prudential needs to start originating business itself," Keith said. "The board wants to operate on a global basis."

Impressed with Pru's ambitions, Fowler pressed further:

"Do you know how much I make?" Fowler asked bluntly. At the time, the banker was making more than $1 million.

"I do," said Keith.

"Do you have any idea what investment bankers make on the Street these days?"

"I do." Keith had worked for an investment firm years before. He had earned his M.B.A. from Harvard and had started in the Pru's corporate finance department. He had formed PruCapital or PruCap, the in-house investment banking arm that dealt primarily with utilities and industrial companies—conservative risks. Over the years, no doubt, Keith had followed Street banking with a mixture of awe and disgust, partly because of the wealth. A junior associate could earn as much as $150,000 in his or her first year out of college; after several years, a star could rake in $5 million or more.

Fowler emphasized his point. "You probably know how much you'll have to pay to attract good people."

Keith nodded.

Securities brokers earned a lot of money, but Street bankers outpaced brokers. To some officers at the Pru, salaries had already become an issue, according to insiders. Now the issue was doubly charged: the difference between an insurance exec's pay and that of a star banker is a significant matter of two or three zeros. As vice chairman of the nation's largest insurance company, Keith himself earned only $865,370, or less than Fowler. Fowler knew that money can divide a house—no matter how sincere or sophisticated the corporate family.

Being a "compensation hawk" himself, Fowler wanted to make sure that he could lure top talent with the promise of top pay.

Fowler tried again: "You don't think there'll be some penis envy about salaries within Pru?"

Keith laughed in spite of himself. "That won't be a problem, I assure you."

Fowler left convinced that the Pru not only was serious about investment banking, but would go the distance to help Pru-Bache achieve its goal. Keith had told Fowler the Pru was committed to Project '89 for the long haul. Without that commitment, the plan would have been doomed and Fowler would never have joined. That support would become crucial in the days ahead.

Fowler joined Pru only after discussing every facet of the job exhaustively with Keith, Ball, Gahan, and Crowley.

And now, not even a year into his post, Fowler found himself in the middle of what, at best, was a colossal misunderstanding. He could not have anticipated this.

Through a securities lawyer he had known, Fowler found an opportunity to advise National Gypsum Co., the nation's second-largest maker of gypsum-coated wallboard, used to build houses. The Charlotte, North Carolina, company was involved in a $750 million takeover bid of another firm. To Pru-Bache, the successful deal would mean between $50 million and $75 million in fees. It was the stuff for which bankers lived.

As soon as Fowler learned about it, he told Ball, and they reviewed the four basic parts to a merger. The first part occurs when one CEO meets another and says, "I want to buy your firm." Chances are, the second CEO says no, and that's the end of phase one.

Next, the first CEO writes a letter repeating his offer to the chairman of the board. The chairman also says no. In phase three, the CEO writes the chairman a second time, only this time, he includes a purchase price. Now the chairman must dutifully disclose the offer to his board, and the takeover bid is seriously discussed.

At this fourth step, the takeover attempt turns either friendly or hostile. If the buyer offers the seller a high enough premium to sell the firm, the deal becomes friendly. If the vulnerable company seeks a competing bid, the deal turns hostile.

Because the Pru didn't want to be associated with hostile takeovers, Fowler was restricted slightly in what he could do. He and Crowley argued that in 1986, all bankers and most financiers, including insurance companies, were involved in takeovers that may have started in an unfriendly mode, but usually ended amicably.

Fowler wanted to deal in what he called unsolicited friendly offers, or UFOs. The Pru restricted the investment bankers to "conditional offers," that is, only those offers subject to board approval. If the board didn't approve the bid, the offer would be dropped. It's hard to understand how such a genteel approach would work in a shark-eat-dog world, but Fowler and his client had agreed to the approach—knowing that in the end *real* bankers do all deals, whether they begin in a friendly way or not.

Still, he and Ball agreed that the firm would proceed on the takeover bids under these conditions. Over the next few days, Fowler guided his client through the three stages of the merger process. At stage four, they haggled over the fine points of a twenty-page offer-to-purchase letter, which was to be delivered to the takeover target. Negotiations continued daily until Fowler was almost ready to send the letter.

Then the rules changed abruptly.

Some misunderstanding arose either between Ball and Fowler or between Ball and the Pru. But the bottom line was that now Pru-Bache was forbidden from doing *any* unsolicited takeover offers, whether friendly or not.

Ball delivered the bad news to Fowler, who couldn't believe it. "What do you mean, no conditional tender offers? That offer is subject to the board's approval. You told us that Newark approved it. Why are you changing the rules on my client in midstream? We've done the deal exactly as you required."

Ball was nervous, but he repeated his instructions. No takeovers. Period. The Pru feared that the phrase "hostile takeover" would sully its reputation. It didn't want to be associated with the vultures and raiders who were circling businesses at the time. It feared that such an association would scare away its corporate clients.

"We are in the Dark Ages if they don't let us go ahead with this," Fowler said.

But the Pru was adamant, Ball said. No hostiles, and forget the UFOs. Fowler's stomach churned as he was forced to accept the fact. Now the question became: what was he going to tell his client?

He called the lawyer and delivered the ridiculous news. "What do you mean you can't do this?" the lawyer yelled. "Aren't you a securities firm? Aren't you an investment banker?"

Fowler held the phone away from his head as the attorney unleashed an earful. Fowler didn't blame the guy. They'd spent hours hammering the deal tight. Fowler himself didn't understand why the sudden change, although he knew that it meant lost business. No hostiles, not even the "bear-hug" conditional hostile offers, meant that Pru-Bache's investment banking unit could kiss off a ton of relatively easy and lucrative transactions—transactions that would make Project '89 a profit winner right from the start. As Fowler pondered the crushing impact of what now was the Pru's policy, he mentally subtracted a number from Project '89's projected revenues.

He figured $200 million worth of humiliation.

Rules were slightly different in the direct investment group. By 1987, DIG seemed to be Pru-Bache's golden goose. That year it would sell $1.128 billion in public limited partnerships and bring in an estimated $110 million in revenues—before taxes and expenses. The phenomenal sales occurred despite the tax laws that made the vehicles less attractive. Still, Wall Street continued to sell LPs, and Pru-Bache sold more than anyone. Business was outstanding.

That year, however, some disturbing news developed behind closed doors. The Pru had quietly stopped investing in Graham's LPs, ending a three-year commitment. When Ball heard about the turnabout, he asked Darr for more information. Why was the Pru pulling out?

The Pru had put its Graham LP oil and gas investment "on ice," even though the insurer had received a better deal than small investors. For example, the Pru did not have to pay the hefty sales commissions and other costs charged to other LP investors. Unlike individual investors who paid acquisition fees on properties, the Pru *received* part of those fees for evaluating the properties.

The Pru had ceased investing in Graham's LP funds in 1986 because it realized the oil market was declining, and that Graham was not such a great deal. When it stopped investing, three Pru executives resigned from the board of Pru-Bache's and Graham's energy income funds. Still, the insurer continued to collect hundreds of thousands of dollars in annual fees for "monitoring" the earlier partnerships. The Pru was supposed to earn those fees by tracking the performance of the LPs, as a safeguard for investors. Yet that effort entailed one meeting a year, and instead of informing the smaller Pru-Bache investors of its concern about the energy LPs, the Pru remained silent. Such a lack of disclosure seemed deceptive and wrong.

Also unknown to Pru-Bache investors, the Pru invested in private deals with Graham in what was a clear conflict of interest. For example, Prudential purchased from Graham an $85 million interest in one of its giant oil and gas properties. At the same time, the insurer sat on the energy income oversight board charged with monitoring investors' limited partnerships. Some later questioned whether the insurer received favorable terms in its private purchase, but the Pru's secretive position smacks of serious conflict-of-interest problems.

The Pru also lent Graham $20 million it needed to complete financing related to properties for a future LP Pru-Bache would sell customers later. The transaction was such that potentially Prudential would not get paid *if* Pru-Bache failed to sell the next series of energy LPs. No wonder the Pru didn't want small investors to become aware of its concerns with Graham's LPs; if Pru-Bache investors didn't buy more Graham LPs, the Pru would lose the money it had lent to Graham.

As it was, the Pru made interest on the loan, another $500,000 in "finder's fees," and the right to 1 percent of the cash flow from the properties, in addition to the return of its principal.

But it would be years before these fine deals would come to light, and once they did, the Pru would decline to explain the deals, saying only they were "private." It would remain mum even as outsiders charged the company with violating its fiduciary responsibilities to Pru-Bache and its clients, who would lose money.

After the Pru ceased investing in Graham, Pru-Bache launched nearly twenty other new Graham LPs over the following four years. Aware of Graham's high expenses and low returns, the Pru did not invest and did not stop the offerings, as it should have. By the beginning of 1987, three of Pru's executives had resigned from the LP energy board, which guided those investments. The Pru doubted the soundness of the LPs. When Pru-Bache learned about the resignations, the news was "met with less than a warm reception," according to an internal memo. One Graham officer wrote: "I believe their reluctance may have more to do with not 'trusting' the Direct Investment Group" than with any other factor.

Distrust of DIG was spreading, and by February 1987 trouble was brewing with the LPs. Yet Jim Darr held forth calmly and confidently at Pru-Bache executive committee meetings with Ball and other directors.

In one such meeting, the twelve-man group racked their brains, as they often did, for new ways to generate income and create new product. It was a common exercise, only this time, Darr had an idea:

"We have a lot of residual values in these limited partnerships, you know." Residual values meant that after LP investors had received back their money, plus anticipated returns, the LPs still contained some value—let's say 10 percent of the total purchase price.

Fowler looked at Crowley. They had both heard Darr's boast of residual values more times than they cared to recall.

"Well?" Crowley said, prompting Darr.

Darr tipped back in his chair, looked up, and said: "We must have about $300 million of those things."

One man whistled. "That's one hell of a number."

"That is," said Ball, looking at the faces of his senior officers to elicit more ideas.

Fowler leaned forward, placed his forearms on the table, and said to Darr: "Well, if you have so many goddam residuals, why don't we package them and sell them?"

Darr stared at him. "That might work."

"Why wouldn't it?" said Fowler. "But first we have to get into the books and see what you have. You know, adjust them for risk, value them to market, give them a haircut."

Ball was enthusiastic. "That's a great idea, Ted." He turned to Darr. "Jim, let's do it."

Fowler continued: "If we repackage them, you can revalue the residuals, investors can buy some product, and George gets to take a profit."

"Absolutely," Ball said. "Great idea." The others concurred. Fowler and Crowley arranged to send a few of the department's oil and gas experts and real-estate specialists to a conference room. DIG was supposed to deliver the relevant books and accounts. Over the next few days, the group would evaluate the accounts to determine their true value. A time was set.

But within two weeks, the "review" was called off. The investment banking specialists hadn't been allowed to examine the DIG books. No reason given. No apologies rendered.

"Fuck it," Fowler thought. He wasn't going to waste time with Darr. But something didn't smell right, and Fowler grew suspicious.

By 1987, at least three members of Pru-Bache's executive committee harbored serious but still-secret doubts as to the exact nature and value of assets Darr and DIG actually held. Perhaps George Ball did too. That March, Ball sent Darr away to a prestigious business course at Harvard University called the Advanced Management Program. The executive development curriculum lasted three months, until the end of June, when graduates earned a certificate. Darr was delighted to go, and at the time, many people in the firm thought Ball was grooming Darr for a promotion, which is what Darr certainly desired. Only later would another equally plausible reason emerge for Ball's sending Darr away.

"It was a way for Ball to get Darr out of the way, so he could look at DIG's books," said one executive. Perhaps.

While Darr was at Harvard, he would call the investment banking department between five and six in the evening. "He'd ask us for help with his corporate finance homework," said Jack Welch, a managing director at the time. Whenever the telephone rang in that department, some of the bankers would scatter to their offices. "There was a joke around the office as to who would take the call that day," said Welch, who shared the duty with two other bankers. For one to two hours, the bankers would help Darr solve his problems. "Then he returned to Pru-Bache that summer and bragged about how he knew all about corporate finance," said one banker.

By 1987, Darr hungered to rise above DIG. "I had hoped to either take over part of investment banking in its entirety or the retail group," he later said. However, in his absence, some senior officers surely learned more about Darr's LP business. Upon Darr's return from Harvard, he did not resume his old duties.

Ball tried to move the entire DIG into investment banking. One morning, Fowler appeared at work after having just stepped off a red-eye flight from Tokyo. Exhausted, jet-lagged, and in no mood for she-nanigans, Fowler flipped through the mail and papers that had piled up in his absence.

His eye landed on a short memo that announced that Jim Darr's group was moving into investment banking and would be reporting to Ted Fowler and Jim Crowley. Fowler went berserk. He stormed out of his office, stomped up the stairs, marched through the thick-carpeted executive floor, and barged into Ball's office.

He stood in the doorway and waved the memo in the air. "What the hell are you doing?" he yelled. "How could you do this, without even asking us?"

Ball was clearly distressed. "It's good for the firm, Ted. Jim's a talented guy. The move will be good for you."

"Bullshit!" Fowler yelled. He rattled the memo like a saber in the air. "This is not going to happen." Fowler didn't share his suspicions about Darr, because he had no proof. But he knew, after twenty years on Wall Street, that a firm doesn't suddenly move one hot-producing department under the supervision of another without a good reason.

By now, Crowley was in the office, as was Jim Gahan, who oversaw all of corporate finance, including investment banking. Crowley didn't want to accept the responsibility of DIG, either, and he said so.

Ball tried to reassure the two men: "Just try it for a while. I'm sure it'll work out."

"What's the point?" Crowley asked.

"This can't happen, George," Fowler repeated.

"Try it," said Ball. "It's not so bad."

Fowler walked up to Ball's desk, glared at him with his bloodshot blue eyes, and growled: "It's either him or me." He turned and stalked out.

Later, Gahan, Crowley, and Fowler discussed the move. Neither Crowley nor Fowler liked or trusted Darr. Plus, he sure as hell wasn't an investment banker, no matter what Darr thought, Crowley told Gahan.

"Besides," Fowler added, "why would someone who made the firm forty fucking million in profits one year suddenly be moved out of that part of the firm? It makes no sense."

Gahan agreed and said he had the solution. "You've been slipped the silver weenie. Don't worry," he told the coheads. "I'll take care of it."

Within twenty-four hours, Darr—the silver weenie—was moved out of investment banking into somewhere in Gahan's division. Darr was given the title executive vice president, but it wasn't clear what he actually did. He later claimed that from 1986 to 1988 he was in the investment banking department and reported directly to Fowler and Crowley, but both men deny that.

"All I know is that after he returned from Harvard, he walked around in a haze for a year," said one woman who worked in DIG. "He had been emasculated. He had nothing to do. He had time on his hands to sit around and joke with the younger guys. It was kind of sad."

As for the investment banking division—PBCF—it plowed ahead. In its first few months, the unit had sold what had been called "the best foreign deal" that year. It had brought public the Australia Prime Income Fund, a $865 million unit, which made millions for the firm and earned kudos for PBCF. It had also raised $125 million for Chrysler Financial—at the lowest possible rate—within twenty-four hours, and another $100 million for the Kingdom of Denmark. Jones Intercable, British Gas, Gilbarco, and Mobile Communications Corp. were among its clients. This was in addition to the swap business that Crowley had created, which made the firm money and raised its profile on the international stage.

In December, its biggest deal would be completed with Reliance Electric—a $1.3 billion leveraged buyout that would put PBCF on the map.

13

A Ton of Positions, a Load of Laundry

CARRINGTON Clark, director of the Pacific North region, pressed the woman to attend Pru-Bache's seminar retreat. She hesitated: the rowdy, drunken, promiscuous affairs had repulsed her in the past. She politely declined. But Clark was insistent. As a top-producing broker, he said, she should make an appearance and help inspire younger brokers. Okay, she said.

In April 1986, the $1 million sales producer arrived at the Marriott Hotel in San Francisco, located near Fisherman's Wharf. She checked into her room and unpacked. Around three that afternoon, her roommate arrived in shocking condition. Kristi Mandt stood in the doorway and swayed unsteadily; her long red hair was disheveled, her blouse half-unbuttoned, and her nylons shredded. Clearly Mandt was drunk and incoherent. Without a word, Mandt flung herself on a bed and promptly passed out.

A half hour later, the telephone rang. A DIG senior officer wanted to speak to Mandt. The roommate carried the phone to her and roused her gently. Mandt didn't rise but listened to the man on the other end of the line; she agreed to go up to his room and asked for his number. Without straightening herself, she rose from the bed and stumbled out the door to meet the DIG officer. A few hours later, she reappeared in even worse shape than when she had left. She was drunker, her eye makeup was smudged, and her clothes were more disheveled. The roommate was appalled.

"I realized that the guys upstairs were using her sexually. As often as they could," said the woman.

That evening, the firm threw a fine dinner. All of the firm's employees were expected to attend. After dinner, the woman left and walked up to her room. She slipped on her modest satin nightgown, turned out the lights, and fell asleep.

At one o'clock she was awakened by loud knocks on her door. She opened the door but kept the chain fastened. There was Kristi, her eyes crossed, her head hanging, her words barely discernible. "Let me in," Kristi slurred.

"Are you alone?" the roommate asked.

"Yeah."

"Kristi. Listen," the roommate demanded. "Are you alone?"

"Yes."

The roommate unchained the door and let Mandt into the room. Four or five male brokers suddenly lunged forward out of hiding, slammed the door open, and threw the roommate hard into the wall. The male brokers burst into the room and began to grope the woman. Their hands were everywhere on her body: her breasts, her thighs, her crotch, her waist. One of the men yanked at her nightgown, which had an elastic neckline. He pulled the nightgown down to her waist, exposing her breasts. She began to hit the men with her fists and screamed for help. Kristi stood in the doorway, frozen like a statue, nearly comatose, it seemed to the woman. By now, nearby hotel guests had opened their doors, alarmed at the woman's cries for help. "What's going on?" they demanded of the men groping the lone woman.

"Okay, okay," one of the men told the screaming female broker. "Give it a rest, will ya?" They filed out of the room.

Near tears, the woman was appalled and horrified. She turned and saw that Kristi had passed out in bed. Meanwhile, the hotel manager had appeared in the doorway. He offered the assaulted woman a bed in his office and promised to do whatever he could to comfort her.

Furious at the inexcusable treatment she had received at the hands of her male "colleagues," the woman complained to a few Pru-Bache managers. Upon her return to her office, she called Clark, but he laughed at her. "You weren't hurt, were you?" What's the problem, then?

The woman was stunned. After a while, she realized what had been going on. "The managers were using Kristi as a way to entertain the troops. They were probably hoping I'd play along, too."

Kristi Mandt was no angel, but she was a talented broker. Like other Pru-Bache female employees, she was harassed by some executives. During the 1980s and 1990s, many women who worked in Pru-Bache's retail network and in New York filed sexual harassment claims against the company, according to numerous sources. One manager in the Southeast was accused of attempted rape; another senior executive in New York allegedly paid $250,000 to keep a woman quiet.

"Let's face it," said one top female broker. "The attitudes on Wall

Street toward female brokers—no matter what firm you're at—is fairly sexist.

"But the attitude at Pru-Bache was worse. The firm and its managers degraded and used women in a deeply personal way. You were treated like pieces of meat. That's just how it was."

According to several women, DIG executives frequently propositioned female employees. The behavior of the men at the top set the tone for the people in the field.

Few men were more egregious philanderers than Bob Sherman, president of Pru-Bache's retail system. Said one director of Pru-Bache's executive committee: "Sherman was a male slut. He'd take his wife on an incentive trip and keep her in one tower of the hotel and his mistress in another side." At Sherman's request, Clark frequently arranged dates for him during Sherman's visits to the West. Clark, a married man, was not above requesting dates for himself.

Many female professionals in the field felt pressured to go along with the social demands of their superiors to the point where some believed it was a part of the job. Indeed by the late 1980s, the situation for some female brokers had deteriorated rapidly.

Then again, the job situation had become pretty wretched for some men, too. Especially for those in Pac South.

One day, a client from the San Diego office walked into the La Jolla, California, office to see the manager. Joe Kett no longer managed the San Diego office; now he oversaw Pru-Bache's La Jolla branch, about ten miles away. Still, Kett listened to the client, who didn't understand the activity in his account. The client explained:

His broker had called him within the month suggesting he buy a closed-end mutual fund. The client said no. About a week later, the client received his statement in the mail. On it was recorded a $100,000 buy order of shares from the very fund he had refused to buy. On his statement was a sell order that had been made the next day. The client had never authorized those trades. He asked Kett what was going on.

Kett told the client to report the problem to the San Diego office manager. A short time later, Kett found a rookie broker in his office who had done the same thing. Kett immediately told the broker to stop the practice, which he recognized as an old trick.

It was a classic "pancake," or flipping of a stock, also known as churning. A broker buys a stock and sells it quickly, often within a day, in order to generate commissions for himself and the firm. The practice could be lucrative for the brokers and the firm, but often hurts the client, who pays the commission. That's why it's illegal.

In the case of these mutual funds, however, the commission was paid by the mutual fund manager, not by the client, and not by Pru-Bache. It was still wrong.

As soon as Kett discovered the practice in his own office, he telephoned the syndicate department in New York, which oversaw these issues. He alerted the department to the problem and assured it he had it under control.

Yet the illegal practice was widely encouraged in the firm. In May 1987, Kett attended an insurance seminar to instruct brokers primarily about Prudential Insurance annuities. The seminar was designed to tap some of the benefits of the insurer's owning the brokerage firm.

Held in a hotel near the Los Angeles Airport, the seminar included every manager from Pac South. Rick Saccullo approached Kett and took him under the stairwell out of earshot. He said, "I was looking at the computer recently. You have a ton of positions in closed-end funds."

Kett explained: "We sell them for long-term. The prospectus says the purchase is long-term, and that's what the syndicate department says, too."

Saccullo said only, "You've got to move them out."

Kett felt certain Saccullo was telling him to flip the funds.

He was flabbergasted but didn't say a word. Still, he knew that his boss, a regional sales "coordinator," was on probation with the SEC: Saccullo was not allowed to act in any management capacity, yet here he was, managing the sales in the region. Compounding the problem, Saccullo was pointedly ordering Kett and others to churn accounts—which was a flagrant violation of the law.

Indeed, the SEC had chastized Saccullo in 1983 for illegal stock trades. In 1985, regulators had slapped Pru-Bache for churning customer accounts. Although Saccullo was not involved in that incident, he too had been penalized at the time for the Captain Crab matter. As a result, the SEC had forbidden Saccullo to supervise brokers for eighteen months. Yet now, sixteen months later, the man and the firm were again violating the rules, only this time from a higher, more visible management position and in a larger, more lucrative region.

Still, Saccullo wasn't the only manager advocating "pancakes." Brokers throughout the system joked about spending mornings flipping stocks as a way to generate income and meet their sales quota. "Hey, how about a pancake breakfast this morning?" was a half-serious clarion call in some offices.

Said Kett: "Several brokers came up to me and said, 'Do you know they have pancake breakfast seminars downtown [San Diego] and talk about how to flip?' Some brokers were angry that I didn't allow it."

Although Kett didn't allow it, other managers did. In a January 26, 1988, memo from the Florida region, flipping was encouraged. "Buy for a flip or longer term."

At the time, Kett had his hands increasingly full with other problems much closer to home. In the fall of 1986, a broker told Kett of yet another potential problem unfolding in San Diego and relayed a story about Randy Schroeder, who worked in the San Diego office.

According to allegations later made in court, Schroeder was laundering drug money from his Pru-Bache office. He was never charged with a crime, cooperated with authorities, then left the firm within weeks. Later, at least one person pled guilty to felony charges.

Kett heard of the allegations months before government agents raided Pru-Bache's office. As Kett was told, Schroeder had recently attended a Mormon church service and, afterward, approached members with a special request. If he gave them cash, say $9,500 or so, would they please convert the cash into bank cashier's checks as a favor for him?

Legally, all financial institutions, including brokerage firms, must report cash transactions of $10,000 or more to the U.S. government. By requesting cashier checks in denominations of less than $10,000, Schroeder insured that such exchanges would not be reported, thus evading income taxes and federal scrutiny. The checks then could be deposited in brokerage accounts that Schroeder managed.

Other employees had heard that Schroeder "washed" cash regularly. Former broker Tim Irish said, "There were stacks of money in his office, and I saw it myself. Every day a mule [courier] would come with more cash from Mexico and the management in San Diego knew it."

Now, however, an attorney in the Mormon Church demanded that a Pru-Bache manager be informed of the problem. So the broker was telling Kett he had to do something about the situation.

Kett called Dave Utter, the San Diego manager, and repeated Schroeder's alleged solicitation of cashier's checks. Utter said, "Is he doing that again?" He sighed. "I'll take care of it."

Two more weeks went by. Kett received another call from yet another employee in the nearby Rancho Santa Fe office. The employee said: "Randy Schroeder's in the lobby of a bank next door. He is yelling and swearing and causing a big fuss because someone won't get him a cashier's check. He's saying things like 'I'm with Pru-Bache, do you understand?' Someone at the bank just called me."

Kett told the caller to telephone Utter; Kett wanted Utter to hear it from someone else this time.

Still, Kett was in trouble. Utter didn't like him, Graner didn't consider him a "team player," and Saccullo did not like his sales practices.

At one point, Graner and Kett discussed the alleged drug-money laundering in San Diego. Graner told Kett, "You let Dave [Utter] run his own office, and you run yours." During that conversation, Graner grew exasperated with Kett and said that perhaps he should consider working in another region. "We keep butting heads." Kett knew that others were getting fired by Graner; Kett kept his mouth shut.

One morning, Graner met Kett for breakfast in San Diego. Pru-Bache was about to defend itself against a former broker in an arbitration hearing. (Such hearings are common when brokerage firms want to settle disputes with clients and employees that otherwise might end up in court. Unlike court hearings, the details of arbitration proceedings are kept secret from the public.)

During breakfast, Graner asked Kett if he was testifying in the case on behalf of the ex-employee. "I am," said Kett.

"How are you going to testify?"

"Well, truthfully."

"What's the truth?"

The ex-employee claimed he had been unjustly fired by Trice with no warning. Kett knew the firm had a ninety-day warning period, and he told Graner: "I know the firm's policy, and it was violated."

Graner jumped in: "Here's how you handle this. Say you didn't know about it."

"I can't lie. That's perjury."

"You are just a branch manager," Graner reminded him. "You don't set the firm's policy."

Kett didn't argue with Graner, but he testified on behalf of the ex-employee, who was awarded $1 million against Pru-Bache.

From that point forward, relations between Kett and Graner deteriorated. Soon Kett began hearing rumors of his own firing. Brokers came up to him and said, "I heard you're leaving," and "Where are you going?" It irritated Kett, and he was just one of a growing number of unhappy managers.

Under Graner, Pac South unraveled rapidly. In addition to the intense sales pressure that New York applied to all offices, on top of the poor product emanating from DIG, compounding the everyday quandaries faced by most managers, Graner bore another affliction.

By 1987, rumors of Graner's cocaine use were common. One regional director said that some people in Graner's office used cocaine. "[Secretaries] were making $50,000 to $70,000 a year and he'd have them working all night until five in the morning, tallying production numbers. It was meaningless work. But Jack was obsessed. He had a fixation on numbers, and I don't think he knew what else to do in order to manage."

Graner wanted his brokers in the office at six A.M. He'd sometimes quiz a broker about his sales figures, for no apparent reason. "Do you know what your production was yesterday?" The questions were meaningless. Meanwhile, Graner worked harder, longer, and later than anyone. People noticed that his health suffered.

One afternoon, Graner called Kett. "I'd like you to move to another region."

"I've been hearing these rumors about my being fired," said Kett. "What's going on?"

"This is a bona fide offer. Bob Sherman wants you to go to Seattle."

Kett remained calm. "I don't want to go. I'm going through a divorce. You know that. I don't want to be separated from my two little kids right now. I can't move and leave them."

"I want you to talk to the director up there. Go see Clark and hear what he's offering."

"If I go up there for an interview, but I don't like it, will I be fired?"

"Absolutely not," Graner said. "Bob Sherman wants you to take this job. But you don't have to take it."

That day, Kett made arrangements to fly up to see Clark in the following week. But the next day, Graner called Kett.

"Sherman is pissed," Graner said. "He wanted you up there immediately. You get your ass on the airplane. Now."

Kett left the office and boarded a plane without a shaving kit or fresh shirt. He flew into San Francisco, and met Clark at his office.

Clark was gracious and understood Kett's uncomfortable position. The men discussed the Seattle office and shared dinner and drinks.

At one point, Clark said to Kett, "I understand you like to have a good time. Do you like to fool around in the office?"

"No."

Clark smiled. "Hey, that's okay. There's nothing wrong with it. I like to have a good time."

Kett spent the night in San Francisco and flew back home the next day. He called Graner and asked if he could see him the following week in Graner's office. Kett desperately wanted to settle the festering problems between himself and Graner; and he didn't want to leave the La Jolla area and move to Seattle.

Kett drove up to Los Angeles, and Graner kept him waiting awhile. At last, Kett was led into Graner's office. Kett began: "Jack, I want to figure out how to get along. Why aren't you getting along with me? How are we going to solve this problem?"

Graner looked him in the eye and said slowly, "Well, I could kill you.

You could kill me. I could have you killed. You can have me killed." He rambled off some more morbid possibilities.

Kett was dumbfounded. Then he turned angry. He felt he had been mistreated for months, and hadn't done anything wrong. He deserved better than this. The relationship between him and his boss was turning bizarre.

Just then, Graner turned around to retrieve a piece of paper from his credenza. He faced Kett again and lifted the yellow sheet of paper in front of Kett, without showing its contents. Graner said, "I got an anonymous phone call the other day. Evidently there's a drug deal going down in your office. Something about cocaine."

"Well, in that case, let's call corporate security."

"No, no! Don't do that."

"You tell me there's a drug deal going on in one of the offices and you don't want me to call corporate security. Why not?" Kett asked.

"Because [a senior executive] does cocaine. It would be an embarrassment to him."

Kett was shocked. He had no idea whether Graner was telling the truth. He had never seen the executive use drugs; nor had he heard of "deals" going down in his office.

Some time later, Graner confessed during a stay at a drug rehabilitation center that a superior had introduced him to cocaine during a New York "meeting" in a hotel room with women. The suggestion that a member of senior management at Pru-Bache not only condoned but introduced employees to addictive drugs discloses a seedier side to the Rock that many employees confirm existed.

But to Kett at the time, the mention of drugs was shocking. The whole conversation was turning absurd and nothing was closer to resolution.

Kett decided not to take the job in Seattle. A few weeks later, he was summoned to Graner's office again. This time, he was told he was being replaced—with no reason given. The firm offered him a demotion to a broker position, which he didn't accept. Instead, with more than a little relief, he left the firm for another brokerage operation.

Meanwhile, the situation in San Diego involving Randy Schroeder and his alleged drug-money laundering had come to a head. In May 1987, government agents had moved into the San Diego Pru-Bache office and seized brokerage records related to the accounts managed by Schroeder. In court papers, the U.S. District Attorney claimed that he had helped a drug-smuggling ring launder money into cashier's checks and had then deposited those checks into a Pru-Bache stock account. By the time agents seized the account, it had grown to $500,000, but by then, Schroeder had abruptly left Pru-Bache.

Within days, the money-laundering and drug-smuggling charge erupted into one of the bigger drug busts in the area. A federal grand jury indicted several Mexican nationals on charges of smuggling thousands of pounds of marijuana into the United States. To assist them, the ringleaders had bribed a $7-an-hour U.S. Customs inspector, who had looked the other way while drugs were driven across the border. The smugglers then carried between $500,000 and $800,000 of cash into Pru-Bache's San Diego office, stuffed in briefcases and knapsacks, according to prosecutors.

Pru-Bache cooperated fully with authorities, and those indicted were convicted. However, Schroeder was never indicted.

Kristi Mandt was excited because finally she had been noticed for her achievements. The green-eyed woman combed her long, curly red hair and made up her face. She was of medium height, and pretty. She wanted to look professional for this meeting.

This time, she promised herself, she wouldn't drink. Growing up as the oldest of four kids, she had always been an achiever: great student, ballet dancer, piano player, campfire girl, softball team player, student council president. The only thing she couldn't do was drink. Because of her severe reaction to alcohol, she had signed up for a treatment center in 1983. Yet she had started drinking at Pru-Bache company functions, where it seemed to be the thing to do.

After the San Francisco trip, she had been harshly reprimanded because of her loud, drunken behavior, and had almost gotten fired over it. The firm now knew Mandt had a drinking problem, but didn't realize that when she drank, she'd black out completely and forget her actions. That's what had happened on the San Francisco trip, and she probably would have been fired by now if Carrington Clark had not intervened on her behalf. Mandt was grateful.

Now he had invited her to dinner, where he and Bob Sherman would meet her while the two were in town. Mandt had reserved seats at a fine restaurant on Puget Sound in honor of their arrival. She had wanted to impress the regional director who had saved her job, as well as the president of the firm, and had chosen Salty's on Alki. While dining al fresco, one can view the city's stunning skyline.

Mandt met Sherman for the first time. She greeted Clark, who had with him a gorgeous woman he had met at a Portland bar. Sherman said, "I hear you're a great broker, Kristi."

"Thank you. My production is going up, and I'm finally on a roll."

"Kristi is a great producer," said Clark. "Have a glass of wine, Kristi."

"No thanks," she said, covering her wineglass with her hand to prevent Clark from pouring the bottle. "Mr. Sherman—er, Bob, how do you like Seattle?"

"Fine."

"C'mon, Kristi," said Clark. "You can have just one."

"No. I don't want any."

Over dinner, the three discussed limited partnerships such as Polaris and Watson & Taylor. Sherman seemed to be impressed with Mandt's sales abilities; Clark kept trying to fill Mandt's glass with wine, but Mandt abstained from alcohol. She began talking with Clark's companion, who was named Peggy. The two women hit it off very well.

When dinner was over, Clark walked Mandt back to her car.

"Don't ever tell anyone you had dinner with us here tonight."

"That's fine."

He smiled. "Perfect."

About two weeks later, Clark was again in Seattle's Pru-Bache office. The blue-eyed, snub-nosed director had thick bushy eyebrows and hairs sprouting atop his nose, which was frequently red. He dressed either impeccably or ridiculously, depending on his mood. His distinctive voice was high and reedy, and Mandt could hear him approaching as he breezily greeted her coworkers.

Clark then came into her office and closed the door, which alarmed Mandt. She wasn't sure what he was going to say.

"You know the only reason you're around is I saved your job," he said. "You know that, right?"

"Yes," she said, looking up at him solemnly.

"Good. I need you to book a flight to Denver. Write these dates down." She did. "I'm going to be there, and Bob Sherman will be there, and another woman."

He looked at her, his pale blue eyes serious. "Don't tell anybody about this. Is that clear?"

She nodded; she knew she was already treading on thin ice.

"Okay. It's Tuesday through Saturday." He repeated the dates. "You'd better make up a story, because I don't want anyone to know where you're going." Then he left.

Mandt did as she was told and made reservations. At the appointed time, she boarded her plane and landed in Denver, where she was supposed to meet Peggy. Peggy, however, wasn't there, and Mandt was scared. She took a taxi to the Hyatt Regency and waited in her room, as instructed, until Clark called her.

When he telephoned, Mandt told Clark that Peggy had never arrived at the airport. He got angry and telephoned Peggy with instructions for her to fly now to Denver, which she did.

Meanwhile, Mandt walked up to Clark's hotel suite, where she greeted Sherman and Clark. She sat down in a chair while Sherman paced nervously; Clark mixed some drinks.

"What'll you have, Kristi?"

"I'll have a diet pop, please."

He turned to her and said, "Oh, no. You'll drink."

"I can't drink. You know that."

"You *will* drink." He began to fix her some alcoholic mixed drink, which he brought over to her. He waited.

Tears welled up in her eyes. She had promised herself she wouldn't drink; she couldn't drink; she would ruin things if she did. She tried to stop the tears from falling.

Clark stood over her, the drink in hand. "Remember why you are still in the firm," he warned.

She shook her head slowly; he handed her the glass; Sherman watched. Mandt sipped the drink. Disgusted with herself, she gulped, then drained it.

From that point on, she blacked out, although she remained standing and drinking.

The next morning, she woke up in the same room, in bed, and naked. The light poured in through a crack in the curtains. At first Mandt didn't realize where she was. She had a terrific headache and knew she was hung over. Then she looked over and saw Bob Sherman next to her. He too was naked. She then noticed blood on the sheets, blood on herself. She realized that rough sex had happened the night before. She felt mortified. From an adjacent room, Clark walked into the room, wearing only his underwear. He stood over her, peering at her face.

"Are you among the living yet?"

She wanted to slink under the crack of the door, she felt so low and dirty. Clark smiled and walked back into the other room. Mandt didn't want to rise from the bed naked, and she surely didn't want to stay.

Clark reappeared again. "C'mon, Kristi. You have to leave now. Let's go. Get up. C'mon."

Cringing, she dressed in a hurry, filled with humiliation. She grabbed her shoes and nylons and walked toward the door.

"Remember," said Clark. "All you have to do is work on staying sober the whole day."

"Don't worry."

"Perfect."

That day was her mother's birthday. Mandt took a long, hot shower to scrub herself clean. Then she telephoned her mother in Tacoma, Washington. As the two women talked, Mandt started crying without a sound. It felt so good to talk, to hear her mother's voice; she couldn't stop her tears. Mother and daughter talked for a long while. Mandt's mother told her how proud she was of her daughter, who was on a business trip, who worked for Prudential, the Rock.

After she hung up, Mandt began to drink, and continued all day long. She wanted to kill herself. The next day, she took a flight home. On subsequent trips, Sherman called her a few times at the hotel, but she successfully evaded him. Meanwhile, her drinking problem worsened, and her work performance suffered. By April 1987, Mandt had lost her job.

14

A New Culture Takes Root

THE most intangible—and vital—part of Pru-Bache's investment banking effort was its culture, separate from that of the brokers. The society of investment banking in America during the 1980s was "little more than a collection of feudal principalities, [hiding] behind their moats and parapets, ready to pour boiling oil on any would-be king" who approached the system, as Pru-Bache investment banker Andrew K. Simpson later wrote. To a Manhattan banker, the terrain from Park Avenue to Gold Street in the 1980s resembled the fields and vales of Western Europe during the Middle Ages. Both featured turf wars and court intrigue.

As a modern banker, Simpson had waged battles in these fields for years. He had worked at large securities houses in the corporate finance division and had specialized in mergers and acquisitions. He knew the drill of ambushing competing battalions of bankers, right at a critical juncture, in order to blow them out of a deal.

By 1987, Simpson had grown disenchanted by what he saw as institutional "dysfunction." He wearied of the petty ways in which one camp within the corps plotted to entrap or trick another camp. The enemy was not always the firm down the street; more often it was the guy down the hall, the one with whom you eventually had to share the spoils of war. At year-end bonus time, for example, the money earned by the various "camps" from victorious deals would be divided among the knights, lords, and pawns. This inevitably led to individual posturing so that each man could obtain for himself the biggest possible check.

Simpson identified those traits belonging to the "gotcha culture." "One of the most prevalent elements of the 'gotcha' behavior is what I call the Wall Street lie," he said. Most bankers don't tell overt lies. But they do tell just part of the story, leaving out a crucial element—perhaps just one undisclosed fact—that, if known, would drastically alter the other camp's decision. "The rules are you don't lie to your rabbi [or mentor]," said Simpson, "you try not to lie to your clients, because they are your meal ticket, but everyone else is fair game. Particularly senior bankers who are competitors with your rabbi."

One treats other senior bankers like demigods, until they walk away. Then, under "gotcha" rules, a man undermines the "other" senior banker by withholding information he needs to service his accounts, or by denying him opportunities easily shared. "The whole gotcha culture is predicated on envy, fear, and anger," Simpson said—the envy of talent and prestige, the fear of humiliation, and the anger that is inherent to the deal-maker's archetype. To catch one's colleague off balance, to spring out from the woods clutching the treasure, to yell "Gotcha," was the object of the game.

In firms weak in leadership, the one-upmanship ploy can occupy more of a banker's time than does actual business. "I've been in firms where 75 percent of the time, department managers deploy defense maneuvers to fend off their colleagues, as opposed to engaging in productive business." By 1987, Simpson had grown so disgusted with the "moral violence on Wall Street," he yearned for something different.

At six feet three inches and 250 pounds, the red-faced descendant of Celts was himself an angry man. Some accused him of taking the moral high ground, even when there was business on the table. Simpson quoted General Patton, read Prussian military history, and studied warrior cultures. He realized that history's best warriors, its most admirable and courageous communities, were those devoted to a cause larger than themselves. Sometimes "the group's *raison d'être* is the fellowship of the group," he wrote. Take, for example, the Knights of the Round Table.

When Simpson founded Project '89, he believed he had finally stumbled upon his own Grail. Molding a corporate culture takes years, and the end result often doesn't match expectations. Even when a company reflects upon its goals, few Street cultures include words such as "competence" and "integrity." Yet those words were explicit in Project '89's original mission statement in March 1986. "We will . . . display personal and professional integrity without compromise and comfort ourselves with dignity and mutual self-respect." Such words might seem hollow in retrospect, but to Simpson and the others who joined PBCF, they struck a chord.

"We really believed in it and were convinced we could achieve those goals," said Jack Welch, a former managing director for Project '89. Even the old guard sensed that this time, PBCF and its coleaders might actually pull off a brilliant coup.

Neither Pru-Bache, Crowley, nor Fowler specifically espoused the Round Table lexicon, but the tag was used by Simpson and acknowledged by others. "I referred to them as Arthurian leaders," said Simpson, and, to some extent, the term fit. In any event, the Round Table metaphor became the unofficial ethos for those who joined this new crusade.

"It was so compelling to me because it was not a commercial mission, it was a mission of values and integrity," Simpson said. "They had a value system and a teamwork that was not the usual cliché." The two men leading the charge seemed more than capable figures. Crowley was the visionary, the father figure, the man who could solve the personal problems. "He radiates an odd kind of earth-sign warmth," said Simpson. "With his bearlike safety zone, you know he's going to take care of the cubs."

Fowler was the strategist. "He was relentlessly fascinated with every deal that was going on and always gave the impression to the guys lower down that he was available to be a champion for any good idea," said Simpson. The two coheads had agreed never to second-guess each other and to stand by each other's decisions. The two shared power and responsibility equally, which was difficult in any corporate setting, and virtually unheard-of on Wall Street.

They clicked like two parts of one mind, which helped PBCF's culture root firmly and, most important, ensured that most deals would be done properly.

To build itself up, Project '89's investment banking unit was allowed to reinvest no more than $113 million of its own revenues (the number had been increased from the earlier-quoted $92.5 million). Publicly, the Pru had claimed it would be willing to invest that much money in the effort, hoping that such an investment would pay dividends down the road. But, in fact, the Pru never spent a dime on Project '89. Fowler and Crowley never tapped that "allowance" because they generated enough money internally to fund the project from the start. That was a tremendous achievement.

The two built PBCF, which engaged not just in investment banking but in traditional corporate finance in addition to activities that fell outside those customary boundaries. Importantly, its myraid units moved as one synchronized piece: bankers called on clients, whom research analysts followed, and for whom traders could buy and sell issues, in offerings that the syndicate department could organize. Everyone rowed together, and the fact that so much fit under the PBCF roof was remarkable.

By year-end 1986, a third component was added to PBCF's ship. The Pru agreed to extend an $800 million line of credit for the Pru-Bache Interfunding unit—the newborn merchant banking arm. This credit allowed PBCF to invest for itself in mergers, acquisitions, and leveraged buyouts (in which a company borrows money to take over a firm whose assets then secure that loan). With the arrival of the merchant banking arm, Crowley and Fowler's operation was now complete: Pru-Bache was now a full-service house.

In December 1986, PBCF began negotiating as a principal in a leveraged buyout of Exxon Corp.'s industrial motors division, called Reliance Electric. With the purchase price of $1.35 billion, PBCF invested its own money. Pru-Bache had six weeks in which to pull off the deal with Exxon, which traditionally had done its banking business with Pru-Bache rival Goldman Sachs. Pru-Bache landed the deal, in part, because former Bache officer Virgil Sherrill was friendly with a key Reliance executive. The economics were such that seven years later the deal would return a compounded rate of 86 percent on Pru-Bache's money.

Reliance was by far the biggest leveraged buyout Pru-Bache had done at the time, and it trumpeted the debut of its merchant banking unit. Unlike investment bankers, merchant bankers invest their own capital in a client's deal. The transactions resemble venture capitalism, because the merchant banker often takes a percent of the company as payment for service. "Merchant banker" conjured images of many-masted ships sailing in the Indian Ocean, flying the English flag, but actually the phrase was now enjoying a modern-day renaissance. "The like of First Boston, Merrill Lynch, and Salomon Brothers are hardly exotic . . ." one newspaper reported, but "increasingly these firms are eyeing the merchant banking arena."

The Pru gave Pru-Bache's merchant banking effort the $800 million line of credit so it could finance more than one deal at a time. The house rules were that no single investment could cost more than $300 million, and the unit couldn't borrow more than $800 million on the credit line at one time. Basically, the idea was to finance companies that needed cash, form an investor group, then obtain some stock or equity in the company as a fee for service, so that a few years down the line, Pru-Bache could sell its stake for a handsome return.

In 1987, PBCF began to do just that. In August, it advised a large investor group in its purchase of Spreckles Industries for $185 million in a leveraged buyout. PBCF received some equity. When a radio broadcaster wanted to sell part of its properties, PBCF formed an investor group called Fairmont Communications Corp. and acted as a principal in the $120 million deal.

In one of the largest deals of the year, a group of managers who worked for CBS Magazines bought from CBS Magazines the consumer magazine publisher Diamandis Communications. The $650 million buyout was for twenty-one consumer magazines, including *Woman's Day,* with its six million subscribers. Pru-Bache's merchant banking arm, along with its sister, PruCapital, arranged the management buyout and invested in the deal. The deal was solid, big, and synergistic, because it involved the Pru family. Here was the financial supermarket in action, the Round Table ethos at work, with everyone working together for the whole. Indeed, the Pru would feature the deal in its annual report, stating that the transaction "represented the largest unsecured leveraged buyout ever financed by The Prudential."

Even though the Pru had neutered its own unit by forbidding "hostile" takeovers—which cost PBCF an estimated $200 million in fees—Project '89 was performing very well indeed by the summer of '87. In addition to its more glamorous business of megadeals, it continued to do brisk bread-and-butter business of underwriting new issues, packaging mortgage bonds, swapping interest rates, and other more mundane activities. The by now routine business brought into the house the profits Project '89 needed to grow and expand.

To his credit, George Ball allowed Crowley and Fowler to make their own decisions. Although Ball and Gahan blessed the major elements of Project '89 and approved the hiring of any banker whose base salary exceeded $250,000, the perception was that the coheads ran their own shop, with the blessings of Mother Pru.

At this time, the competition moaned that Crowley and Fowler were throwing money around the Street in reckless abandon, in efforts to lure talent to their project. Actually, the duo never paid any investment banker even $2 million in total compensation, which was a paltry sum by Street standards in those years.

Around July of that year, Ball wrote a twelve-page memo to welcome the new hires who had joined the effort. He encouraged employees to assist and "integrate" the new hires so they could begin producing revenue as quickly as possible. Importantly, many of the new faces were not destined for Project '89. Rather, the bulk of them were research analysts, traders, municipal finance experts, and other capital markets professionals that the firm needed regardless of Project '89.

In 1986, the number of investment bankers numbered 143; by year-end 1987 it would climb nearly 50 percent to 207. That staff was less than half the size of ones employed by its then major competitors. "After a while, we were working seven days a week, sometimes around the clock. It was exhilarating and exhausting, and rather unbelievable," said one banker.

In his welcoming epistle, Ball encouraged the bonding of bankers to the brokerage firm. He understood the danger that existed because of all the new hires: so many members of outside firms could potentially cripple Project '89 only because they brought with them old habits. "We had new people who had come from different firms and cultures and everyone had a different view of how a deal should be done," said one female banker who recruited new hires. A midlevel person hired from Goldman Sachs had been taught to "deal" in a fashion that might be entirely different from the lessons imparted at Merrill Lynch. At its extreme, the result could be a Tower of Babel, with no one understanding what anyone else was saying. The situation was fraught with pitfalls, but the project was still young.

Some new hires later realized that they were not as aggressive as the new enterprise required. "Many people came from well-established firms and had been used to having the business come to them," said one director. "At Pru-Bache, we had to go out and hustle aggressively to get business. We were the newcomers." The unit purposely didn't hire "stars" from competing firms, precisely because it intended to create its own stars from within. The focus was that the house of Pru-Bache, as a team, would win business. As Ball's memo indicated, everyone at the firm had to help newcomers in the acculturation process for the sake of company profits.

By now, Ball's memos had achieved cult status. "Ball-o-grams," they were called, or "Ballisms"; they elicited strong opinions from the troops, but they were rarely ignored. "George uses words like this," said one woman, stretching her arms wide to indicate size, "to mean this," she said, pinching forefinger to thumb. Brokers appreciated his creative and erudite musings. Indeed, his letters were considered so quirky and unusual they were featured on the front page of the *Wall Street Journal*, with the officious headline addressed to Ball: "Re: Your Messages. Sir: They're Weird."

Once a month, Ball wrote a three- or four-page memo ruminating about the industry. He delivered bad news with panache, and good news with puns. "Avail Yourself" was the title of a memo from a Colorado ski resort. "But let me depart from the Chairmanesque veils of obliqueness and pin myself down in a hall of specificity" was a line from another memo. His style was fun, light, and self-deprecating. "They were like snowflakes because they didn't carry much weight," groused one executive.

During his eight-and-a-half-year tenure, Ball wrote eleven thousand memos that were distributed to seventeen thousand employees—all signed simply "George," in his loopy, expansive scrawl. He flourished as a writer perhaps because he stuttered as a speaker—a trait that grew pronounced when he was nervous or upset. Perhaps he wrote as a way to order the hugeness of the firm that was now "bigger than life."

He once explained that he wrote memos because it was an "act of faith." Writing of any kind assumes the existence of an audience that cares about what you have to say. The impulse to express himself and his private thoughts was stronger than fear of criticism from readers. Ball believed that his legions of brokers, bankers, and staffers were interested in his words and musings, and by the summer of 1987, that was still true.

The year 1986 had been a good one for Pru-Bache. The bullish stock market had buoyed earnings to a whopping $82 million—or double 1985's $42 million income. According to internal documents, PBCF had contributed $35 million (before allocated costs) to 1986 earnings, or a third of its income. Most important, the project hadn't lost money in its first few months. That amazing feat was not well known outside of Pru-Bache's executive committee, but it demonstrated the enormous potential of Project '89. Ball had made a sound decision to build an income stream from investment banking, and it could augment the cash flowing from DIG, which over the years had also proved to be a gold mine.

The summer of 1987 would be remembered as a time when Pru-Bache seemed to be on a roll. The troubles in the field had yet to mount, and DIG's woes were inconceivable then. The bull market was climbing, deals were swelling, and in Project '89, Pru had the potential to score even bigger profits than before.

PBCF's new hires and old hands gathered for a four-day conference at the Rye Town Hilton Hotel in Westchester County. The resort, located north of New York City, was surrounded by forty acres of woods and lawn. Golf courses, horseback trails, tennis courts, and swimming pools offered opportunities to meet and relax with coworkers.

That summer, all of the people from all of the offices—from as far away as Australia and Hong Kong—flew in for the occasion. The purpose was to build confidence and spirit among the scattered staffers and to cheer on the group. As at most corporate functions, the morning and early afternoon hours were devoted to educational and training seminars. The late afternoons were devoted to play or free time.

"It was the first time we had all come together. People wanted to celebrate—I mean they were really psyched—because of what we're doing," said Carol Curley Kelly. She had talked to fellow bankers from offices in London, San Francisco, and Sydney, but only on the telephone. That summer, she met them personally. "It was neat to realize they had lives outside of Project '89," she said. "It was a real bonding experience."

That Friday evening, the group anticipated a particularly festive evening with dinner, drinks, entertainment, and a speech from the vice chairman of the Pru, Garnett Keith. He would address the bankers and signal that the Pru was observing their performance.

By now, Keith had lost the chairman's position, which had naturally disappointed him, according to those who knew him. He had vied for that post with Bob Winters, who earlier that year had become chairman of the Pru. Nonetheless, he stayed—Keith was still young and had a chance to secure the top position at the world's largest nonbank financial corporation, once Winters retired in eight years or so. "Keith had to make sure he looked good," said one executive, "in order to be in line for that post."

That Friday night, Keith arrived late to the party from a prior engagement. After dinner, Fowler stood at the front of the group and auctioned bids for the golf Calcutta pool. The entertainment was scheduled for ten o'clock; Fowler was still taking bids at ten-twenty. Bankers bid about $45,000 that night. "The next morning, after we sobered up, we all felt kind of bad," said one bettor. The group later donated most of the money to charity.

While Fowler acted as bookie, Crowley noticed that Keith frequently checked his watch. The hour was late, and Keith was anxious to deliver his speech and leave. Finally, he spoke. He didn't say much, but complimented the group's efforts, according to half a dozen listeners. "He was very serious," said one woman. "He had been a big supporter of our organization and the Pru was pleased about what we had done so far."

As the vice chairman left the dais, the lights went down and jungle drums beat out a loud, urgent, hard-driving rhythm. A shrill whistle overpowered the drums. Then a Brazilian troop of male and female dancers ran into the room, wearing native costumes and headdresses and carrying musical instruments. Some of the women wore bikini tops and G-strings; some of the men were bare-chested. Gay samba music flooded the room as the troupe performed for the bankers.

The reaction to the entertainment was mixed. Some of the women didn't mind the scantily clad women at all; others remembered the music. Some men said they were deeply offended, especially on behalf of their female colleagues. Many people saw Keith bolt from the room during the performance and assumed the worst. "It was so un-Pru-like," said Welch. The big money laid on the golf tournament, the tipsy camaraderie, the women in G-strings. Some people believed that Keith was offended, even though the men who sat with him at the table said that he was simply eager to go.

Whatever the reason, Keith's abrupt departure would later be remembered by some as a watershed event in the fate of Project '89.

Harry Jacobs, the avuncular former head of Bache, understood Wall Street's volatile cycles. He used to say that for four years, a brokerage house loses money; for four more years, it makes a modest amount of money; and for two years, it makes a bundle. That, in a nutshell, is the cycle of the retail securities business: eight out of ten years, a brokerage firm doesn't earn much money.

In the fall of '87, the downside of the cycle was about to hit with a bang. On Monday, October 19, the stock market plunged 508 Dow points, from 2,246 to 1,738. It was the worse one-day drop ever, and traders, analysts, and investors were dumbfounded, even hysterical. One investor that day said, "I'm scared. Should I sell? Tell me, should I sell?"

Pandemonium ran wild as people attempted to save their own portfolios, their own firms, and their own deals from disappearing altogether. The Great Depression was a reoccurring image at the exchange. The 1987 decline, tallied over a few days, accounted for a total of 743 points, or 30 percent. By comparison, the total drop in the market over two days on October 29 in 1929 had been 69 Dow points, or 23 percent. An editorial the next day prophesied that "the record-shattering losses would seem to predict an unpleasant future indeed."

Ball, Crowley, Fowler, Gahan, Darr, Sherman, and others of the twelve-member executive committee gathered later that day to list the damage—just as directors of every other broker-dealer firm around the city were huddling over boardroom tables in vain efforts to stem the financial hemorrhage. Pru-Bache had lost only about $10 million that day, according to a few executives, but other houses got pummeled far worse than that. "Gahan had performed a minor miracle" by hedging smartly, said one observer.

The firm's arbitrage department had lost money, but its head, Guy Wyser-Pratte, was still regarded as one of the best.

Arbitrage evolved in fourteenth-century Venice—the term is derived from the Italian verb *arbitrare,* meaning "to referee." In that medieval trading port, merchants swapped currencies and pocketed the difference. Arbitragers evolved to equalize the fluctuations between foreign currencies and to referee arguments.

In the eighties, risk arbitrage came to be associated with unwanted connotations such as corporate raiders, vultures, and Ivan Boesky (whom Guy Wyser-Pratte had nicknamed Piggy). When following SEC rules, these professionals perform legitimate functions. For example, an "arb" buys stock in companies that are being taken over or reorganized, on the theory that if the transaction is successful, as such transactions usually are, the arb will hold stock worth more than he paid for it. Unlike those who trade on insider information, reputable arbs wait until a deal is agreed upon and "hedge" their bets based on their knowledge of the deal, the people involved, and the company's valuation. It's tedious, arcane, specialized work that can be very lucrative.

Guy Wyser-Pratte is a handsome, blue-eyed, French-born American who was highly regarded on Wall Street and somewhat feared by corporate executives. He believed in corporate democracy, by which shareholders take an active part in managing companies they own. At Pru-Bache, Wyser-Pratte managed as much as $375 million for the house account (with the firm's own money) and about $125 million more for clients. For Pru-Bache, he made millions with his small, twelve-person staff. From 1981 to 1986, his division had returned as much as 35 percent a year on investments. The lowest annual return was 17.4 percent—still a healthy rate in any year.

Yet, on the day of the crash, he lost money. That morning, while the market was still falling, Ball walked into his office and asked, "How do you feel?"

"Fine," said Wyser-Pratte. "I think I know what's going on." He explained that a congressman's proposed ban on interest deductions for acquisition loans (as in leveraged buyouts) was responsible for a significant part of the market crash. (His understanding would later be verified by a congressional study.)

Ball nodded, then asked, "Would you like to double up?"—meaning, go back into the market and double the bets.

"Sure." Wyser-Pratte did. In the next few weeks, he turned the department's 20 percent loss into a gain. "We made a killing," said Wyser-Pratte. The arbitrage department ended the year with only a 3 percent loss, which would have been much worse if Ball hadn't suggested doubling up.

However, in the weeks after the crash, business on the street withered. After nearly collapsing, E. F. Hutton was sold for about $1 billion to Shearson; Ball was still answering questions regarding his role in E. F. Hutton's check-kiting scam. Investors ran scared from the stock and bond markets, and sales were tough. Mergers and acquisitions slowed down, initial public offerings died, and arbitragers lost as much as 80 percent on their portfolios.

Ironically, the year 1987 would be the best ever for Pru-Bache's limited partnerships, which sold a total of $1.128 billion in public LPs bringing into the firm about $100 million before expenses. But because of investors' jitters following the crash, the expensive retail brokerage division—the salespeople—were not producing the profit the firm had projected. Ball needed revenue to close the year with a profit. He had already budgeted some $125 million for the Pru, which was anxious to recoup its investment. In 1985, Pru-Bache had scored $42 million, and doubled this the next year. Ball had budgeted a profit of close to $125 million for 1987, which the Pru was expecting. The earnings momentum had to be maintained, but how?

In November, Ball froze all new hires across the board and began to cut back on staff. Thus, Crowley and Fowler could not complete negotiations with about fifteen key people they had planned to hire for Project '89. In the first full year of the five-year plan, the project was already emasculated. Crowley told Fowler to be patient as it was only a temporary situation.

The two men looked at their record to date. The total amount of money PBCF had raised by sales in the public sector had tripled in two years to reach $6.1 billion by year-end 1987. Its market share had nearly doubled to 1.9 percent—within reach of the firm's 2.4 percent goal it had vowed to meet by 1989. But most important, the firm had finally landed on the prestigious deal-makers' list. It ranked number ten among all investment bankers, according to Securities Data Corp., which was the first time ever for Pru-Bache.

Incredibly, PBCF had—in its first full year, in the wake of the worst-ever stock market, in spite of the odds against the ambition in the first place—reached one of its key goals. Plus, it had made money. After expenses, PBCF had contributed $28 million to the firm.

Ball needed that money, so clearly, there would be few bonuses that year for investment or merchant bankers who had achieved so much. In 1987, the brokerage firm recorded a loss of $164 million, which was a stunning loss for its owners across the river. It would have been steeper had it not been for Project '89. For the bankers, the issue was clear. "It was a question of trying to get something to work for the firm and, at the same time, to deal fairly with people," said one banker. None of them liked the situation, but they all understood they had to weather bad times together.

15

RISERs and Departures

By the end of 1987, Mike Kudlik's Pac South region ranked at the top of the limited partnership list. In 1987, the firm had sold an enormous $1.12 billion in public LPs; in 1988, it would sell another $1.1 billion—even after the historic stock market crash. Pru-Bache had beaten the odds and now dominated every other LP sales firm. And, of all the nine regions, Kudlik's region had sold 24 percent of the firm's total—or the bulk of the firm's LP sales.

At the time, Kudlik believed in the products, especially the oil and gas partnerships. "Later I saw problems with VMS and I'd speak out. I got beat up a few times for doing that," he said. But he spoke his mind. He thought that because he was making so much money for the firm, he was invincible, and they would never fire him. "We were chasing the dollars, all of us." Top salesmen were gods.

Yet Kudlik slowly learned that just because one excels at a job doesn't mean one is held in high regard by the home office. Not in DIG, anyway. Kudlik had repeatedly asked what it would take for him to participate in the special pool that included a select group of men: Darr, Proscia, Pittman, Defur, Clancy, Jim Parker (regional director in Florida), Mark Harper (regional director in Texas), and some others.

Said Kudlik: "I don't know who knew about this pool, but even before limited partners [investors] received a payout, they got a payout." This is confirmed by other employees as well as by Grattarola from Graham, who wrote quarterly checks for the special Pru-Bache fund.

Neither Kudlik nor others saw the bonus pool explicitly described. According to a man who received such monies, the arrangement worked like this:

All limited partnerships paid management and other fees to Pru-Bache entities such as Pru-Bache Properties. A portion of these fees flowed to the bonus pool. At year-end, Darr decided who received a bonus and how much (Darr said that staff people made those recommendations). The thinking behind the pool was that it would help retain talent who might otherwise go to the sponsor's side of the LP business.

"Many people could go, for example, to the VMS group, where they would have made substantially more money," explained a former manager. In DIG, one earned his bonus by auditing books, visiting properties, and generally reviewing records. Said the pool member: "It was legitimate." Although the fees paid to Pru-Bache entities were properly disclosed in prospectuses, neither Kudlik nor others saw the bonus pool explicitly described.

Yet because some of the fees were used for executive compensation, that fact should have been fully disclosed to investors, according to attorney Jeff Dennis Ferentz. In the case of Polaris Limited Partnerships, for example, Ferentez claimed that investors paid due diligence fees equal to 5 percent of the total $1.1 billion raised (on top of the 15 percent already discussed). That's $56 million in "fees" meant to help safeguard investments that, on the whole, didn't perform as expected. "Where did the money go?" Ferentz asked.

Most of it, according to Ferentz and others, went to the thirty-third floor, where Darr and the "guys in the inner circle" profited.

By 1986, the protocol of DIG became apparent to Kudlik. At the time, the boundaries of the two Pacific regions were redrawn slightly, which meant that Kudlik would no longer cover Utah. He had spent two years developing contacts in the Mormon state and had finally gained their trust. He had a home in Salt Lake City and would eventually settle there; Kudlik didn't want to let go of his hard-won sales region.

He talked to his counterpart in the Pacific North region, Larry Forness, who agreed to let Kudlik keep the state as his sales territory. In return, Kudlik would sign over all of his commissions from all the sales he made in Utah. Forness heartily endorsed that idea. Now all Kudlik had to do was get his boss's approval.

Kudlik called Jim Darr, who agreed to take the matter up with his boss, Bob Sherman, the man who had rejiggered the retail divisions' boundaries. After three months and no response, Kudlik called Darr again. "Don't worry," said Darr. "I'll handle it." Kudlik still did not get a response.

For advice, he turned to Graner, who suggested that Kudlik talk to Sherman while Sherman was in Los Angeles for a Pru-Bache party. "Sherman was Graner's best friend, so I figured Graner knew best how to handle this," said Kudlik.

Over cocktails, Kudlik approached Sherman: "By the way, Bob, what's the possibility of me keeping Utah, and working it—you know, making sales—and not getting paid for it. I'll give Larry [Forness] all the commissions. Jim [Darr] said he was going to talk to you about it. But I thought I'd bring it up with you."

"That's ridiculous," said Sherman.

Kudlik explained how long it had taken Pru-Bache to develop the Mormon contacts, and how he had a home in the state. But Sherman indicated the matter was closed.

The next day, Darr telephoned Kudlik, shouting at the top of his lungs. "How dare you go over my head," he screamed. "Who the fuck do you think you are?" He was livid with rage and cursed a stream of profanities.

"Wait a minute now," said Kudlik. "I don't know what story you got, but here's what happened. All I did was ask Bob an innocent question. I don't think I did anything wrong."

Darr paused. "Listen," he said. "That was not the way to handle it. Now you'll never see it."

Kudlik didn't speak.

"I want you on the plane. Now. I'll have someone call you." Darr slammed down the receiver, leaving Kudlik bewildered. Darr later said he had no recollection of berating Kudlik over this incident.

Kudlik recalled that next, Proscia called him: "You'd better get your ass on the next flight to New York, buddy. Quick, before you get fired."

That Sunday, Kudlik boarded a red-eye flight to New York. In the morning, he took a cab to One Seaport Plaza. He rode the elevator to the thirty-third floor and waited for Darr. After two hours, Proscia called him into his office. Proscia closed the door and lit into Kudlik: "How could you do this?" he screeched. "Who the hell do you think you are? You think you're hot stuff. But pal, you're nothing." He read a list of transgressions that Kudlik had committed. They all seemed to be minor, petty, and nonexistent infractions.

Proscia held forth: "We told you we'd think about Utah. But no. You had to keep pressing, and pushing. You're always going above us. You never follow the chain of command.

"Obviously, you can't dance to our tune. Although your numbers are good, you're not following commands. Darr's probably going to fire you."

Throughout the scolding, Kudlik acted humble and kept silent. When Proscia was finished, he led Kudlik to Darr's office, where Kudlik was scheduled for another meeting. For the next three hours, Kudlik patiently waited.

Finally, he was ushered into Darr's spacious office, which had a bar, a few couches, and a breathtaking view. Darr was calm. Without raising his voice, he said: "Mike, maybe you should reconsider your commitment to the firm. Maybe you don't like working here." Darr repeated the same infractions that Proscia had listed, such as insubordination, and again warned Kudlik never again to reach beyond Darr's domain.

Chastened, Kudlik left Darr and One Seaport Plaza after what amounted to a twenty-minute "conference" with his boss. He realized he still had a job, but he wasn't so sure he needed the aggravation. He had wasted $1,000 in travel money, a full work day, and five hours of waiting, just to be treated like a bad schoolboy? Kudlik was disgusted.

"They played with my mind," he thought. The political setup was too bizarre for him to fathom. He boarded another red-eye flight back to California, which landed in time for him to arrive at work the next morning.

Still, even after his humiliating trip, Kudlik didn't bend completely. He was stubborn. Sister Theophilia had told him that years ago whenever he was caught scuffling, he'd rather slug it out with a boy than "turn the other cheek," and Sister Theophila disapproved. She'd be right behind him, grabbing him by the ear and leading him to the cloakroom, where she'd knot his blue uniform tie to that of the other boy. "You want to fight?" she'd say. "Go right ahead." She'd throw the boys into the closet to punch it out for half an hour. Usually, the boys would just sit in the dark and cry.

Now, some thirty years later, Kudlik felt as though he were still getting into fights, only this time with guys who outranked him.

From time to time, officers such as Proscia and Clancy called Kudlik to ask a favor. Could a buddy, secretary, or female assistant attend one of Kudlik's seminars? Kudlik ran a tight budget; he made more sales than anyone else, and had fewer expenses. If there was money left over from a due diligence trip, he'd return it to sponsors, which was unusual. "For every dollar raised, the firm said it took fifty cents in expenses," said Kudlik. In his region, expenses amounted to a dime per dollar. So when Barron Clancy called and asked if a friend could fly in, Kudlik asked, "To do what?

"To be an observer."

"Fine."

"Well, you need to pay for his airfare and room."

"Look, my budget is really tight. Unless this person is going to add value to the event, I can't pay for him." Kudlik thought, "I'm not going to shell out $2,000 so some guy can go on a boondoggle. No way."

Aloud, he said, "It doesn't make sense, Barron."

"I find it very important to have this guy there."

They argued, but in the end, Clancy won, Kudlik paid, and the guest played golf during the "due diligence trip."

Kudlik learned to submit, but not to kowtow.

In January 1988, Jack Graner walked into his office in downtown Los Angeles and had a heart attack. A secretary screamed; people rushed to his side; a broker drove him to the hospital. Graner spent three days in the intensive care unit. Eventually, he was moved to another hospital, where he rested in a private room. Flowers, plants, and get-well cards streamed into his office, and someone hired two vans to transport the presents from Pru-Bache's office to Graner's hospital bedside. One friend sent him 120 pounds of tropical fruit and a stuffed monkey with the greeting "You're driving me bananas! Get well."

To those around him, Graner appeared overwhelmed by his job, the firm, the market, and his life. His wife was not happy; he was not happy; his life as a regional director in Sherman's company was hard. Despite his region's high sales of DIG product, Pac South by 1988 was coming undone.

Saccullo took over as "acting" regional director. By now, Mr. Crabs, as he was known after the Captain Crabs incident in Atlanta, had completed his SEC-imposed probationary period. He could legally assume a management position. His title remained regional sales coordinator, but his power increased. In Graner's absence, Saccullo supervised all the employees who worked in the region—but not Kudlik.

Every January, Kudlik treated the top fifty sales people in his territory to a three-day ski trip in Snow Bird, Utah. The sponsors paid for it: VMS, Polaris, Graham, and others. Kudlik staged his due diligence meetings in the morning so that brokers could ski in the afternoon.

A few days before the meeting, Saccullo made the by now routine request: "By the way, I want my secretary to go."

"Rick, I can't do that," said Kudlik, sighing. "I can put her to work, but if she's not going to do anything, I can't afford to accommodate her. Sorry."

"No," Saccullo said. "This is something I promised her. And she's not going to work for it."

"I really don't have a place for her."

"Oh, you'll find one."

"I'll get back to you, but I don't have the budget. I'm telling you."

"Find it." Saccullo hung up.

A few days later, Saccullo telephoned again, requesting tickets to an upcoming Super Bowl football game, which was scheduled in San Diego. San Diego Chargers' football team owner, Alex Spanos, was a general partner for some Pru-Bache LPs. Kudlik said he couldn't get the tickets.

Before long, Clancy called Kudlik: "What happened with you and Rick? He's talking to Sherman. He wants you fired."

"I don't know what you're talking about, Barron. He wanted his secretary to come to Snow Bird. Fine, she's coming."

"Listen, I don't know what the problem is, but you'd better solve it. Quick. Do whatever it takes."

On the eve before the seminar started, Kudlik went up to Saccullo.

"Rick, I apologize for the way we weren't getting along. What can I do to make it up to you?"

Saccullo retorted, "You're doing it."

Kudlik ignored the sarcasm and attended to his guests and the sponsors. After the event, he flew to New York for the quarterly DIG meeting and party. Darr congratulated him for his great sales figures and awarded him two achievement awards. Later, Kudlik heard from Clancy that he was about to be fired, but he didn't pay it any mind. How could they both reward him and fire him?

Kudlik boarded a red-eye back to Los Angeles and showed up for work at six-thirty. Then, Clancy called.

"I'm sorry, Mike, but I need your resignation."

Kudlik laughed. "Are you joking? Stop it, will ya?"

Clancy continued, "Bob Sherman called, and I want you to resign."

"Didn't you see all the awards I won yesterday? Why do you want me to resign?"

"I don't know yet. But for right now, I need your resignation."

Kudlik learned that Sherman and Darr had been fighting a political battle for a few months. Kudlik concluded that he had gotten caught in their crossfire. By now, Kudlik could no longer disguise his contempt for the factional politics.

"Look, Barron. I'm not going to resign, but you're really ticking me off. I'm tired, I've been working all weekend, and I'm going home. I don't need this shit." Kudlik hung up.

On his way out, he stuck his head inside Saccullo's office and said, "Hey, Rick. They just asked for my resignation."

Saccullo looked up. "Gee, I'm real sorry. Why don't you go home, and I'll have your stuff delivered."

"No, no. Don't do that. I'll be back."

Kudlik went home. Three hours later, a limousine pulled up to his doorstep. The driver delivered cartons of Kudlik's papers and belongings.

Over the next four months, Clancy and DIG would not fire Kudlik, and he would not resign. Payroll kept printing his checks, which he never received, and the receptionist kept taking his messages, but he hung in limbo. In April, Pru-Bache fired him retroactively to January.

Kudlik found a job at Graham—but Kudlik was soon "let go." For the next five years, Kudlik strove unsuccessfully to find a position that matched the level and pay of his former job. During that time, his salary dropped by 70 percent, his savings disappeared, and his anger swelled.

Where Sherman and Darr had once been friends, sharing good times and trips, they now were bitter enemies. Part of the problem stemmed from their nature, according to those who knew them. Both were strong-willed, arrogant managers in a high-powered corporation. But in 1987 other factors ignited the already volatile relationship.

In 1987, during Darr's stint at Harvard, senior officers in the firm learned more about Darr and his business deals. That summer, George Watson and Starke Taylor, two Texan real-estate developers, met with Pru-Bache officers, and not Darr. Their company, Watson & Taylor, had sold through Pru-Bache about $100 million in public LPs. The officers wanted the two men to relinquish their management role in several LPs that were not performing. Instead, they wanted outside managers to run the LPs. According to one DIG employee, Watson thought that the officers knew about some of private deals he had with Darr. Watson said: "Now, here I am taking care of your boy Jim and giving him deals. Why can't you all take care of me?" The cosponsor didn't want to step away from the LPs after all he had done for Pru-Bache.

Shortly thereafter, Schechter and another attorney, Frank Giordano, walked out of the meeting. "Frank was white-faced," said one eyewitness. The firm promptly hired a law firm, Locke Purnell Rain Harrell, to investigate Darr's deals with the sponsor. The resulting report was completed in February 1988, when Locke Purnell delivered these findings:

Between 1983 and 1985, Darr had participated in at least seven private deals with the sponsor, at least two of which were profitable. In one deal, Darr doubled his money in about seven months. In another he did not pay for his 20 percent interest, in a third, he earned a 42 percent return on his money in one year. In some deals, Watson & Taylor invested its own money for Darr. By the time Darr's personal deals were investigated by Locke Purnell, the firm could not locate many agreements and other supporting details; they were either missing from the files or had never been documented.

In addition, Darr had received a favorable home loan in 1984 and another in 1985. Watson helped him secure those loans from a small

Arkansas bank. Watson owned more than 25 percent of the stock in that bank and introduced Darr to lending officers. Darr then took out a $1.8 million home mortgage with no money down, no points charged, and an interest rate a point above prime—uncommonly generous terms not accorded the average executive homebuyer. Later, Darr denied that he had received special treatment and claimed that in June 1984, he told both Sherman and Pru-Bache's attorney Schechter about the loan. According to Darr, Schechter only said: "That is fine as long as the mortgage is at market rates."

A year later, in 1985, Darr received another $345,000 loan from the same S&L. He used the money to buy 8,300 shares in the S&L after an officer of the thrift called him to ask if he'd like to purchase the shares from a private party. "It was a very good buy at the time," Darr later told attorneys. He bought the shares through his Pru-Bache account.

None of these side deals were disclosed to investors in a 1985 Watson & Taylor prospectus. Yet Darr later said that he had disclosed these arrangements to his boss, Sherman, as well as to the firm's legal department. "They were out in the open," he said, adding that a Pru-Bache accountant took care of Darr's personal investments. Still, the firm's attorneys apparently were surprised by Watson's disclosures in the summer of 1987.

In August, after consulting with Giordano, Darr rewrote at least one of his arrangements with Watson & Taylor. According to Darr, the new rewritten contract better reflected his original intent with the LP sponsors.

Later, Ball would say that the Locke Purnell report "didn't find anything criminal, but it found too cozy relationships between Darr and the sponsors."

Darr and George Watson invested $100,000 each along with a few other people in a leveraged buyout fund that involved a Swiss bank. Watson said that this deal was not disclosed to Watson & Taylor LPs sold by Pru-Bache because it was not related to the warehouse deals the two firms were selling to Pru-Bache clients.

Perhaps if it had been disclosed, some investors might have questioned the objectivity of a deal in which two top officers of the cosponsors had a personal investment on the side. To a prudent investor, such information might seem pertinent.

Some DIG employees also knew about a $10,000 rifle that a Graham senior officer had given to Darr as an unwrapped birthday gift. "It was the type of thing where someone told him, 'There's a gun in your closet and if you like it, keep it,' " said Grattarola. Plus, many brokers and managers had long seen what they considered to be obvious conflicts of interest in Pru-Bache/VMS deals. Still other private deals surfaced later.

The Locke Purnell investigations soured the relationship between Sherman and Darr. By now, Darr was actively lobbying for his boss's job, in addition to those held by other top executives. In his deposition, Darr later said: "I had hoped to either take over part of investment banking in its entirety [sic] or the retail group."

There was no way Ball was going to promote Darr to his boss's job. By 1988, Sherman resisted cooperating with Darr in his new special product responsibilities. All civilized communication between the two had snapped, and their mounting personal attacks undermined business.

By now, Pru-Bache executives—including Ball and Loren Schechter—surely should have known about Sherman's alleged improper conduct. Sherman was involved in the Barbizon deal with one of the firm's LP cosponsors, and his extramarital affairs with female employees were widely known.

Around Thanksgiving 1988, both Darr and Sherman left One Seaport Plaza. In an amicable settlement, Darr collected salary, bonuses, and benefits from Pru-Bache for a while. He left feeling proud of what he had built. He said he had filled DIG with the best talent he could find, and with Pru-Bache lawyers. "They offered product to the world that they were proud of, that was unique for limited partnership offerings." It should have been a legacy of pride, but years later, he said, it "has been gravely distorted." For two years after his departure from Pru-Bache, Darr was self-employed. In December 1990, he joined Robert Todd Financial Corp., but according to his NASD record, he left that firm a few weeks later.

As for Sherman, he too parted amicably from Pru-Bache and reportedly collected a generous severance package. In May 1989, he became CEO of a hot dog company, but left that position before the year ended.

The Friday after Thanksgiving 1988, Ball initiated a conference call with the regional directors and informed them of the two executives' departure.

"I stress," Ball said, "that these two moves are unrelated. Prudential values the contributions that both Bob and Jim have made to the firm. We will surely miss them."

Jim Trice and other regional directors didn't for a minute believe that the moves were unrelated. Many of them sensed that there was more to the story than Ball was sharing. In the next sentence, however, Ball announced that Richard "Richie" Sichenzio was the new chief of retail. Trice, for one, was not impressed.

A few months before, the firm had introduced a new product, called RISERs, standing for Residual Income Stream Equity REITs, or real estate investment trusts. The investments were potentially volatile and would swing dramatically if interest rates changed. Pru-Bache claimed it had found a way to hedge against those swings so that the RISERs would provide a stream of income. The firm touted returns as high as 18 percent, but it couldn't clearly explain the product to its brokers. Few understood how they worked.

During a conference call about RISERs, one manager questioned the product. He said a Pru-Bache research analyst had just forecast a change in rates. "If that guy's right, we shouldn't be selling these things to our customers. We should be getting them to liquidate [sell] them."

"We didn't realize he had said that," Sichenzio said. "We'll get back to you."

A few days later, the analyst spoke on the firm-wide squawk box. He explained to brokers that his earlier comments about interest rates had been misunderstood; he indicated that the RISERs should perform well for clients. To Trice, the analyst's "backtracking" smelled bad.

Neither Trice nor his managers in the Southeast liked the product. Yet, as the number-two man in the retail sales force, Sichenzio wanted it sold. He called Trice:

"Why aren't you pushing RISERs in your region?"

"I'm not pushing them because we don't know what they are. We're not due diligence experts; you guys are."

"So why aren't you selling more?"

"Frankly, a lot of the guys in my region don't understand them."

"Well, that's your job. To make them understand."

"Hell, Rich, I don't understand them. And I don't think the firm does. We have a problem."

Sichenzio didn't appreciate the comment, even though it was true. For the past year or so, Trice had noticed that senior management often evaded questions from brokers and managers in the field. If someone asked why an LP wasn't performing, the New York "experts" provided few clear answers: We don't know. We'll get back to you. Adjust it for taxes. It's too complicated. Don't worry. Trust us.

RISERs were just the latest example of questionable product. In October, despite skepticism from the sales force, the firm offered the product at $10 a share; nine months later, it would drop to $2. But after the 1987 stock market crash, the sales force was pressured intensely to sell "special" firm products, regardless of their real value. Clients were nervous about the stock market, the reasoning went. Pru-Bache had to sell, and RISERs were the chosen flavor of the month.

On December 1, Thursday, Trice flew to New York. The next morning, he addressed a group of people who had just graduated from the firm's management training class. Ball addressed the group, as did Sichenzio, the new chief of retail.

That afternoon, Trice walked up to Ball's office and asked if he could speak with him. "I want to talk to you about Bob Sherman and certain events that have occurred in the last three years," said Trice. He intended to tell Ball about the cronyism between Graner and Sherman, which had resulted in Graner's shift to Pac South. To Trice's way of thinking, Sherman too often had made decisions based on what was good for him and his buddies rather than on what was good for the firm. Ball needed to hear that.

But the CEO was running late. "I only have a few minutes, Jim."

"Well, I'll need an hour."

"Let's do it later. You're going to be back up here later in the month. We're having a meeting of all the regional directors. Let's talk then."

Trice agreed, and flew back to Atlanta. The following Monday, Trice was in New York again and Sichenzio wanted to see him. Trice arrived at Sichenzio's office shortly before lunch.

A man of medium height and stocky build, Sichenzio had thick black hair and black eyes. Some executives admired his quick mind and considered him a well-organized administrator.

Sichenzio, who was by nature a fast talker, escorted Trice to his office. Sichenzio was tripping over his words and appeared nervous. Once in his office, he moved behind his desk and sat down.

"Look. You're a direct guy. I don't know how else to say this other than bluntly and directly. I've made a decision to remove you."

"Is this open for discussion?" Trice said.

"No."

"Why?"

"I don't want to discuss it."

"I've been here at the firm for twenty-five years, and I think I'm entitled to an explanation."

"Call it a change of direction," he said, his voice high. He raised his open palm over his head and quickly moved it from one side to the other in a slicing motion. It signaled the end of discussion.

"Now," said Sichenzio, "I'd like to take you over to Loren's office."

The two walked down the hall, and Sichenzio left Trice in Loren Schechter's office. Trice sat down.

Later, in arbitration testimony, Schechter described the meeting.

"He was distraught; [I thought] that it was not good for him to do that. Frankly, he ought to calm down, compose himself, be with friends. I offered to get him a psychiatrist, if he wanted one. He told me, instead, that he had a priest or a minister in San Antonio who he thought he should consult with. . . . He was crying.

"He was sitting there crying and asking me, in effect, what was wrong with him. And it didn't seem productive to me to tell him, at that point, that people thought he was ineffective. . . . I urged him, at that time, to go home to his family."

Schechter repeated, "He was crying."

Trice claimed he wasn't crying. "But the firm later tried to show that I was weak."

In that meeting, according to Trice, Schechter told him that Trice was losing his job because of the currency trading problem he had found in Richmond, Virginia. "It wasn't your fault, but it had happened on your watch," said Schechter.

Trice told Schechter he was concerned about whether the firm would continue to uphold its agreement to provide medical coverage to his first wife, from whom he was now divorced, but who remained an invalid. Schechter assured him the agreement would remain and that Trice would receive his salary until the firm found him another position.

Trice was not surprised the firm had taken away his job. "I wasn't happy. But by now, I knew these people well."

Still, he wasn't quite prepared for the battle that ensued over the next few years. Trice was offered one position that had already been filled behind his back. He was offered a few branch management positions that were beneath his ability, position, and salary level. For five months, he was left to flounder with no position and no real job—and no good reason for his demotion.

In July, Trice took another job. Still the firm hadn't completed the details of his "settlement." During 1989, Trice wrote letters to Pru-Bache to verify certain matters regarding his medical and pension benefits and to request information. He never received a response.

Finally, at the end of 1989, the twenty-five-year veteran filed an arbitration claim against Pru-Bache. He sought the compensation and benefits that Schechter and Pru-Bache owed him—the similar ones that Schechter had promised Trice back on that bleak December day in 1988.

Rather than settle, Pru-Bache began to fight Trice and many other "outside" men and women who had helped build the company's fortunes. Meanwhile, the firm gave "insiders" such as Darr and Sherman lucrative severance packages.

In early 1988, George Ball agreed to be censured by the New York Stock Exchange for violating exchange rules and securities laws in the illegal check-kiting scheme that had occurred while he was CEO of E. F. Hutton. That firm, which had been acquired by Shearson Lehman Brothers, consented to the findings and agreed to pay $400,000 in fines.

In consenting to the findings, Ball neither admitted nor denied guilt and paid no penalties. At the time, a spokesman for Pru-Bache said that Ball had agreed to the action because he had been found to be unaware of improprieties. "It was thought it was best to agree to the settlement and put the matter to rest," said the spokesperson.

But privately, the Pru began to question its investment in Pru-Bache. It had moved John Murray, a senior vice president of Prudential's Investment Services Department, over to One Seaport Plaza to unofficially oversee Ball, said some observers. By the end of 1988, the Pru had seen too much. It had witnessed poor returns on Graham's LPs; it had paid for investigations of a senior officer regarding undisclosed, and therefore illicit, deals with LP sponsors; it had been told to expect brokerage profits in 1987 and instead received a crushing loss; it had watched a cataclysmic stock market crash erode its own holdings of investments; and it had watched in fear as one of the biggest financial scandals in history slowly developed right under its nose.

Most of Wall Street by now was under attack because of "insider trading" charges and other alleged securities crimes committed by some of the Street's most reputable firms and leaders. In December 1988, Drexel Burnham Lambert agreed to plead guilty to six felony counts stemming from private knowledge of details about public companies involved in takeovers and restructuring. The large firm, which was a top member of the "bulge bracket" on the top-ten banking list, agreed to pay $650 million in a deal that would eventually jail a "star" executive, Michael Milken. This was not the securities industry the Pru had bought into, back in 1981.

By 1988, these factors coalesced to cause acute anxiety in Newark. No one felt the pressure more keenly, perhaps, than Ball. Said one director: "Ball was starting to lose his credibility with the Pru."

16

"Perception vs. Reality"

D URING a Pru-Bache executive committee meeting one day in 1988, Loren Schechter announced that there were some "minor" problems with the limited partnerships packaged by VMS Realty, the firm's second-largest LP sponsor. As he would say two years later, a "vocal minority" was complaining that the investments weren't performing as promised. Fowler shot Crowley a knowing look. Today was not the first time Pru-Bache's executive committee had discussed VMS Realty.

Schechter detailed some of the claims and indicated that at worst, the troubles could cost Pru-Bache about $34 million.

Fowler quipped, "Sounds more like $1 billion to me."

No one spoke, but Fowler's figures would prove to be closer to the mark. Over the decade, Pru-Bache had sold about $1.2 billion of VMS investments to clients, who by 1994 had recouped only half of their funds.

VMS Realty had been discussed in this conference room prior to this, when Darr had boasted he could "roll up" some of the real-estate investment trusts; that is, he had proposed gathering VMS investments and pooling them into one big fund to sell again. At the time, Fowler had wondered why anyone would want to bundle these investments if each of them were performing so well on their own, as Darr and DIG had claimed. If the LPs were appreciating so nicely, why repackage them? To Fowler, "the idea didn't spell Mother."

Now, VMS's board had embraced the roll-up plan. A due diligence team from another brokerage house, as well as from Pru-Bache, were dispatched to review VMS's books. The team's consensus was that "insiders at VMS were doing funny things" that undermined the value of the funds. The roll-up plan died quietly.

Problems had festered for years at the Chicago-based realty company, and by March 1988 Pru-Bache knew of those problems. Senior managers at DIG knew that VMS Realty was short of cash and that some properties in the sponsor's LP funds weren't making enough money to pay loans. Indeed, years later, DIG executive James Kelso admitted as much to arbitrators, saying that "the mere appearance that the properties were not sufficient to serve loans does not, in and of itself, set off a fire alarm that the fund is going down." However, the fund would go down.

Many of the firm's brokers and clients had complained about the VMS deals. In 1986, when the tax laws changed, VMS officers realized they had trouble pending. In February 1987, Xerox Corp. injected about $80 million of cash into the troubled company in return for a 25 percent equity stake. At the time, at least one market analyst warned Xerox and other big investors about the investment. Years later, Scott Miller, an independent real-estate analyst in Houston, said, "VMS is not now and never has been worth anything."

Here's why. The firm in the early 1980s had played the tax shelter game, paying high prices for properties, such as resorts, hotels, shopping complexes, and apartments. Some of these assets were inferior properties, which were then ladened with debt and high fees extracted by VMS. What VMS had really sold in the early 1980s were tax write-offs. The general partner often didn't invest its own money in the deals, although it did secure outside financing to complement investor funds. For example, in the Boca Raton Hotel and Club LP, limited partners would later claim that VMS had contributed only $100 to the LP— while taking as much as $50 million in assorted fees.

In addition, without consensus from its limited partners, VMS in 1988 acquired the Boca County Club golf course and an attractive piece of development property, known as the marina parcel. "There was no vote, they just did it," said one broker. The two properties were encumbered by mortgages payable to Banyan, a VMS affiliate, and each mortgage was collateralized with the other property. By 1990, the mortgages had grown to about a $21 million debt and were in danger of foreclosure; the LP had defaulted on the payments and was in danger of losing the underlying assets.

At the same time, the Boca Raton LP was also straining under the third "wraparound" mortgage, which allowed the VMS entity to siphon off more money. Although it didn't lend any money to the LP, the loan carried a 13 percent interest rate—or about 7 percent above the prime rate. The net effect of the above-market rate loan was that, by 1990, the $8 million debt had ballooned to about $21 million—all shouldered by investors.

In a letter to limited partners, VMS would later state that the wraparound mortgage—and its projected growth—was fully disclosed back in 1983 at the time of offering, which was true. VMS also stated that in 1988 it "refinanced" the large wraparound loan at a lower rate. What it didn't say was that such a move had been projected in the 1983 prospectus.

By 1989, VMS entities were making even more money by "lending" in similar fashion to its other limited partnerships. Why? When the tax laws changed in 1986, the real-estate market began to slip. To keep its earlier private, tax-shelter limited partnerships afloat, VMS turned to raising public "mortgage" funds, which were lent back to its private properties. (Public deals require more disclosure than do private offerings.) "Essentially, public investors in VMS were used to pay off private VMS deals, just like a Ponzi scheme," said Zahn. According to many brokers and branch managers, this tactic allowed VMS to publish glossy brochures that pointed to great track records from earlier programs, which in turn enticed less sophisticated investors to fund later public programs.

By the late 1980s, some brokers began to privately blast these deals as self-dealing. The interest rates on the loans were inordinately high. To an increasing number of salespeople, the deals clearly benefited VMS at the expense of Pru's clients—the investors. Yet the outrageous self-dealing transactions were disclosed in prospectuses, which were rubberstamped by regulators, who were not required to issue opinions on any stock offering.

All the while VMS helped itself to enormously high fees for "management" and other services it charged limited partners. Pru-Bache also earned millions of dollars in fees, commissions, and other charges. By 1993, many of VMS's $1.2 billion LPs had dropped so steeply in value that Pru-Bache clients would lose about $600 million.

In the spring of 1988, Pru-Bache and DIG officers knew VMS LPs and funds couldn't make their loan payments, as DIG executive Kelso testified years later. But in 1988, Pru-Bache's due diligence people didn't consider it a problem, Kelso explained. The mere hint of a problem is usually enough to stop a prudent investor from pumping more money into a troubled venture. But not DIG. It went ahead later that year and sold the VMS Mortgage Investment Fund, which raised about $395.6 million in small, $10 units. People with net worth as little as $50,000 could invest a $5,000 minimum. They were promised "guaranteed" annual returns of 12 percent for the next two years.

Unlike the private offerings, this fund was targeted at the middle-class investor. Based on the representations from Pru-Bache, brokers sold the funds aggressively to senior citizens, who were told it was as safe as a "bank CD."

By now, Pru-Bache and DIG had blitzed its sales force with more dazzle and fewer facts. The direct investment group frequently organized seminars and events to convince the top one hundred brokers to sell, sell, sell. Some brokers, however, were bored because all the products looked alike: double-digit returns; "safe" harbors; "guaranteed" returns; 7 percent sales commission; backed by the "rock-solid" reputation of Prudential. Some even carried the cosponsor's "personal" guarantees, as did Memphis millionaire Avron Fogelman's LPs. "The only way Pru could get us to sell any particular fund was to promise better awards and prizes," said Gary Zahn, a top broker at the time.

A weekend in San Francisco no longer cut it for brokers, nor a trip to an island paradise. "Do you know how many times I went to Maui?" whined the wife of a senior executive. "Nine times! I finally said, 'No more.'" DIG and its cosponsors were forced to create bigger, better, and more exotic lures to hook the sales squad. By 1987, Pru-Bache offered a cruise to the Baltic Sea, a Concorde ride to Paris, and a vacation in Monte Carlo. "It got so out of control that the next logical step would have been a trip for two on the space shuttle," said one salesman.

Even broker meetings boomed into lavish affairs. Salespeople no longer shared rooms with colleagues but enjoyed their own suites, stocked with baskets of fruit and buckets of chilled wine. Big-name entertainers appeared, such as singer Lou Rawles and comedian David Brenner. The sales meetings took on the evangelical fervor of church revival meetings, except instead of the preacher rolling a religious statue down the aisle, a marketer wheeled out a six-foot-long model of a cruise ship, as was the case at a 1987 sales meeting in Dallas. The audience cheered, and DIG officers raised their hands in the air like prize fighters. "The corporate propaganda bordered on brainwashing," said one attendee. "The firm made it seem like we were the geniuses for selling the stuff. Even secretaries got the glow."

But no Pru-Bache unit propagandized better than DIG "marketeers." In May 1988, about one hundred of the firm's top brokers gathered for a seminar in Vancouver, British Columbia. The event, held at a fine hotel, included a presentation called "Perception vs. Reality." DIG officers attempted to persuade the elite sales force that the root cause of poor-performing LPs was not the LPs themselves; it was public perception. The lights dimmed, a screen unfurled, and an overhead projector flashed slides on it. A senior DIG officer stood in front of the audience and discussed some of the firm's struggling LPs, including VMS Realty. Watson & Taylor was featured in that discussion, because it was a hot topic. By year-end Texan developers would no longer manage the LPs and investors were not receiving anticipated cash distributions.

To quash the snowballing fears, DIG claimed that things were not as bad as they appeared. Said the executive: "If you believe that this LP is worth half of its original value, but it's really worth 60 percent, well then, hey! The investment is actually a better value than you perceive."

No one challenged the speaker.

A few brokers walked out of the meeting, disgusted at the cavalier attitude toward investors and brokers. "Who are they kidding?" said Zahn. "We were livid that they would talk down to us like children."

That spring, the firm sold the VMS Mortgage Investment Fund for $10 a share. A year later, the shares traded at around $7. In May 1991, they were listed at sixty-two cents. Money from the mortgage funds was lent to VMS's struggling real-estate funds in what, to many employees, smacked of a blatant conflict of interest. "It was fraught with potential self-dealing and fraud," said one broker. Yet the bare necessities were disclosed properly in prospectuses, which were approved by regulators and bore the imprimatur of the Rock.

In another part of Pru-Bache, reality was better than forecasted. In March 1988, the two coheads of investment banking wrote a long, fact-filled memo. It summarized the group's accomplishments to date and encouraged the bankers to keep up the momentum and not be distracted by the company's recently announced loss. For 1987, Pru-Bache had announced a stunning $164 million loss, but "the [investment banking's] system and the culture are working," wrote Crowley and Fowler.

By now, the names of the two were transposed in a dyslexic hybrid: "Fowley" for Fowler, "Crowler" for Crowley. They had become one unit and had grown even closer by virtue of serendipity. Fowler had married Crowley's sister and so had become his brother-in-law, in addition to his comrade-in-arms. "That violated the natural checks and balances of the department, I thought," said Christian Wyser-Pratte. It certainly bonded the two men tighter.

The division had its share of human peccadillos, and employees sometimes had personal problems. A married elder was known to chase skirts. A talented banker struggled with a drug problem. Another sometimes threw junior associates against the wall in a temper tantrum. A range of human failings and weaknesses ebbed and flowed in the unit—except fraud.

By now, PBCF appeared strong and confident, especially when compared to the post-crash identity crisis afflicting its competitors. Wall

Street was suffering a "firm-by-firm crisis of culture," Crowley and Fowler's memo explained. "Fortunately, we are not caught up in this frenzy of frustration and disappointment." Pru-Bache did not intend to be a "big mamma" banker but resolved to consistently rank at number seven or so on the top-ten list. "We have a chance to be the first and only wire house in recent decades to become a respected investment and merchant banking firm," the memo concluded.

Yet the best news was this: gross revenues for the group topped at $276 million in 1987, or triple the gross revenues the unit had collected in 1985. The figure represented fees and commissions earned by deals completed that year. In the first three months of 1988, Pru-Bache ranked ninth in underwritten offerings. Wrote Crowley and Fowler, "We can all be proud."

By now, PBCF could point to specific successes. It underwrote a $600 million closed-end fund, which moved the firm that year into the fifth spot in common stocks managers. Its customers included Ryland, Southern California Edison, Honeywell, Itel Corp., and Transamerica Financial Corp., all of which represented a higher caliber of client with larger financing needs than the firm's clients of four years ago.

That January, PBCF acted as financial adviser to Northgate Exploration Ltd., a Canada gold miner that sold some business to the Australian Western Mining Corp. in a $160 million deal. In March, it initiated Ahnert Enterprise's $180 million sales of resorts to the Rank Organization, an English conglomerate. In a monster international deal, PBCF initiated and advised its client, Hong Kong Telephone Co. Ltd., in its $9.2 billion sale of Hong Kong Telecommunications.

By June that year, the unit had hit two more home runs. One was the second leg of the management buyout of some CBS-owned consumer magazines. Back in the fall of 1987, Pru-Bache had advised Diamandis Communications in its $650 million leveraged buyout effort, then assisted Diamandis in selling its holdings, which included *Car and Driver* and *Woman's Day* magazines. Now, in April of 1988, Hachette of France bought the group for $712 million. "The sale brings the total proceeds generated by the properties to more than [$1.25 billion] in only six months," an industry magazine reported. For its services, the merchant banking group received an equity stake in the deal. Within two years that investment had returned $600 million cumulatively to the firm, which was sweet indeed.

Another whopper was socked out of the park when Pru-Bache agreed to pay $600 million for a 49 percent stake in the Dr Pepper/Seven-Up Cos., which was a $1.3 billion deal. The properties from the two holding companies had been married during a leveraged buyout back in 1986, when Hicks & Hass had bought that stake for a piddling $45 million. Again, Pru-Bache received an equity interest, which by 1994 had returned 27 percent.

Certainly, there were bad deals, unraveled deals, and deals that never grew legs. In one contentious episode, an Indonesian investor group proposed to buy from Ralston Purina its Chicken of the Sea tuna brand. Indonesia is rich with resources and poor in jobs, including those in fishing. The country is a thin string of islands about 2,500 miles long, in the midst of many oceans and seas, which are home to migratory tuna. However, for years the country's tuna schools had been pillaged by foreign fishermen, such as the Americans and Japanese. Indonesia had enforced its fishing rights and wanted to raise money to buoy its fishing industry. The idea was to lend its people money for boats, and to buy freezers on land, so that at the end of the workday, fishermen could unload their catch in freezers. The fish would be processed in Indonesian plants, canned, and distributed as Chicken of the Sea product.

"It was a great deal, as the Indonesian government would win, the workers would win, and the consumer would win," said a banker who was close to the deal. At the time, only three other "name" tuna brands existed in America, where Chicken of the Sea would be purchased. Because of cheap Indonesian labor, the brand was expected to be cheaper than its competitors.

However, one competitor got wind of the deal and stuffed the distribution pipeline with his discounted product by placing it on sale. As a result, cans of Chicken of the Sea sat in warehouses, and Pru-Bache got stung. Its leveraged buyout deal became a "work-out" deal that had to be financially restructured.

Still, after the 1987 crash, PBCF wrote deals and chased business, from both Fortune 500 companies and midsized businesses.

That year, Crowley and Fowler traveled across the river to the Pru to present Project '89's accomplishments to date. Through regular meetings with Ball, who belonged to Pru's six-member executive office, the Pru had kept abreast of the project. Crowley and Fowler had appeared before the committee on previous occasions to present data on PBCF's market share and deal developments. Winters and Keith were keenly interested in the project, although other committee members would be present: Ball; Joseph Melone, president; and Edward Zinbarg and Richard G. Merrill, both executive vice presidents.

For this presentation, the two bankers prepared a summary of their development to date. It included for the first time the project's gross revenues, direct expenses, contributions to the firm's profit line, and allocated overhead. The detailed presentation represented an accurate picture of the unit's progress.

Crowley, Ball, and Fowler joined the Pru executives at a large polished table in one of the meeting rooms. Crowley began to speak while distributing copies of the project's figures to executives, who studied the handouts assiduously. Fowler explained the figures, but was interrupted.

"Jeez!" said Winters, frowning. He looked at Fowler, then Crowley. "I've never seen these numbers before."

"What do you mean?" said Fowler. "These are the numbers we always use."

Ball tried to diffuse the situation. "Well, those numbers are certainly one way to look at the unit. We use different numbers to look at different things."

Winters scowled behind his glasses. He looked at Fowler. "Where did you get these numbers?"

"Those are the numbers we always use," he said. "They're the ones the executive committee sees regularly." The figures were simple and showed the gross revenues, or fees, the unit collected. Deducted from that number were its total direct expenses: salaries, bonuses, benefits, rents, and direct unreimbursed business expenses. The balance, or "gross contributions," was the cash produced by PBCF's bank.

"What do you mean?" Winters demanded, truly puzzled.

Fowler and Crowley explained that Pru-Bache internally kept five different sets of books to evaluate business. Ball used many accounting systems to reflect different, arbitrary allocations of expenses on various departments.

Winters went "ballistic." "Goddammit, George," he yelled. "You have got to get yourself on one system. There are too many sets of books. I want you to find something you can be held accountable to—and stick with it!"

Ball agreed, but the issue was now on the table. In the minutes remaining in the meeting, Crowley and Fowler ran through the complicated figures quickly. The session dissolved into a mass of frustration because the Pru officers kept referring to the "new" set of figures, and Fowler insisted that the numbers were the *only* accurate ones to use.

As the meeting broke up, the two coheads remained outwardly civil, although inside Fowler was seething. If Prudential had never seen the "right" numbers before now, what numbers had it been reviewing? Even more important, what in the hell were those numbers showing—a dismal failure? Without accurate figures, how could the Pru accurately judge the results of its expensive, arduous, high-profile commitment?

It couldn't.

Fowler left with a sinking feeling, but Crowley felt great. Finally, he thought, the "pure" numbers were out. Now the decision-makers at the Pru would finally understand the dynamics of Project '89 and couldn't help but be impressed. "It's great," he told Fowler.

"Right," Fowler growled. He didn't think Ball had been delivering the unit's good tidings over the last eighteen months. And now, in the wake of a market downturn, while attempting the improbable, at a crucial point in the project's development, PBCF had to contend with either subterfuge or sabotage. Neither suited him.

"Allocation" is a dirty word on Wall Street, because it's tied to bonuses and money. "Allocated overhead is a very touchy issue," said one former board member. At Pru-Bache, approximately five departments, or pistons, generated income: retail (which included direct investments), mutual funds, arbitrage, corporate finance, and institutional sales and trading. Each of those divisions shared the benefits—and costs—of corporate headquarters. Research, the computerized back office, telecommunications, overhead, and whatever other sundry costs a manager declared must be shared, or "allocated," among the departments. The process is rarely equitable to all, and therefore is often seen as arbitrary.

One Street truism has it that if the CEO of a securities firm used to be a trader, you can bet his firm's trading division will always report income; if a CEO came from corporate finance, corporate finance will always appear healthy, no matter reality; if a CEO, such as Ball, came from retail, retail will always show the profit. Yet how can a division that loses money show a profit?

The answer lies partly in allocation. In the extreme, accounting can triple the rent charged to one division and halve the figure charged to another "pet" department. By arbitrarily and, some might say, inequitably allocating company costs, one can turn a black or profitable business into the red, and create a winner out of a loser.

"We paid a certain percent that we called 'George's charge,' because there seemed no better way to describe the category," said one banker. For example, in 1988, the investment and merchant banking—IMB— division paid half of its pretax, preallocated revenue to the firm, or $85 million. No doubt that helped Pru-Bache report a $111 million profit that year. Without the banker's cash contributions, the firm's earnings would have been 76 percent lower. The implications of allocation were crucial.

"Usually, a firm has two sets of books, one for GAP [general accounting principles] and the other for taxes," said a CEO from another securities firm.

But Pru-Bache's executive office kept five sets of books, according to four former executives, and each set reflected radically different situations, largely as a result of allocation. Said one executive: "George would like to look at different results using different systems. There was a book to account for every scenario he wanted."

For example, Pru-Bache kept books called Management Operating Report (MOR); Actual versus Budget (AVB); 100–0; 90–10; and 80–20, which reflected the percentage of IMB revenues that went to retail compared to the percentage kept inside the unit. Originally, Fowler and Crowley had agreed to the one simple method they had shared with the Pru. Revenues minus direct expenses. Period.

But as Project '89 made more money—and as other units suffered anemic earnings or losses—Ball needed to allocate more of IMB's cash to struggling units. In one memo, Crowley and Fowler wrote to Gahan: "IMB had been good in managing its direct period costs but has been absorbing very high allocated costs."

At the pivotal Newark meeting, the Pru's executives didn't appreciate the existence of so many books. But the books, and the issue of allocated overhead, triggered more outbursts later and was simply a sophisticated form of "Bache-ball," according to one insider.

The existence of conflicting figures was destructive in that they were used to mask the real success of a fledgling unit—such as investment banking. They also whittled the bonus pool earmarked for bankers as part of their total compensation.

Conversely, the system buried troubles in the retail division. Either way, the use of multiple non-GAP sets of books did not transmit to the parent company a clear, consistent picture of its subsidiary. Said one CEO at a competing securities firm: "Listen. The last person you want to bullshit is your parent company, because they will find out sooner or later. And when they do," he warned, "your credibility is shot for good."

That fall, Crowley and Fowler appeared on the cover of an industry magazine issue that ranked deals for 1988's third quarter. The magazine grieved over the one-year anniversary of the crash and bemoaned the weak and listless market. Inside, it quoted pundits who predicted various degrees of gloom, although everyone agreed that the deal business had been profoundly changed.

Pru-Bache ranked well in the quarterly issue, landing number eight on the list (as measured by all domestic issues). Crowley said the firm would "continue its philosophy of being the best of the rest," or "edge of the wedge," as he would later call it.

By year-end 1988, Project '89 had achieved success one year ahead of schedule. It had raised nearly $12 billion through global public underwritings, grabbing 4 percent of the market share, up from 1 percent in 1985 and in excess of its 2.4 percent goal, as outlined in its 1986 strategy paper. The firm now ranked number eight among Street bankers, which meant essentially that its original five-year goal of "overtaking whoever else may be number eight" had been accomplished. Globally, it ranked tenth, up considerably from its number thirty-five spot in 1985.

To many, the project's achievement was incredible—especially given that it had occurred during the worst stock market crash in history, and considering that the project in its second year had been forced to cut staff and freeze hiring. Project '89 had scored in spite of being precluded from "hostile" takeovers. Moreover, it had reached the finish line on its ambitious five-year plans in only two full years.

People inside the unit were jubilant.

IMB that year had raised $11.8 billion for its clients, compared to DIG's sales of $1 billion. IMB's gross revenues totaled $500 million, versus an estimated $100 million from DIG.

IMB was becoming so successful, it was about to be punished.

Crowley and Fowler met with George Ball at One Seaport Plaza. The coheads detailed their accomplishments and ticked off the merchant banking equity deals they had finessed for the firm. When the conversation turned to bonuses, Ball grew nervous. Bonuses were often negotiated over a course of several discussions.

"I'm not sure about those numbers," Ball said.

"What do you mean?" Fowler asked.

"We're having a tough year in the market, and we need everyone to pitch in."

He explained how the firm needed "a few million dollars" to cover the general and administrative costs. Although both Crowley and Fowler expected to share their spoils, Ball wanted to whittle deeply into their profits.

"Wait a minute," Fowler said. "We agreed to an allocation system. Remember? Based on our agreement, we've made a fortune for the firm."

Crowley tried to assuage his partner. "It's temporary, Ted."

Fowler pressed: "George, what are you doing? We agreed to account for Project '89 on contributions *before* allocations. That was the deal before we even started this thing. Now," he yelled, "you want to change the rules?"

"I have other factors to consider," Ball explained. He wanted to give the Pru a dividend that year after the monstrous 1987 loss.

But Fowler continued: "I've got people to pay. What about the guys who worked their butts off to bring in this money?" His staff's bonuses hadn't been good in 1986, when the project had started; they hadn't been good last year, because of the crash. But now the banking division excelled, and the project had been completed ahead of schedule.

"Ted, calm down," Crowley said. "Let's try to figure something out here."

Fowler glared at Ball. "Does the Pru know about this?"

Crowley wasn't happy with the situation either, but he swallowed his complaints for the good of the firm. In the end, his compassion for Ball's situation overrode his gut instinct. As for Fowler, he protested fiercely, claiming that the unit carried an unfair burden. Besides, the bankers' total compensation was nowhere near the standard.

Out of all sixteen investment banking firms, Pru-Bache ranked well except in the category of compensation. In domestic underwritings and initial public offerings, it ranked third that year, according to *Investment Dealer's Digest*.

In sharp contrast, its bankers consistently ranked around twelfth or fourteenth in total annual compensation. Try as they might, Fowler and Crowley never did pay "Wall Street" scale for their professionals. Said Christian Wyser-Pratte: "Crowley and Fowler fought hard for us to get a bonus, and I give them credit for that."

The Pru had grown increasingly uncomfortable about paying Street scale when their own professionals earned far less. "They couldn't see paying a twenty-eight-year-old asshole $150,000 when their own fifty-year-old insurance veteran was making $110,000," said one associate. Clearly, "penis envy" did exist in Newark.

That winter, Fowler and Keith flew from Tokyo to New York on business. After that frustrating meeting at the Pru, Fowler and Crowley had pleaded with Ball to allow them to return to Newark and explain clearly and accurately the numbers behind Project '89. At the time, Ball had agreed, but a meeting was never scheduled.

Now, Fowler had a captive audience in Keith. He broached the topic. "You know," he started, "it occurs to me that you guys at the Pru probably don't understand what we're doing with Project '89. Jim and I would really welcome the opportunity to go through the plan, from soup to nuts. It'd take maybe half a day to show you what we're doing and where we're going."

Fowler explained that during the last presentation, he hadn't been given much time to explain the plan. He thought the Pru's board would find Project '89 worth understanding.

Keith was amenable. "That sounds like a great idea. Let me talk it up with the board and I'll get back to you."

A month passed. Fowler called Keith. "Do you remember our conversation in which I offered to bring our numbers across the river?"

"Yes."

"Are you ready to schedule a time?"

"Not yet," Keith said. "I'm still trying to set it up. I'll call you."

However, he never called back on that subject, and an invitation was never extended. After a while, Fowler gave up.

In a curious move, the Pru was building its own in-house corporate finance unit, which directly competed against Project '89. In April 1988, Prudential Investment Corp., headed by Garnett Keith, reorganized its management and positioned it in direct competition with a unit from another subsidiary, Pru-Bache. At the same time, Prudential Capital Corp., or PruCap, was expanded. The Pru's subsidiary had grown from a straight-debt lender to a merchant banking arm that was widely regarded on the Street for its leveraged buyouts and project finance. Supervised by Ball and owned by the Pru, the unit actively participated in big complex deals financed by the insurer's bountiful coffers. In 1987, for example, the subsidiary did $4 billion in deals through its network of thirteen regional offices; in 1988, that number boomed 35 percent to a new high of $5.3 billion.

The intent, according to some executives, was for PruCap to work with Pru-Bache—and its burgeoning investment and merchant banking unit. Why Project '89 was even fed at the same table as its rival sister, PruCap, is a mystery. But by 1988, the Pru's corporate finance siblings were mired in their parents' political jockeying, mutual distrust, and a bit of envy. Any dream of the two working together harmoniously would be cruelly dashed.

Pru's reorganization angered many Wall Street firms, including its own. The expansion meant the company was now making—in addition to taking—deals. Bankers at Pru-Bache were among those criticizing the Pru because some saw it as a clear sign that the parent company was not supporting Project '89.

"We felt shunned by the parent," said Wyser-Pratte. "We were kept in the basement like a retarded child and left alone." He and others recalled a PruCap executive who addressed a Wharton class of graduates, some of whom were considering joining Wall Street. The executive announced that he would never show favoritism or throw deals to Pru-Bache's corporate finance unit because it would scare away other Wall Street firms. "I wanted to say, 'Why the [hell] did you buy us, then?' " mused one insider.

The speech was repeated inside PBCF. Other corporate parents, such as General Electric, gave business to their securities subsidiaries. What's the matter with us? Pru's apparent lack of support for its broker-dealer banking group struck some as not only odd, but self-defeating. "At least give us the most-favored-nation status," said Wyser-Pratte.

By 1989, the salaries, politicking, and internal squabbling for lucrative deals became obvious. Then, when the slew of insider trading scandals continued to dominate the evening news, some insiders believed that the Pru made a decision.

In hindsight, some bankers would recall the infamous Project '89 banking party at which Brazilian dancers shimmied while Pru officer Keith Garnett hastily departed. Aha! the bankers later realized. The insurance executive's retreat had signaled his disgust with Wall Street's Gomorrah-like ways. When Keith left the show that night, the party was effectively over.

This logic was roundly scoffed at by Project 89's officers, but it made sense to others. By now, bankers were searching for any reason to explain their corporate parent's strange lack of support.

"At the time, investment banking was getting a black eye," said John Marcus, former Pru-Bache banker. "Suddenly the Pru realized that the staid old Rock was going to be associated with the public's idea of gangsters."

Soon the Pru would cut the cord.

17

Murders and Inquisitions

THE year 1988 marked the 150th birthday of Pru's founder, John Dryden. Had he been alive, he wouldn't have recognized the company he had founded in 1875, which he had first christened as the Widows' and Orphans' Friendly Society. By now, his firm was called the Prudential Insurance Co. of America, and its assets outstripped the gross national product of many developed countries. The Pru now counted among its clients not just women and children but trusts, pensions, endowment funds, institutions, corporations, and international governments.

For the Pru, the 1980s were a decade of mushrooming growth unmatched by any other period. Total consolidated assets in 1988 exploded 143 percent to $152 billion, compared to $62.5 billion in 1981 when Pru bought Bache. Despite the market downturn and the advent of a slower economy in 1988, the year had rung in excellent sales figures for many of Pru's main subsidiaries: group policies, mortgage finance, asset management, investment banking, reinsurance, and mutual fund operations—all sectors that the steadfast Dryden could never have envisioned for his modest start-up, back in the 1880s.

In its 1988 annual report, the Pru shared its "Vision Statement," which was "to remain the No. 1 insurance company in America; to become the nation's No. 1 financial services company, and to become a leader in global financial markets." One analyst from Moody's Investors Service said at the time: "Its major strength is its size and its ability to be competitive in many different areas that smaller companies can't compete in."

In its annual letter to customers, the Pru for the first time that decade mentioned its "new" statement regarding business ethics. Given the times, the move was no doubt a reaction to the corporate scandals then unfolding. By now arbitrager Boesky had been jailed, bulge-bracket player Drexel Burnham had admitted to felonies and agreed to a $650 million fine, and clean-cut mergers and acquisitions guru Martin Siegel had admitted to accepting suitcases of cash for his insider tips. In the Reagan administration, more than one hundred officials faced allegations of fraud, perjury, and impropriety on grand scales. "Hypocrisy, betrayal, and greed unsettle the nation's soul," headlined a special ethics issue of *Time* magazine on May 25, 1987.

The Pru was concerned about upholding its own reputation. Its codex, "The Prudential Way: Making the Right Choices," was distributed to all employees, which included, presumably, executives and directors.

But the primary goal of the sprawling, ambitious corporate conglomerate was to muscle its way into the world's pockets, from corporate finance to mortgage lending. In 1988 it hired more bankers in its effort to globalize its financing divisions, and that expanding operation fell under the purview of Garnett Keith—not George Ball.

One prominent banker who joined Prudential at this time was Paul A. Volcker. He was intimately familiar with Pru's securities operations, Pru-Bache, as a result of his time spent as chairman of the Federal Reserve Board during Carter's administration. Back then, he had huddled with many of the nation's bankers to stave off a financial crisis in the wake of the Hunt brothers' foray into the silver market, which was aided by Pru-Bache's predecessor—Bache Halsey Stuart Shields. The weekend before April Fools' Day, 1980, the Federal Reserve City Bankers Association had assembled at the Boca Raton resort in Florida, which provided an opportunity for Volcker and his central bankers to resolve the calamity caused by the Hunts and Bache. At the time, the bearlike Volcker negotiated in the Boca Raton Hotel, moving from one meeting room to another, wearing pajamas and puffing his ever-present cigar.

Now, almost a decade later, Volcker sat on the Pru's board.

In its annual report that year, the Pru noted one other unusual development. Pru-Bache had reported stellar earnings of $111 million, which was the result primarily of its "nonindividual" business. LPs, mutual funds, and other products were still sold through retail brokers, but those sales were less profitable than investment and merchant banking. Indeed, Pru-Bache's capital markets and investment banking units achieved "record trading revenues"—mostly from junk, mortgage-backed, and tax-exempt securities. That unit's $538 million global offering of shares in Hong Kong Telecommunications had buoyed results, as had fees from the merger and recapitalization of Dr Pepper/Seven-Up companies.

What the annual report did not disclose was that by now, Pru's directors had been "surprised" by Ball on more than one occasion, according to Pru-Bache insiders. By then, Darr had left Pru-Bache, and the firm's internal investigation had found many "cozy" ties to LP sponsors. The first lawsuit on the limited partnership fiasco would soon be filed, and Pru's senior officers had learned about the existence of multiple bookkeeping records over at Seaport. Although Ball claimed he didn't know about the check-kiting fraud at Hutton, he had by now gracefully accepted the stock exchange's censure.

In February 1989, Ball hired W. James Tozer, a former banker from Citicorp, as president of Pru-Bache. He reported to Ball. Tozer, in turn, hired a consulting firm to study efficiencies within the firm. At first, the executive committee welcomed the consultants, as many thought that outside advisers could help guide the firm in a plan for the coming decade. Yet over the ensuing months, as consultants delved deeper into Pru-Bache's operations, some executives wondered: Had they been given a foregone conclusion to reach?

In January 1989, Garnett Keith addressed another class of Wharton graduates and spoke of Project '89: "The first goal has been accomplished a year ahead of schedule. The first phase of the goal has been to move Pru-Bache out of the second-tier pack [those below number ten] and stand clearly above [them]." In other words, to break into the top ten and be the "best of the rest" as ranked in the sixth through tenth spot.

Now Pru-Bache ranked eighth, higher than Bear Stearns (ninth), Kidder Peabody (tenth), and Smith Barney (twelfth). Its goal had been to accomplish that in five years, but in June 1989, Crowley said: "Miracle! We did it in two and a half."

And the deals rolled in, albeit more slowly now. The merchant bankers secured stakes, or equity positions, in more and more firms. Some of the investments were stellar, as in York International (compounded return rate of 46 percent) and Gilbarco Inc. (89 percent). Others, such as Marketchief and Van Camp Seafood (the Indonesian venture), lost money. Still, the unit swept fees into the door, raising $12 billion in the first nine months of 1989.

In May, the consultants, Strategic Planning Associates, arrived to review Pru-Bache. Crowley and Fowler were a step ahead. They had already accomplished their mission in Project '89, and it was time for a new plan. They saw dramatic shifts taking place: trading volume was declining, the volume of new issues was dropping, and competition was escalating, especially in the coveted merchant banking arena.

Although Project '89 had been declared a success internally, the two men predicted rough times ahead. Crowley and Fowler proposed to reorganize PBCF by splitting the division into two main sectors. One would handle traditional capital markets functions, such as mortgage-backed bonds, swaps, bonds, and securities offerings. The other was to be the investment and merchant banking group—IMB.

Now that the capital markets functions had been built up sufficiently, they could stand on their own. In the past, that group had generated money and connections to initiate, build, and stabilize the nascent investment and merchant banking efforts. But now Crowley and Fowler believed that the tougher economy ahead demanded that they focus solely on maintaining IMB so that when the Street rebounded in 1992, Pru-Bache's bankers could collect big dividends.

In the dark days ahead, Fowler and Crowley saw opportunities. Corporate America would need more help to "work out" debt-laden, troubled deals. Companies would need bridge loans to help refinance onerous loans. In down economies, leveraged buyouts, mergers and acquisitions, and straight investment banking business are scarce. Yet, with a sharp focus, Pru-Bache could still compete, even thrive.

The plan was approved and applauded.

On June 8, 1989, Ball circulated the detailed eight-page reorganization memo and attached his own summary. "Project '89 was a success by any measure," he wrote. "Let me commend [the attached] for your reading pleasure and commend the architects for its design." The redesign meant that instead of 450 people reporting to the two men, about 200 professionals would now work for them. The rest simply moved to where they should have been originally: in capital markets.

The next day, a story in the *Wall Street Journal* began: "Disappointed by its lackluster performance in investment banking, Prudential-Bache Securities is launching a major reorganization today."

Ball was quoted as saying that the changes had been planned months ago, but "people close to the firm" were quoted as saying that Ball was dissatisfied with Project '89's results. A securities analyst added that he "suspect[ed] some people will now be phased out and a new cadre of corporate professionals will be installed." The article detailed how Pru-Bache lagged behind the top five.

The piece triggered departmental angst. Over the next few days, staff members came to Crowley, clearly upset by the rumors. They feared that they, like many of their counterparts on the Street, were about to be laid off. As Crowley pointed out in a June 15 meeting, PBCF's competitors employed as many as nine hundred professionals, and most of the bracket firms employed between six hundred and eight hundred people. PBCF never employed more than 437 people, and that included the capital markets folks, who typically did not belong in investment banking. "Two-thirds of our people are terrified there [will] be massive layoffs," he said in a meeting then. Relax, he told his group, which had already downsized. No more layoffs were scheduled.

"I'm getting terribly frustrated with our children because they're all confused and nervous and don't know what's going on. And I [say], everything is going to be all right, children. [Go] back to work."

Still, more distortions leaked out, and in that June meeting, Crowley repeated some of the more ridiculous forms. One report had it that Crowley was "out" of Pru-Bache; another that he was leaving invest-ment banking; another that he had landed in the hospital after an es-pecially gloomy story. Actually, there was some truth to the last rumor, as Crowley underwent surgery to remove his gallbladder, and while he was recuperating, a reporter had found him. "How they found out that my room had two telephones and a fax is beyond me," he told his staff. But "the leaks to the press have been disturbing. . . . Never have so many talked about things they knew so little about."

In one way, PBCF had brought upon itself the innuendo and distor-tions. In recruiting brochures, Fowler allegedly had claimed in 1986 that PBCF would rank among the top five by 1989; he doesn't recall the quote, nor do other sources. In newspaper accounts as early as 1987, Project '89's goal was mistakenly reported as becoming part of the "bulge bracket," or top five. "Prudential-Bache hopes to elbow its way into the ranks . . . of the bulge bracket . . . in four years," said a leading newspaper. Although the "hope" was inaccurate, it became Street lore, and neither Fowler nor Crowley corrected the record at the time.

Whatever the root cause, by 1989, it was generally accepted in the public view that Project '89 had failed because the firm had not cracked into the top-five league. Crowley encouraged the troops to focus instead on the work at hand.

In another part of headquarters, more plans unfolded. In June, Ball announced a bold and risky move to expand the firm's retail brokerage operations, despite the industry-wide slump. Pru-Bache intended to ac-quire a small rival, Thomson McKinnon Securities, whose assets were valued at the time at $120 million. The buyout would make Pru-Bache the third-largest broker on the Street, directly behind Merrill Lynch and Shearson Lehman Hutton, based upon the number of brokers. At the time, Pru-Bache ranked fourth.

A month later, however, the deal was abruptly canceled as Pru-Bache discovered an $80 million shortfall between reserves and potential lia-bilities of Thomson McKinnon. In August, Pru-Bache bought only Thomson's 158 branches, customer accounts, and related assets for $60 million. Ball, the former stockbroker, was back at it—building the retail division.

By late August, the consultants had worked their way through the firm and had arrived in the IMB department. Crowley and Fowler spent time with the outsiders explaining Project '89, what the unit had, and where the division was now headed. They shared figures that showed that about 43 percent of the firm's profit came from investment banking. "The executive office [knows] that we've done really well as a bank," Crowley had told staffers in his June address. But somehow, the consultants weren't getting the message.

Fowler, for one, grew frustrated with the corporate advisers' confusion as to his unit's real numbers. Early drafts of their findings were flawed. Again, the two men explained their operation, and the actual "real" figures. By September, the two coheads believed that the consultants were making conclusions unsupported by the facts.

One night, Fowler developed a theory for the communication snafu. He thought, "The CEO had given the consultants an agenda, a conclusion to find, and they were going in that direction."

Then, on October 13, 1989, the market crashed again. The Dow dropped 190 points on Friday the 13th, which, at first blush, was not as damaging as the October crash of 1987. Still, the "crashette," as Ball called it, would maim junk bonds and squeeze traditional investment and merchant banking business. Since this was the prime business under the supervision of Crowley and Fowler, their challenge would be formidable. So would be the Pru's.

Privately, Ball worried. He had just committed to buying a retail firm, even though his own retail division was sluggish. The arbitrage department, headed by Guy Wyser-Pratte, got battered by investing in the failed United Airlines merger, which Ball said cost about $50 million of the firm's money (Wyser-Pratte put it at $15 million). Ball had projected earnings for the year, but he watched as the income turned to loss.

By now, Crowley and Fowler believed that IMB was endangered, and they took the offensive. Earlier in the year, they had predicted tough times ahead and had even planned for it. They had reorganized and believed that under the current plan they could weather the storm.

Crowley and Fowler took their case to Ball and asked to be left alone. That November, they produced their own report, which demonstrated their success. Project '89 had brought to the firm $300 million in gross contributions. It had engineered eight investments from the merchant banking unit, which at year-end 1988 were valued at close to $200 million. Later, that investment would grow to $581 million in net gains.

The bottom line: over the last rocky three years, the two had created a franchise that, in November 1989, had already contributed $500 million to Pru-Bache and the Pru.

Based on their track record, the two forecast conservatively that the unit could bring to the firm another $554 million over the next three years. But the plan needed "active board participation to ensure success," not the undermining that Fowler, for one, was witnessing.

It was a last-ditch effort to save IMB. But neither Ball nor Gahan was happy to receive Crowley and Fowler's offensive report, not while the consultants had yet to write theirs.

By now, the Pru was on the defensive. It owned more real estate in the world, and real estate began to fall. It owned one of the largest junk bond portfolios ever—$280 billion—and the junk bond market crashed in the wake of its "king" Michael Milken's indictments. The Pru had invested in every sector of the economy, and the economy dropped. The savings and loan crisis, foreclosed mortgages, a glut of overleveraged assets—all of it came crashing down around the Pru. The eighties were closing with a whimper.

Shortly after Crowley and Fowler had presented their plea to "stay the course," Ball came to Fowler.

They talked of bonuses. The department had $12 billion in deals, had tripled its market share in the last three years to almost 5 percent, and had contributed $60 million to the firm. This year, Crowley and Fowler were firm. They wanted to reward their staff with bonuses. They had $50 million with which to pay about 220 people, or on average about $227,000 a person. Big producers were supposed to be paid more.

"The firm's had a tough year. I need $25 million from the pool," said Ball.

Fowler sputtered, "I can't do that. We had a great year."

"Pay out the contracts you have to pay. The firm is retrenching and you'll have to fire seventy-five people."

Fowler argued ferociously against that. Neither he nor Crowley saw the wisdom of such a massive cut. Mass firings would in effect kill their plan.

Ball listed his concerns and described his rough position.

Fowler argued, "Look, you can have all of our bonus pool. Here, take $50 million." In return, he asked Ball to agree to one allocation system and stick to it. Fowler and Crowley also said they'd pay their staff out of a percent of departmental profits—using the agreed-upon accounting system—instead of tapping the traditional bonus pool. The two men argued that this was more efficient, and fairer than this annual disagreement.

"I can't do that," said Ball. "It's too complicated. I don't have the time."

For the next few days, Fowler moped around the office. He vacillated between two courses of action. He couldn't fire seventy-five people, and too many hard workers had waited patiently for rewards. One day, as he sat racking his brain for a way to save the unit, the futility of the situation struck him. He felt as though he had been hit in the knees with a baseball bat and told to run home. "This sucks," he thought.

He walked to Gahan's office and shut the door.

"Jim, you and George have put me in a position in which I have no choice. I'm being ordered to do something that makes no sense. This mass slaughter is unreasonable when we've done everything we've said we would do and more. I can't do this.

"I resign."

Gahan sighed. "I thought you'd do something like this. And there's no sense in me trying to talk you out of it. You've got to do what you've got to do."

Fowler left and walked into Crowley's office.

"I've just resigned."

"What?" Crowley bellowed and rose from behind his desk.

"I quit," Fowler repeated.

Crowley shouted, "Why did you do this? You can't leave now. How could you do this to me at a time like this?" He yelled and cursed; then he considered a solution.

"Look," he said, more calmly. "Walk up there right now and tell Jimmy you've changed your mind. Let's see if we can't work something out."

"Wake up, Jim," said Fowler curtly. "The dream is over."

"No, it's not," he said. "Come on. There's got to be a way to save this." He tried to coax Fowler to change his mind.

But Fowler left. That night, when he walked out of Pru-Bache, he felt deeply betrayed. He had trusted the Pru, had believed it was committed to the plan. He had set goals and exceeded them—in spite of market crashes, slowdowns, and restrictions. He was convinced that after this slowdown, investment and merchant banking would roar back in 1992 to 1994, and Pru-Bache would be rich.

Fowler grew embittered. "I'll probably go to my grave believing they made a big mistake."

That weekend, Pru-Bache's last junk bond conference was held at the Phoenician, which had been built by Charles Keating's savings and loan customers. Most of the senior people of IMB were present, and Fowler's absence was noticeable. Still, no one mentioned his resignation.

The following week, Crowley scheduled an IMB meeting at the UN Plaza Hotel overlooking the East River. He required all remaining managing directors to attend. In a meeting room, Crowley and the so-called Gang of Twelve assembled around a table. Looking haggard and depressed, he told the group that Fowler had resigned. The directors looked shocked. "Everyone started asking questions," said Welch, who was present at the meeting. "What does this mean? What's going on?"

Then he announced more bad news. The unit had to fire or "let go" at least fifty people in the next few weeks. That amounted to a quarter of the staff of the core investment and merchant banking group, and the directors shook their heads in disbelief. Others couldn't help but notice that Crowley looked personally wounded. Someone asked what had happened to the Pru's commitment. Crowley just shrugged.

One banker muttered, "Rock Solid, Brain Dead."

In January 1990, a story appeared in the Sunday *New York Times* that featured Pru-Bache and its investment banking rout. John Marcus opened his morning paper, turned to the business section, and nearly choked on his bagel. On the front page was the piece "Deadline Time for George Ball," which "pretty much heralded George Ball's imminent demise," he said. Adding to the shame was Pru executive Garnett Keith, who, according to the reporter, "went to great lengths to distance himself and Prudential from Mr. Ball's expensive foray into investment banking."

Basically, Keith said that PBCF had been Ball's idea. Without being asked a question, the executive told the reporter that he could "only comment as an observer" about Project '89, which he approved and oversaw. At best, Keith's efforts to distance himself publicly from his own child seemed callous and unstately for a man of his position. After the beating they had taken in the last few months, the remaining Pru-Bache bankers weren't enthralled by the corporate chief's response. It simply inflamed old wounds of feeling like the "retarded kid kept hidden in the family basement," a sentiment that not a few bankers had shared in the past.

The piece indicated that Pru was reluctant from the beginning about the project and that "after 1987, it refused to put any more of its money into the banking effort." The story killed at least one deal. Marcus, after three months of negotiating with a client's deal, walked into work that Monday only to get a call from his client, a CEO who said: "Sorry, the board won't support me working with you after that disastrous piece in the paper."

From then on, the "failed investment banking effort" was frequently inserted into feature stories on Pru-Bache.

Inside, murmurs and distrust affected morale within the skeletal staff. More numbers and facts were leaked to newspapers, according to some employees. "The place became paranoid," said Christian Wyser-Pratte, as people began to spend more time covering their tracks and second-guessing management than they did actually working. In the early part of the year, Pru-Bache announced a $51 million loss for 1989, even though the IMB division itself had added about $60 million in gross revenues.

That March, Crowley tried to counter his staff's growing pessimism in another address, only this time his heart wasn't in it. "In spite of what you may have read, PBCF is very much in business," he said. His terse, four-page speech was much shorter than his prior year's chatty, forty-four-page exhortation. "I believe in you and I believe that together we will prevail in the decade ahead," he said, then walked out. Few believed he meant it. By now, the remaining cohead felt emotionally drained.

The final blow came that summer. The consultants completed their study, and the executive committee gathered in a room atop One Seaport Plaza to learn the results. Crowley listened as the outside advisers' report called for a gutting of the investment and merchant banking unit. He was stunned.

He looked out the window. A movie was being filmed on the rooftop across the street. He watched the actors and half-listened to what he believed was a canned, foregone conclusion. He thought, "This result is inescapable, and I can't create a scene that will make any sense to these goons."

His mood darkened after that. People began to divine the division's fate by reading Crowley's face. If he arrived grouchy in the morning, the rumor was that Ball had just told him to cut more people, and in late 1990, that's exactly what Crowley was ordered to do.

Andy Simpson knew ahead of time that he was about to be fired. As he walked into the last meeting with his boss, the six-foot-five Simpson crowned himself with a stage-prop arrow that appeared to pass through his brain, à la comedian Steve Martin. Although some of the shell-shocked staffers had just been fired, they couldn't help but laugh, watching Simpson lumber down the halls, "lanced by Pru's arrow."

In his exit interview, Christian Wyser-Pratte warned the firm of pending doom. The former Navy officer told the young attorney, "You're new to this organization, and you're not going to understand what I'm going to say. And you may think I'm exaggerating, but mark my words. In the time I've been here, Pru-Bache has been operating an organized criminal conspiracy to defraud the public. And Jim Darr has been taking (favors). . . . It will cost $1 billion to erase it clean," he said. "Mark my words."

In December Crowley quit because he couldn't stomach the mass firings. As for the remaining sixty members of IMB, the staff continued working, and for the next three years, the firm managed to remain ninth in the league tables. But those years were like "working in a morgue," said Marcus. "Everybody spent a lot of time talking about how awful it was but knowing that if we improved, we would have something again."

In 1989 and 1990, Pru-Bache reported more than $300 million in cumulative losses. By then, the firm had been pruned back to its retail bone.

In June 1994—after a two-year dearth of merchant and investment banking business—Prudential Securities announced that it was "beefing up its investment banking effort." In an internal memo, it said that the new unit "will strategically align many of our proven analytical, origination and distribution capabilities in order to strengthen the firm." New hires were afoot.

18

In the Mouth of the Rat

AROUND the time Project '89 was extolled and then impaled at One Seaport Plaza, DIG held its annual meeting in Dallas. In May 1989, it unrolled the carpet for the cream of Pru-Bache's crop—the top-selling one hundred brokers.

By now, Paul Proscia had replaced Jim Darr as president of the newly christened specialty finance group. Although some brokers believed that with the changing of the guard the quality of the group and its offerings would improve substantially, DIG had dug too deep a hole for itself to ever change its course alone.

During the conference, the salespeople broke into smaller rooms for more intimate discussions. In one, DIG's senior officers held a "Meet and Greet" open-door forum around a table. Proscia sat at the head of a conference table flanked by Clancy, DeFur, and attorney Frank Giordano. Proscia addressed about thirty of the firm's top brokers, who sat in chairs packed around the table and stood against the walls, crowded close. Among them was top broker Dick Hechmann, a former chairman of the Small Business Administration during the Carter administration and a man who flew his own jet to soirées, such as the birthday party of his friend King Gustav of Sweden. Hechmann was a rainmaker, worth $3 million a year in commissions, and a model for the other brokers, including $1 million producer Gary Zahn.

Zahn and the others listened as Proscia read a prepared speech detailing the slower real-estate market, the aftershocks from the 1987 stock market crash, and other factors that had hindered the LPs' performance.

Then, Hechmann spoke: "I want to talk about VMS. When are we going to stop denying there's a problem there?"

"Well, Dick," said Proscia, his voice soothing and calm, "I don't think this is the right forum to address such problems."

"No," said Hechmann, perturbed. "This is the right time, and I'd like to discuss it."

Turning to Giordano, Proscia appeared calm except for the panic and dread in his eyes. Giordano caught the look, as did some brokers. "When I saw that, it chilled me," said Zahn. "It was clear Paul was pleading for someone, anyone, to get him out of the mess." The look lasted a second, but it carried in it the sum total of DIG's knowledge of long-running problems with VMS Realty.

DeFur spoke up. "I think you're exaggerating the problem, Dick," he said lightly.

"No, I'm not," said Hechmann. He brought up a private VMS LP, which in 1988 was not performing. Wealthy clients who had invested in the deal had been required to pay taxes on their principal as well as on money they had never invested but had written off on their taxes, prior to the 1986 tax law change.

Obviously, Hechmann said, VMS couldn't pay its loans. Conspicuously, he added, Pru-Bache had known of its sponsor's cash problems. Why was the firm now selling to its clients yet another VMS product, this VMS Mortgage Investment Fund?

The attorney spoke: "We don't have a right to stop VMS from selling their funds," said Giordano. Speaking legalese, he said that VMS hadn't broken its contract with Pru-Bache or exposed itself in any legal way that would allow Pru-Bache to cease acting as sales agent for the firm.

"Bullshit," Hechmann said. He detailed how he believed investors were getting nailed. Hechmann wanted to know: was Pru-Bache going to sit by and watch?

Giordano repeated that VMS hadn't broken its contract with Pru-Bache, so the brokerage firm was obliged to maintain its part of the contract. Giordano didn't mention investors.

The room was quiet. After listening to the sharply differing sides, brokers considered the quandary.

Zahn spoke up: "We can't do anything."

"Yes, we can," said Hechmann, turning to the roomful of producers. He said that if Pru-Bache brokers could persuade 75 percent of their clients who had purchased a VMS LP to oust VMS, investors could regain control of the LPs, refinance them at lower rates, and turn their own investments around. It made sense to Zahn.

"Whoa, now, Dick," said Giordano. "We can't change the scope of the partnership like that. We are bound by the letter of the law." DeFur, Proscia, and Clancy jumped in to diffuse the situation. Some brokers continued to ask questions, and the DIG officers artfully attempted to quell the situation. They intently wrote on memo pads. Their brows creased, their heads nodded, and they mouthed promises. "We'll look into the matter," they said that day.

The brokers accepted the leaders' words at face value, but management never did come through. The issue wasn't resolved to the satisfaction of many salespeople in the field, and investors were left hanging on their own.

Still, at the time, no broker took the revolutionary step suggested by Hechmann, at least not right away.

No one riffled through the pockets of Hollywood television producer Michael Dubelko. But in his office high above Sunset Boulevard, he felt he was being shaken down like some "chump" in the alley below. As producer of *The Rockford Files, 21 Jump Street,* and *Hunter,* Dubelko was arguably the most respected, most consistently successful producer of hit television shows—the president of Cannell Productions. Tall and muscular, Dubelko could have been a movie star himself with his square jaw, grass-green eyes, and elegant manner. But he wasn't. As a former accountant who now regularly dealt with slick fast-talkers, Dubelko could spot a financial morass before meltdown.

Usually. But now, in 1989, as he stared at the latest investment letter from VMS, his jaw clenched and his throat constricted.

In 1984, Dubelko had bought $600,000 worth of Boca Raton LP units from his Pru-Bache broker, Rob Hughes. Over the years, Dubelko had matched VMS's original projection of LP revenues and operating income with the actual figures, but the two didn't match. "They were growing farther apart," he figured. Dubelko would call the investor relations people at VMS, who would obfuscate the issue. He never received clear answers to his questions.

The Boca LP results had eroded to the point where now he was genuinely worried about whether he'd ever see his money again. Sometimes he'd discuss the problem with Hughes, who in turn had called Pru-Bache. After all, the securities firm in 1983 had collected in fees $1 million in nonaccountable expense allowance, which it didn't have to explain, and a consulting fee of $506,000. That totaled $1.5 million.

On top of that, from 1983 to 1988, Pru-Bache had collected annual "monitoring fees" that had totaled $759,000. All together, the brokerage firm had charged investors $2.2 million for the cost of supervising its customers' investments.

Yet as evidenced at the "Meet and Greet" forum in Dallas that year, Pru-Bache officers said they couldn't take cautionary action—even when VMS appeared to be violating its fiduciary responsibilities. And Dubelko believed that VMS was running roughshod over its Boca Raton LP investors.

For example, VMS had surreptitiously bought a third of the company whose sole function was to manage the Boca Raton Hotel's day-to-day operations. Under that company's hotel management contract, it collected a bundle every year: 2 percent of gross revenues; 10 percent of gross profits; plus 10 percent of net profits from a special membership club. In a good year, that could total a few million dollars.

The partnership already paid the salaries of the capable, on-site hotel managers who operated the hotel; that wouldn't change, no matter who owned the hotel management contract. What could change, however, is that the owner of the management contract could pile on even more fees for "fiscal and asset management" of the hotel—which wouldn't necessarily improve the hotel.

Clearly, the contract's fate was crucial.

At the time, Boca's LP investors were not asked, let alone informed of, VMS's self-dealing arrangement, as they should have been. As part of its fiduciary duties, VMS should have alerted limited partners to the opportunity so that they could buy the lucrative contract for the LP itself, and so enjoy more income.

But VMS grabbed the opportunity for itself.

Then, in April 1986, VMS mailed to Dubelko and other limited partners a strange document. Dubelko had read the thick onerous package, which was written in convoluted jargon. With difficulty, he figured out that VMS was telling partners that they could buy one-third interest in Boca's hotel management contract. As it should have done initially, VMS was now recommending that the partnership buy the contract.

The value was such that if the LP ever sold the hotel, the management contract would be part of the deal and could conceivably fetch as much as $50 million.

But in order for investors to buy that contract, 51 percent of the LP needed to vote yes. If they did buy it, the partners would have to assume the $3.6 million loan that VMS had procured to buy part of the contract. The loan's terms were not disclosed.

At the time, Dubelko believed that VMS had made it tough for the LP to buy the management contract. For one thing, the enormous tome was written in mangled English. "Most people are going to throw this in the trash," Dubelko had told Hughes then. Second, although VMS had owned part of the contract for about two years, it gave investors less than a month to evaluate the proposal, consider alternatives, and vote.

But the strangest aspect of the proposal was this. Normally, when management recommends an action and an investor doesn't vote, silence is counted as a yes, concurring with the recommendation. But VMS had turned that time-honored practice inside out. If an LP investor didn't vote, silence was counted as a no. In other words, no vote was counted as a vote against the LP itself.

Despite these obstacles, half of the investors actually voted eight-to-one in favor of buying part of the contract. But because of the way VMS had stacked the deal, investors lost; not everyone had voted.

At the time, Dubelko thought, "This is outrageous."

Later, when the issue was openly contested, VMS "unequivocally" denied that it breached its fiduciary duty. It consistently said that it had purchased the management contract in a "fully disclosed arm's length" transaction. It also reminded partners that VMS had recommended that the LP purchase the lucrative contract, but partners rejected that proposal—which was true.

By 1989, VMS had disclosed that it owned the entire management contract. In time, VMS would claim that the contract was worth $100 million, which VMS—not investors—could pocket upon any future sale.

"The entire deck was stacked against us investors," thought Dubelko. Still, whenever brokers complained about VMS's tactics, Pru-Bache told salespeople to remain "neutral."

In Montreux, Switzerland, during the second week of September 1989, Gary Zahn and Paul Proscia were relaxing on yet another rewards trip.

Zahn and Proscia walked up the hill with their wives in tow after touring the six-block fairy-tale city. Suddenly, a woman who worked with Proscia ran down the hill. She told Proscia she had to talk to him, and he walked toward her, out of earshot of the others. The woman whispered her message in his ear. Immediately Proscia's shoulders slouched. Zahn thought someone in his family had died.

Proscia returned and announced: "I have to go to New York."

"I'm really sorry," said Zahn. "Is everything all right?"

"Oh, yeah," Proscia said, realizing what Zahn must be thinking. "I've got some serious problems with VMS I've got to deal with."

Proscia caught himself, but it was too late. He realized he was talking to a broker who owned VMS, "a broker with a big mouth who was going to tell everybody what had just happened." The two stared at each other; Zahn knew then that Hechmann had been right all along. VMS was troubled.

Upon returning from the European awards trip, Zahn saw that VMS

Mortgage Investment Fund was trading at $3, down from $10. Two months later, VMS Realty, one of the nation's largest real estate firms, replaced its top management, laid off five hundred employees, and admitted to cash-flow problems in an unexpected announcement.

At the time, management said that chances for bankruptcy were "very, very small." An executive with Xerox Corp., which now owned 25 percent, took over as president. In February 1990, the firm stopped paying lenders and investors, and shares of VMS Realty's public funds fell steeply to as low as $1.25. Meanwhile, some one hundred private LPs were in limbo. Xerox considered sheltering the firm by filing Chapter 11 bankruptcy.

Then, three months later, the Xerox executive was forced out and Joel Stone took over. For the next five years, Stone and other executives of VMS would remain connected with some VMS partnerships even after investors had tried to boot them out.

What neither Zahn, Hughes, or other brokers knew is that by year-end 1989 the firm was facing a slew of court and arbitration cases. Many investors claimed fraud, breach of fiduciary duty, and other wrongdoing on the part of both VMS and Pru-Bache. In arbitration, some investors claimed that Pru-Bache misled them about the VMS partnerships and that they had been pressured to move pension funds, IRAs, and Keogh accounts into VMS LP shares, some of which cost as little as $1,000 a unit. For example, one elderly couple, Dom and Shirley Miele, had trusted their broker, who in turn had trusted Pru-Bache and VMS.

In 1987, the Miels moved a bank certificate of deposit into an LP; by year-end 1989, they watched their life savings of about $300,000 dwindle to half that amount. They filed an arbitration claim, and in 1991 won $553,309, which included punitive damages.

In its sales sheets, Pru-Bache had advised brokers to close with this pitch: "Mr. Investor, all you are doing is lending money to a major company that will borrow at established rates, give you a floor of 12 percent return for approximately 27 months, and give you a share of the upside in real estate that they own or are developing. How much would you like in your account?"

As many other investors around the country began to file arbitration claims, Pru-Bache fought its cases aggressively—too aggressively, according to some critics. The firm earned a reputation for using "scorched earth" tactics and "hardball" methods against its clients. One litigant said that Pru-Bache used a "gangster ploy" when it threatened to reveal damaging information about him if he didn't settle.

While some investors sought relief through arbitration, others pleaded their case in court. By December 1989, one of the first lawsuits against VMS and Pru-Bache surfaced publicly; many more followed in rapid succession. These suits were consolidated into two class actions—one for the private LPs and another for the public LP funds. In 1991, some VMS private LP investors settled a class action suit that returned to them only two cents on the dollar. Their attorneys, however, reaped $6 million and VMS retained the rights to sell the properties underlying the LPs. So instead of earning income on their savings, investors lost all but a few pennies of every dollar they had entrusted to VMS's care. Instead of a stake in some valuable, income-generating property, they had next to nothing. "It was a pretty lousy deal for investors," said a real-estate consultant at the time.

In 1992, a class action settlement was approved for public LP investors, which also returned a fraction of investor funds. Indeed, some people—such as the Mieles—won more money in arbitration than they did from class action settlements. However, many investors didn't understand that they had the right to "opt out" of these class actions and to pursue arbitration instead.

And here was another rub for Pru-Bache clients. Later, some claimed that Pru-Bache falsely told them that their only hope of recovering any money from their VMS funds was to participate in the class action settlements. Upon settling and later learning otherwise, some class members were furious and sued the firm again—this time alleging that Pru-Bache falsely advised them of their rights. In its defense, the brokerage firm explained that it instructed its brokers not to offer any advice concerning class action suits.

However, in 1994, an Illinois judge allowed investors in the VMS Mortgage Investment Fund to proceed with their claims that Pru-Bache gave them unauthorized and improper legal advice. Importantly, that decision reopens Pru-Bache's and VMS's potential liability in the sale of some $357 million worth of product.

Still, few investors have recovered all of their money plus the returns once projected by VMS. Certainly no partnership attempted to kick out VMS as general partner in quite the same way that Hechmann had so cogently outlined back in 1989.

No one, that is, except for Dubelko and gang. The Boca Raton limited partnership would prove to be the only one of ninety-five private LPs to break away from the "settlement." What appeared to be a radical act was actually quite sensible. Investors were simply trying to control their own assets. But there was nothing simple about the process, as investors would soon learn.

By 1991, Dubelko was furious with the stonewalling from VMS regarding his investment. By now, VMS had breeched its fiduciary duties further. In 1988, VMS took for itself the remaining two-thirds interest in the hotel management contract, and now owned it all. VMS had another faucet from which to draw more fees from the Boca Raton LP. In 1990 and 1991, VMS took $7.4 million in management fees—even though the LP *lost* $9 million during this time. "It was now beyond outrageous," Dubelko fumed.

The LP had become a pocket for the cash-strapped VMS. By now, the LP's "wraparound" third mortgage of $8 million had exploded into a $20 million debt. Before investors would receive a dime of their money, they'd first have to pay VMS that amount. Plus, in 1988, VMS principals had added another $20 million debt owed to its affiliate, Banyan. All told, the LP was now straining under $186 million in debt.

By 1991, Hughes had left Pru-Bache, disgusted with the "rancid" corporate culture. He had sold many units of VMS limited partnerships and in the early 1980s had become one of the best salesmen of them. He had never suspected that the investments would prove to be as disastrous as they ultimately became. During the ensuing battle for control of the Boca LP, VMS would point out: "Mr. Hughes now has joined with those who question many of the essential business elements of the same transactions he recommended to some of the LPs when they made their investment." Still, how was Hughes to know that two of the nation's largest financial firms—VMS and Pru-Bache—would behave so questionably with its own clients?

While VMS began to fight fraud charges in class action suits, Dubelko and Hughes settled on a different battle plan: Dubelko and other investors would "opt out" of the suits altogether and wage their own fight against VMS. Along with another large investor, the Oakland-based Liquidity Fund, Dubelko mounted an attack.

He arrived early at his Hollywood office to telephone other limited partners. The idea was to convince investors to exclude themselves from the class action suits, or "opt out." Dubelko talked to farmers in North Dakota and doctors in Kansas in his straightforward, persuasive manner. "They didn't know me from Jack," but eventually, Dubelko and Liquidity Fund produced enough LP votes to exclude the Boca Raton LP from the beggarly class action settlement.

By now, Ted Fowler had joined the fray. As the former cohead of Pru-Bache's investment banking unit, Hughes had briefly met Fowler while the two men worked at Pru-Bache. Fowler knew of VMS, knew how to restructure deals, and was trying to do just that with his own New York investment banking firm. In Fowler, the Boca Raton LP investors had found a deal man who could match wits, point for point, with the dealmeisters at VMS.

In 1991, at the behest of the two largest investors—Dubelko and Liquidity Fund—Hughes, Fowler, and others formed the Boca Raton Management Co. (BRMC) in order to replace VMS as general partner. The new firm helped investors wage a hostile proxy war to force VMS out of the partnership altogether and replace them with BRMC.

In January 1992, Fowler, Hughes, and investors tried to cajole VMS representative Joel Stone into working with limited partners to turn around what had become a money-losing operation for investors. By now, some $150 million mortgages encumbering the hotel were about to come due and needed to be refinanced. Talks between VMS and LP investors had deteriorated to the point where it became clear to Dubelko and the others that Stone was not about to budge from his position. A fire sale of the lovely Boca Raton Hotel was not unlikely, which meant that investors could conceivably lose most of their original investment—after paying VMS's fees and mortgages. Dubelko grew increasingly frustrated.

"After diddling with VMS for so many years and talking with Joel [Stone] in conference calls," he said, "I felt that the only way to get his attention was to hit him with a two-by-four."

Dubelko found an attorney willing to work on contingency. He and other investors filed suit against VMS, charging them with breech of contract in their purchase of the management contract. In March 1992, the investors claimed that VMS had "concealed, retained, exploited, and failed to offer to the limited partnership certain lucrative business opportunities. . . ." The suit chilled any potential sale of Boca Raton Hotel for a time.

However, by some great misfortune, that suit ended up in the same Chicago courtroom that had just settled claims from all the *other* VMS investors, who had joined in the infamous class action. At first, Dubelko's suit was thrown out, aided by VMS's false declaration that claimed that Boca Raton LPs had never "opted out" of the class action, had already settled with VMS, and so could not sue the firm again. "They flat-out lied," Dubelko realized.

He continued to fight his case on appeal, while Hughes and Fowler tried another tact to save the LP. They helped mount a second suit, claiming that VMS was basically bankrupt and so could no longer fulfill its LP duties.

VMS denied that it was bankrupt, even though it was working with creditors to liquidate VMS properties and pay off its debts. However, VMS claimed that its financial problems didn't mean it could no longer remain general partner. The battle lines were drawn.

Yet nothing was smooth. For example, on the day they had planned to file suit in 1992, investors nearly missed their deadline when Hurricane Andrew ravaged the Miami law firm that was to have filed their suit. Frantic, Hughes found another law firm up the road in Palm Beach, which filed the documents in the nick of time.

Meanwhile, the mortgages secured by the Boca Raton Hotel were about to be auctioned by the Resolution Trust Corp. (RTC), which had taken over the lender, a failed savings and loan. Come the fall of 1993, some $150 million would come due. Investors had to either refinance the loans by the end of 1992 or suffer a potential total loss once the RTC sold those loans.

Throughout all this, VMS fought bitterly to keep its "crown jewel." However, in October 1992, 80 percent of the limited partners voted to oust VMS as general partner in a proxy fight. Still, the sponsor continued to claim it was the LP's rightful partner. Finally, in January 1993, VMS bowed out and BRMC was voted in as the new general partner. As part of the settlement, Joel Stone of VMS Realty became a director of the new general partnership, along with Hughes, Fowler, and two other men.

Now the new general partner had to scramble to salvage the limited partners' interests. On the eve of the auction of Boca Raton's mortgages, general partner BRMC found some lenders willing to refinance the loans at a lower rate. This allowed the LP to pay off the RTC. The move also saved the LP about $20 million, reduced its interest expense 20 percent, and extended its loans for ten more years. Dubelko and investors now had some breathing room.

In October 1994, VMS settled with limited partners the lawsuit concerning the management contract. The LP agreed to pay VMS a reduced $10 million payment for the contract, rather than VMS's original $22 million claim. That settlement removed the cloud hanging over the Boca Raton LP and returned to limited partners the valuable hotel contract.

In December 1994, the LP also settled with VMS's affiliate, Banyan, the $22 million claim regarding two property loans. The partnership agreed to pay Banyan $4.5 million for one encumbered property and return to Banyan the other piece of real estate.

By the start of 1995, investors in the Boca Raton LP had finally achieved what they had set out to do back in 1989. It had taken about five years, enormous financial resources, a few strokes of luck, and much persistence just to safeguard their investment. No wonder this LP would prove to be the only VMS partnership to stake its own claim.

Now, after more than a decade, investors are still waiting for a return on their $50 million investment.

19

"Rock Solid, Stone Broke"

B<small>Y</small> 1990, troubles with the limited partnerships had mounted and distrust of the brokerage system was running wild. The complicated RISERs—which Jim Trice had complained about—had dropped in value from $10 a share to nearly zero. VMS Realty had suspended dividend payments, and according to one work-out expert, investors were left holding "piles of shit" for which they had paid $1.2 billion. Fogelman, Polaris, Spanos, the Related Cos.—the bulk of Prudential's partnerships were troubled. One Fort Lauderdale investor, who had lost $200,000 in Pru's products, suggested a new motto for the company: "Rock Solid, Stone Broke."

Even the $1.4 billion limited partnerships of Graham Resources—once the pride and joy of Pru-Bache's retail and DIG system—were not performing, despite the surreptitious and illegal bank borrowings that sponsors had used to prop up the Ponzi-like investments. Many within Pru-Bache's system, it seemed, fired questions to company managers, who responded with disingenuousness and outright lies.

The smooth and polished answers no longer satisfied the disgruntled sales force. Wrote one Graham insider in mid-1989: "Brokers were getting tired of the fact that even though we always seem to have answers why our programs are not meeting projections, the fact remained that only two of our programs were at the 13 to 15 percent level we projected." The memo pointed out that "any salesman cannot sell effectively unless he has complete faith in his product . . . and complete confidence and trust in management. . . ." Graham's situation by now had deteriorated to the point where the writer suggested that its energy funds be consolidated, or rolled up, before the firm exited the retail market altogether.

In June 1990, Prudential Insurance installed one of its top executives, Arthur H. Burton, Jr., as vice chairman of Pru-Bache. He oversaw the crucial areas of mutual funds, risk arbitrage, and administration. That move clearly signaled that Ball had lost some authority over Pru-Bache. By now, the "poor performance of the investment bank" was widely—and erroneously—publicized and blamed for "the enormous sums of money poured into Pru-Bache." The purchase of Thomson McKinnon was applauded for augmenting Pru-Bache's retail core, even though that division had been secretly struggling for years.

Prudential Insurance now found itself defending Pru-Bache and Ball for the first time. This was a dramatic change for the securities broker-age chief, whose new defensive posture with the press broke sharply from his customary offensive stance.

Ball had long enjoyed a favorable, visible position in the business press. He gave great quotes, and was frequently prescient with industry forecasts. For example, in January 1987, he cautioned readers about the stock market's frenzied rise: "about as sustainable as the afterglow of a third martini." He knew the business and was well-read and pleasant. He was so accessible that he sometimes answered his own phone and occasionally returned reporters' telephone calls while traveling in Europe. Some correspondents had elevated him to mythic status during the early to mid-1980s. He had been called the "golden boy," a "cheerleader," one part "choirboy" and one part "Boy Scout," whose energy and optimism inspired tens of thousands of people. Courting the press was a part of Ball's job, which he did well. Even in 1990's unglamorous market downturn he opined in clear, colloquial terms: "Business stinks."

But his own retail force began to question him and the firm's credibility, and so too did the press. Rumors surfaced that Pru-Bache was for sale. Stories appeared with headlines such as "Prudential's Ball Gets Parent Firm's Vote of Confidence." In any other firm but Pru-Bache at the time, such a development would not be considered news.

Ball was privately hurt and stung by such reports. He continued to withstand the mounting criticism "without flinching," as he would later say. The firm had lost $51 million in 1989. By the end of 1990, Ball surely knew Pru-Bache was about to suffer a financial loss with no hope of an eleventh-hour rescue. That year's $259 million loss would be its worst ever.

By now, the investment banking unit was limping along, still trying to wring forth some income after "the slaughter." DIG was constricting, although mutual funds were profitable. Another main piston, risk arbitrage, offered both good and bad news, Ball said. The bad news was that "business hasn't picked up any more than the markets have," but the good news was that Pru-Bache "has the best arb people around."

Guy Wyser-Pratte had gotten clobbered in the stock market crash of 1987, when, according to Ball, the department had lost about $100 million. In 1989, after the junk bond market "crashette," Wyser-Pratte's risk arbitrage department had gotten hit again with the collapse of a takeover bid for UAL Corp., the parent of United Airlines. Like most arbs at the time, Wyser-Pratte had been counting on the successful deal. He said its failure cost Pru-Bache about $15 million.

That summer, however, the Pru drastically cut back the arbitrage department's earning power by slicing its credit a whopping 90 percent. Instead of using $375 million to play the market on behalf of the firm's portfolio, Wyser-Pratte now had only about $25 million—and that miserly allowance occurred just as the takeover market collapsed. It should come as no surprise, then, that the division's returns would not be as substantial as it had been in prior years.

Since 1967, when Guy Wyser-Pratte's father had married his firm to the predecessor of Pru-Bache, Wyser-Pratte himself had made a substantial amount of money for the firm. In return, he had been treated well, even though such treatment was spelled out carefully in a contractual arrangement. Wyser-Pratte had secured an oral employment agreement with Pru that was extended automatically each year unless the Pru canceled the contract in writing by November 30.

The firm had also agreed that Wyser-Pratte's compensation would be structured in such a way that Pru-Bache's "allocation shell games" would never touch his pay. Since the arb department was a lean, twelve-person unit, its overhead was relatively low, as were its expenses.

Yet its returns were high. Since 1967, the department had made for the firm an average return of 31 percent a year. One year, Wyser-Pratte doubled the firm's portfolio. In 1988, he had made 45 percent on the firm's capital, and he had made some $319 million in gross trading profits over a twenty-year period.

Guy Wyser-Pratte knew he was a major contributor to the firm. He knew Ball counted on him for profits. Because of those two factors, Wyser-Pratte believed the Pru's executive Arthur Burton, Jr., who had told Wyser-Pratte that the 90 percent cutback in his credit was a temporary condition. Because of the assurances given by Pru-Bache's new vice chairman, Wyser-Pratte was led to believe that his credit—and power—would soon be restored.

On December 4, 1990, Burton told Wyser-Pratte that he had to "terminate" the arb chief and his division. Wyser-Pratte was angry that Pru-Bache and Pru had not told him this six months before, when the firm had cut back his credit so drastically. "We could have worked it out gracefully and together," he told Burton.

Instead, he said, he had been reading in the press about losses in his division. Wyser-Pratte added: "You know, I'm not the reason for the firm's cash problems."

"Still," said Burton, "we're having capital problems."

At the time, neither Wyser-Pratte nor Pru-Bache's other employees knew just how serious were those problems. In November, the New York Stock Exchange had placed Pru-Bache on its credit watch list, said Wyser-Pratte. The stock brokerage's capital was so low that the exchange was worried about the firm's financial health. Unknown to many people throughout the firm, the firm's position was precarious and the exchange could close the firm anytime. Ball was in a tough spot; he needed $255 million in cash in order for the exchange to release the firm from its watch list.

In addition, Pru Insurance feared it might lose its high rating from the credit agencies. Standard & Poor's Corp. and Moody's Investors Service, among others, assign ratings to indicate a company's ability to repay its debt and obligations, including bonds. In general, the higher the rating, the more attractive or safer a company's bonds are to risk-adverse buyers. Issuers of high-rated bonds tend to pay lower interest rates on their "safe" bonds. However, in 1990, Pru held a large portfolio of junk bonds and a substantial amount of real estate. According to four executives, rating agencies pressured Pru to whittle down its higher-risk holdings or lose its AAA credit rating: The Pru could potentially pay higher rates of interest on its lower-rated bonds. Said one executive: "The board of directors had been given a mandate to not lose its high rating. But they could give it up if they wanted to." Clearly, the board didn't want to.

However, Burton didn't share that news with Guy Wyser-Pratte at the time. The arb chief thought that the company's chief problems stemmed from Pru-Bache's bitter limited partnerships, rather than from a rating crisis at the parent company. Wyser-Pratte asked Burton how much money he thought the LP woes would cost the firm.

Burton looked heavenward, squinted, and then replied, "About $34 million." That was the amount of a pending lawsuit against Pru-Bache and VMS.

Said Wyser-Pratte: "I thought it was closer to $1 billion."

Burton's face turned red and he left.

Wyser-Pratte returned to the business at hand. He had a few weeks to wrap up his business and consider alternatives. That night at home, he discussed with his wife the possibility of reviving the family business by starting his own arbitrage firm.

The next morning, one of his staff people called him at home. The staff member was upset.

"We've been locked out of our offices."

"What?"

The caller repeated himself.

Enraged, Wyser-Pratte immediately called the legal department. "How dare you?" he said. "You'd better open those doors now or I am going to have the press down in front of your building in two seconds."

With that, the company unlocked the doors, and the department was allowed back in to work. Still, the "dean of Wall Street arbitrage" was appalled at the treacherous treatment of his department. He realized he could no longer trust the firm or its executives.

Over the next three weeks, he and his staff smuggled out of the office their more important personal papers. In the evenings before they left, designated "mules" stuffed their backpacks and knapsacks with documents that would be key to business, and, later, would be used in a legal dispute with Pru-Bache and the Pru.

"They treated us like they were street-corner gangs," said Wyser-Pratte. So much for gratitude, he thought. After twenty-three years of providing Pru-Bache with spectacular financial returns, Wyser-Pratte felt he had been thrown into the street like a knave. In 1990, as the firm's losses mounted, he was used as a public scapegoat to explain embarrassing losses. About six months later, Pru-Bache blamed its poor financial performance on "unprofitable business lines, such as investment banking, and risk arbitrage." In the Pru's annual report for that year, it indicated that it had exited the arbitrage business, among others that "were losing money.

"We are now focusing on those businesses where we consistently make money and we want to broadcast loud and clear that we expect to keep doing so," it said. Still, a year later, the Pru lost its treasured top rating from Moody's.

To clear his name and reputation, Guy Wyser-Pratte filed an arbitration claim against Pru-Bache with the National Association of Securities Dealers (NASD). He claimed the firm had defamed him by blaming its losses on him. Later, he would drop that point because it was too difficult to show malice on the part of the Pru.

Significantly, he filed the claim against both the securities firm and its parent, Prudential Insurance. Wyser-Pratte claimed the Pru had induced Pru-Bache to breach many of its promises. Pru-Bache had effectively tied his hands and prevented him from doing his job. He and the securities firm had agreed that it would "not impose any restrictions or limitations which would prevent or substantially impair the continuation of arbitrage activities," which Pru-Bache had clearly done by emptying his arbitrage purse. He claimed that the Pru-Bache had wrongfully terminated him and had misrepresented its intentions.

According to NASD documents, Pru-Bache represented that his employment agreement was expressly terminated in 1985 and not renewed. Yet Wyser-Pratte produced a taped conversation in which he and a Pru-Bache executive agreed that his employment contract was in force at the time and would continue indefinitely.

For its part, the brokerage firm claimed that risk arbitrage had lost $70 million in 1990. Yet, before he had left the firm, Wyser-Pratte had smuggled out of the office financial results that proved otherwise. According to internal numbers used by Pru-Bache, Wyser-Pratte had produced $251 million in gross profits from the period 1981 to 1989, while the firm during that period had *lost* $62 million. Later, Pru was forced to admit that the firm's losses in 1990 "were not the fault of Mr. Wyser-Pratte."

Upon hearing testimony from both sides, the NASD harshly reprimanded Pru-Bache for "the egregiously improper manner in which [it] defended itself." One executive was sternly reprimanded by the arbitrators for flat-out lying, as were other employees. During the proceedings, the NASD noted that Pru-Bache had failed to produce some documents demanded by the hearing panel and had actually destroyed others.

The claims against Prudential were dismissed, yet Pru-Bache lost its case; Wyser-Pratte won about $1 million in awards. In a highly unusual move, the NASD sanctioned Pru-Bache "for failing to comply with this panel's order" to produce documents. It would not be the last time that the firm would be accused of such unethical and underhanded tactics.

"Despite the seduction of easy money in the '80s, we managed to stay away from some of the risks that now haunt others," the Pru boasted in its 1990 annual report. "We think our focus on integrity had a lot to do with that."

During the 1990s, some former employees experienced firsthand Pru-Bache's brand of integrity. Jim Trice, for example, filed an arbitration claim against his former employer and fought a long and bitter battle just to recoup essentially what attorney Loren Schechter had promised him back in 1988. The settlement was only that which Pru-Bache legally owed Trice after nearly three decades of loyal service. On New Year's Eve 1991, Trice received balance due from his pension and medical benefits for his invalid ex-wife.

Michael Kudlik, who had been responsible for selling about $1.5

billion worth of Pru-Bache product, found no justice in his proceedings against Prudential. During the hearings, Pru-Bache lawyers produced a personnel file memo Kudlik said he had never before seen. The April 1986 memo summarized DIG's New York meeting with Kudlik, in which he was chastised because he "did not follow the line of command" and did not sell all of DIG products. He was also told that "it is not his decision to pick and choose what offerings he wishes to emphasize." His attitude of "continuously questioning various decisions" irritated senior vice president Paul Proscia, who wrote the memo. Unlike most other Pru-Bache memos, this one did not include the initials of the secretary who had typed it.

Kudlik, challenged his firing in arbitration and lost. The arbitrator denied him the back wages and benefits that he believed he had earned during his tenure.

Joe Kett, who also had questioned the sales of certain products, filed arbitration against Pru-Bache for being fired by Graner without just cause. While still employed at Pru-Bache, Trice and Kudlik were both asked by Pru-Bache officers to lie in those proceedings, which they refused to do. Kett won his claim against his former employer.

Still, not all former employees of Pru-Bache were so shabbily treated. When James Darr left the firm, he amicably collected a fine settlement from Prudential-Bache and an agreement that his enormous legal fees would be paid by the firm. Sherman, for his part, collected a seven-figure settlement, and his legal bills were also footed by Pru-Bache. Jack Graner and a number of other executives who had overseen questionable and unscrupulous efforts were all awarded healthy severance pay and defense costs in Pru-related suits and arbitrations. They testified on behalf of Pru as "friendly witnesses."

During the 1990s, the "rattlesnake" policy of Pru-Bache was firmly intact: keep happy those who could bite you. As for the other, less threatening ex-employees, the firm's "hardball tactics" became infamous. Kristi Mandt, for example, in 1992 filed a claim against the brokerage firm for having to "engage in sexual relations with [its officers] as a condition of continued employment." The securities firm fought her arbitration claim on technical grounds rather than on any grounds related to the sexual harassment issue. This forced the case into court, where it became public record. In 1994, a New York appeals court ruled that Mandt had the right to pursue her claim behind the closed doors of an arbitration proceeding. She was seeking $3 million for "outrageous" conduct of former Pru-Bache officers Robert Sherman and Carrington Clark.

In the nineties, some employees bypassed Pru-Bache altogether and took their complaints to Prudential Insurance. In March 1990, Trice wrote a letter to Bob Winters, warning the then insurance company chairman of numerous problems at its subsidiary Pru-Bache. "Although current management might dismiss me as a disgruntled ex-employee, I believe a thorough investigation would lead you to a different conclusion. . . . I do not understand how the Prudential can put at risk the goodwill and reputation that the company has so carefully nurtured over the years. . . ." Trice never received a response, but his warnings that the Pru could face a set of "very embarrassing problems" would prove to be prophetic.

In February 1991, a seminal article appeared in *Business Week* that detailed some of the LP woes at Pru-Bache. The article also discussed some improper dealings related to Darr, which publicly put Ball, and the Prudential itself, on the defensive.

On Valentine's Day, Ball resigned from the firm. After spending nearly a decade trying to build a securities firm for one of the world's largest companies, he was forced to step aside ignobly. All told, the firm had lost $62 million during his nine-year reign. Including its original purchase price of Bache, the Pru had spent $1.3 billion on the securities brokerage unit in order to become one of the biggest and richest financial powers in the world. And that didn't include the costs that would snowball from the LP fiasco.

By 1991, Ball had reorganized Pru-Bache, at the command of the Pru. It, in turn, had been induced by pressure from rating agencies that had threatened to drop a letter from its AAA rating. To satisfy the parent, Ball cut back on investment banking, arbitrage, and direct investments. Only the last of these made any sense to some Pru-Bache insiders. Yet, the reorganization saved money and helped the firm earn $16.4 million in January 1991. It also allowed Ball to exit with some sense of dignity.

For the Pru, Ball had built up the brokerage unit in one long, expensive gambit. He had overseen a valuable mutual fund division, which earned about $90 million a year. He had helped strengthen PruCap to become a diversified merchant banking investor, with annual profits of $50 million. In what would prove to be one of the best-kept all-time secrets on the Street, Ball had overseen the buildup of a successful investment and merchant banking unit—and then had quarterbacked its defeat. Also, he had built up the most successful limited partnership sales team on the Street.

Of all his accomplishments, the last one would become his legacy.

True to character, Ball resigned in a memo. Entitled "All Good Things," it explained that his track record had hindered the firm from moving forward. "The hubris of what happened to the securities industry in the 1980s, and as a result, to the firm, led to some bad results in several areas," he wrote. "The net of it is that someone unencumbered by the aftermath of those past results should lead the firm into the future."

Years later, Ball would say both that he was fired from Pru-Bache and that he voluntarily resigned—a classic Ballism. After his departure from Pru, he would disappear from the Street for about eighteen months, after which time he would resurface at yet another securities firm, Smith Barney.

For a time, Ball and the Pru were well matched. Said one former executive: "Prudential represents middle America, the pilgrims, Plymouth Rock. We're not talking Wall Street raiders, at least not in the minds of Congress or regulators." The Pru represents widows and orphans, WASP America, a friendly society. According to its own account of history, the company was "known for the three P's: Princeton, Presbyterianism, Prudential. (Some added a fourth: Prissiness.)" Said the former executive: "The company has the imprimatur of the United States on it."

And what better figurehead for such an institution than George Lester Ball, a descendant of the country's first president, George Washington. Washington's mother was a Ball, and her family traveled to America on the *Mayflower*. They were Puritans who landed at Plymouth Rock. Born generations later is Ball, the son of a college professor, an Ivy League graduate, an Illinois-born, Jersey-resident, fair-haired, blue-eyed perennial optimist. A salesmen's salesman, whose favorite book was the classic tome *Extraordinary Popular Delusions*.

How did Pru-Bache get into so much trouble? "We weren't smart enough to ask naive questions," Ball said. The man who once said that Wall Street is greed later explained that "we didn't understand that some temptations were too big for some people." Ball claimed he knew nothing was amiss with the LPs' sales practices or DIG until sometime "in 1987, '88, '89, or '90," even though some professionals around him had warned of potential problems.

As its subsidiary's problems began to surface publicly, Prudential Insurance ignored what some termed "the mess." In the opening line of its 1991 annual report, it told its customers that "1991 will long be remembered as a year when truth was stranger than fiction." Prudential Insurance asked its retired ex-chairman, Robert Beck, to step forward and act as temporary president of Pru-Bache Securities while the insurer searched for a permanent chief. Beck had been chairman and chief executive officer of the insurer in 1981 and the one who had decided then to buy the Bache Group. In 1982 he had hired Ball, and over the next five years he had been Ball's champion and chief supporter during Pru-Bache's costly expansion period. Now, a decade later, Beck surveyed the wreckage.

A week into his new position, Beck changed the brokerage unit's name to Prudential Securities. By dropping "Bache," Prudential signaled its attempt to break from the past and start anew. Three months later, Beck stepped aside as a new man took over.

In May 1991, Hardwick ("Wick") Simmons became CEO of Prudential Securities. A great-grandson of a cofounder of the investment banking firm Hayden Stone, Simmons had spent his career at the family firm. When the firm had been acquired by Smith Barney Shearson, he had headed Shearson's retail brokerage unit until May 1990, when he quit in a fury because he had been passed over for a top job. He had not worked at a brokerage firm until Prudential hired him in May 1991.

By now, the Pru had trademarked the term "Rock Solid," even as its customers derided that phrase as empty and hypocritical. In its annual report that year, the Pru claimed its rock "image is worth more to us than any single entry on our balance sheet." Replacing its former oft-stated ambition of becoming the biggest, the firm pledged that its new focus was to be "worthy of trust."

In 1991, the Securities and Exchange Commission, the National Association of Securities Dealers, numerous state regulators, and the U.S. District Attorney's office in Manhattan all initiated investigations into Prudential Securities. Over the next few years, the regulators began to unravel an astonishing array of abuses that had become commonplace in the 1980s: brokers had lied, churned customer accounts, and flipped securities, cajoled customers into signing agreements they didn't understand, and sold risky partnerships using system-wide tools of fraud and deceit.

Simmons, meanwhile, attempted to polish the Rock's new face. He blamed the firm's past problems on "rogue brokers" rather than rogue chiefs. Among the first things the chief executive officer did was install a confidential "ethics" hotline so Prudential employees could report suspicious and improper behavior. As it turned out, that hotline wouldn't be so confidential.

20

History Repeats Itself

In the fall of 1991, Susan Clayton boarded a plane from Los Angeles to return home to Phoenix. She worked in the Pru-Bache brokerage office and was a young, bright broker-trainee who wanted to become a portfolio manager for high-income clients. Petite, blond, green-eyed, and freckled, she had a simple blunt haircut and wore tailored work suits.

As the passengers boarded the plane, she recognized Carrington Clark, the director of Pru Securities' Pacific South region, in which she worked. Clark spotted Clayton sitting alone in the back of the plane, and walked toward her. "Here's an extremely attractive woman," he said, sitting next to her.

She thought, "Uh-oh. He's picked up the scent."

Clark was new to his position and had just replaced Jack Graner, who had been demoted to head the Beverly Hills office. The twenty-five-year-old Clayton felt nervous around the older man, partly because he oversaw the entire region; he was her boss's boss. But there was a more personal reason for her discomfort.

For the past few months, Clark had been calling her at the office, as well as at her home, sometimes leaving messages on her telephone answering machine. He'd invite her out socially on dates. She never returned the calls or went out with him. She was not interested in dating anyone, primarily because she was still recovering from a painful divorce. Even if she were dating, however, she would not have been interested in a man like Clark. His reputation for womanizing repelled her.

"Do you have a boyfriend?" Clark asked her.

"Yes, I do," she lied.

The two chatted on the plane amicably, and upon reaching their destination, said good-bye.

A few weeks later, Clark called Clayton at home and left a message. When she heard his invitation, she grew extremely uncomfortable. She was trying to break into the firm's elite training program to become a top-tier broker who managed wealthy clients' accounts for a flat or "wrap" fee rather than earning income on commissions from individual transactions. To enter the prestigious program, Clayton needed the recommendation of her manager as well as the support of Clark. Now she found herself in a tough position, as Clark was trying to develop a personal relationship outside of work.

Should she confront Clark and tell him to knock it off, possibly jeopardizing her career? Or should she ignore it, and not "rock the boat"?

For a time, she tried the latter approach.

Around the same time, Wick Simmons wrote a memo admonishing employees to beware of sexual harassment. In October of that year, Anita Hill testified before a Senate committee regarding the sexual harassment she had experienced while working for Clarence Thomas, who at the time had been nominated for a seat on the Supreme Court. In light of the controversial hearings, Pru chairman Bob Winters had also written a memo exhorting all employees to report improper behavior.

A confidential hotline was set up so employees could report such complaints.

One evening, Clark called Clayton's home and left a message on her machine. "I've got an airline ticket for you. You can fly up to San Francisco and meet me. There will be another manager and his lady friend, and we'll have a good time."

Clayton knew this was serious. "He's not asking me. He's telling me, and this has gone too far."

Clayton confided her problem to a coworker, a woman. Somehow, Clayton's boss, who managed the Phoenix office, heard about Clark's harassing telephone calls. The manager discussed the problem with her one day at work.

"You must be doing something to invite his attention," he scolded her.

"I'm not!" she protested. "He's a pig. You've even told him he ought to be cast in bronze. Don't do this to me."

"C'mon, Susan," he said. "A guy doesn't just call a woman at home uninvited."

"Well, he does," she said, trying to stop her tears. She was angry with her boss for accusing her of "inviting" the phone calls.

Another woman, who handled office administration, overheard the conversation. She took the office manager aside and told him he was handling the situation poorly.

Later, the office manager returned and apologized to Clayton. He gave her the company's policy on sexual harassment and said: "Call this number. It's confidential. No one will know you've called, but they'll investigate the matter."

"I don't want to make a big deal out of this," she protested.

"I can't protect you if something else happens. You have to disclose it. They'll keep it confidential."

"Thanks." At his behest, she went into his office, closed the door, and dialed the number. An attorney answered the phone at One Seaport Plaza.

"I'm trying to stay anonymous," she began. She identified herself as a broker-trainee in Phoenix and explained that the regional director had been calling her at home for some time. His latest message instructed her to fly somewhere to meet him and another man and his "lady friend." She hadn't returned the phone call, didn't want the invitation, and wanted advice on how to handle the situation without harming her chances for advancement at the firm.

"Just a minute," the attorney said. He put her on hold.

Then Loren Schechter picked up the telephone. "We are going to investigate this immediately."

"No, we're not," said Clayton. "I simply want some advice. I'm trying to defuse a situation." She added, "My manager told me to do this."

Schechter grew angry. "Look. If Carrington Clark is bothering you, we have to investigate. You have to talk to somebody and detail what happened."

"Forget it," she snapped. "I'm not talking to anyone. I didn't want this to happen."

"I'm sending someone out there tomorrow," he said.

"I refuse to talk to anyone."

"Look. They'll meet you across the street for coffee or something. No one will know what's going on. This will remain confidential." He continued to assure her that she would not be harmed and that all discussions would be kept in strict confidence.

"Okay," she agreed. Upset, she left early that Friday afternoon.

On Monday, she walked into the office. "Well, aren't you popular?" a male broker said, with raised eyebrows. It turned out that everyone in the office knew about her "sexual harassment charge" against Clark. An attorney from Pru Securities had flown out from New York and had interviewed all of the employees in her office. Clayton was floored by the violation of trust.

Someone told her she had a visitor. "There's an attorney in the conference room waiting to see you, Susan."

Clayton walked into the conference room, where she found the firm's attorney.

"I don't believe you guys have done this," Clayton told him. "You have lost all credibility with me. Loren Schechter said you'd meet me across the street. He assured me no one would know about this. My call was supposed to remain confidential!"

"Can I have the tapes?" the attorney asked.

"What tapes?" She walked closer to him.

"The tape from your home telephone answering machine. The one where Carrington Clark left you a message." He stared at her expectantly. "I can't fly back to New York empty-handed," he explained.

"You know what?" she said, leaning into his face.

"What?"

"Fuck off!" She turned and walked out of the room.

From then on, attorneys from Pru Securities began to harass her, calling her both at the office and at home and leaving urgent messages for her to answer. Coworkers were told that Clayton had filed a sexual harassment claim against the regional director, which was untrue. She was ostracized and shunned. Her branch manager began investigating her telephone calls. Suddenly, she was under investigation.

At one point, she relented and talked to Pru attorneys. "You guys have really screwed up," she told one man. "This is no way to handle this."

They asked her to fly to New York over Christmas holidays. Her understanding was that she and the attorneys would discuss a new position for Clayton, who wanted to be transferred out of the region. She met two attorneys, who asked her questions about Clark. Twenty minutes into the meeting, Clayton realized the discussion had little to do with her transfer. "They don't care about me or my situation," she thought.

She politely excused herself, walked out of the room, and continued walking out of the building. From a nearby telephone booth, she called the attorneys and told them she wasn't returning.

Now she felt she needed her own attorney, and she had engaged one by the time she returned to Phoenix.

A week later, Clayton was suddenly transferred to a smaller, more isolated brokerage office in Mesa, Arizona. "They took everything I owned and threw me out of the office." She could not even collect her personal mementos from her office.

Overwhelmed by the bizarre situation, she did not report to work and stayed in bed for the next two weeks. She reviewed the situation over and over. She had never filed a formal complaint against Clark, yet now she was branded as a troublemaker. "I thought I had done something wrong, that somehow I had gotten myself into this mess."

One morning she woke up angry. "All of a sudden I became, excuse the term, a royal bitch from hell. I started sticking up for my rights."

Her attorney sent a letter to Pru Securities' legal department, accusing it of placing her in the untenable position of complying with company policy by reporting a problem only to find herself now defending herself and her job. "Susan was desperately embarrassed by the enormous response to her simple inquiry and the resulting rumor and innuendo. . . . She sought help from the legal department, which ironically was responsible for her predicament."

The letter was copied to Pru chairman Bob Winters.

By now, the alleged "sexual harassment" filing was known throughout the entire system. That spring, Clark addressed a regional meeting of all male branch managers in Pacific South and assured them that the firm "is behind him and is helping to fight the allegations," according to one source. He apologized to his branch managers for any embarrassment he may have caused the firm.

Quietly, around the same time, several other female employees at the firm began to complain to New York about Clark's inappropriate behavior toward them. Things started to move. Clark had reportedly been docked $40,000 in bonus pay the prior year because of his misconduct.

Meanwhile, Clayton filed a claim with the Equal Employment Opportunity Commission, accusing Pru Securities of retaliating against her for reporting Clark's phone calls and then transferring her to an undesirable office. "My confidence was violated . . . and my professional reputation was damaged."

In May 1992, Carrington Clark was asked to resign, and Clayton's former branch manager in Phoenix became the new regional director. A month later, Clayton received a $100,000 secret settlement from Pru Securities and resigned.

In January 1995, the "new" regional director left Pru Securities amid allegations that he, too, had sexually harassed a female employee.

By 1992, investor lawsuits and claims against Prudential Securities were threatening to bury the firm. Although Pru-Bache had, during the 1980s, violated SEC rules on five occasions, it had paid scant attention to compliance.

Yet the firm now supplemented its army of seventy-four in-house lawyers with outside attorneys in order to wage battle on the mounting claims from clients and employees. Some of the thousands of investors who had purchased $8 billion worth of limited partnerships during the 1980s began to state that they had been defrauded and deceived by

Prudential's securities unit. The investors tried to recoup their money, as Pru Securities denied all wrongdoing.

In Phoenix, two lawsuits were filed that claimed Pru Securities had lied about possessing a crucial consultant's report, the stated existence of which would have damaged its case. The report concerned Polaris Aircraft Income Fund, whose assets were nearing the end of their useful lives. The report said that the Polaris LPs were taking severe financial risks by extending credit to airlines with poor credit ratings.

Pru Securities denied it had ever seen the report, let alone commissioned it. Therefore, investors couldn't use the report to examine Pru Securities lawyers, which caused investors to lose the case. Actually, the firm did indeed have the report and had turned it over in another arbitration case. A Pru Securities spokesman explained that local counsel in that case had never seen the report. Added a Pru Securities attorney: "We simply made a mistake. It was made in good faith."

By 1993, Prudential Securities had expended a large amount of time and money on defending itself in cases related to one of its two largest limited partnership sponsors, Graham Energy. Prudential had raised about $1.5 billion in a series of thirty-five oil and gas partnerships sponsored by Pru Securities and Graham Energy. Most of that money—about $1.3 billion—had flowed into twenty-six partnerships known as the Prudential-Bache Energy Income series.

In about forty other arbitration cases pending against Pru, investors' attorneys claimed that Pru Securities had deliberately lied about its oil and gas partnerships in sales material—a claim that Pru Securities denied vigorously at the time. By now, the units were illiquid and so not readily salable; many investors—retirees—appeared closer to death than they were to recovering their lost funds. The investors had received only half of their original investment—sans the interest or return that they had been promised a decade ago.

By 1993, about 137,000 investors had joined a class action lawsuit in federal court in New Orleans. At first, Prudential Securities had offered to pay investors $37 million in cash. After paying attorneys' fees of $22 million, plus expenses, the settlement would leave investors with a meager cash settlement of $11 million, or slightly more than a penny on the dollar. In addition, as part of the settlement, Pru Securities and Graham would roll up, or consolidate, the partnerships into a company. That company would issue to investors new shares, which would be traded publicly. Overseeing the new corporation would be Graham Energy, the same entity that had run the partnerships into the ground in the first place.

The new company would be incorporated in Delaware, giving it more power over partnership affairs than it had wielded during the 1980s. For its troubles, Graham would be reimbursed $13 million in reorganization costs if the settlement went through, and it would ask that limited partners pay more than half of $9.2 million in severance payments to Graham employees. Whatever remained could go to investors.

About twelve thousand investors opted out of the settlement and pursued their claims in private arbitration, where they had a better chance of recovering more money. In February 1993, a judge temporarily blocked the settlement, which was widely criticized as "a cruel joke," according to one attorney. In his opinion, the judge wrote that some 125,000 investors could lose as much as 90 percent of their money from the so-called settlement; he wanted to wait for pending state investigations of Prudential Securities.

That spring, two of Graham's executives, Anton Rice and Mark Files, failed to appear for their scheduled depositions. John Graham, the chairman of the oil firm, lamented the stalled settlement in an interview with a regional newspaper. His company, which had long been bloated with high general and administrative costs, was in danger of shrinking dramatically from its current size of 250 staff people, he said. He and his wife, Suzy, who had been paid as the company's interior decorator, objected to what they called attorneys preying on their company. "They literally have dragged our name through the mud," she said at the time. Her husband added: "I have been victimized by the trial lawyers."

Indeed, the attorneys and the sponsors stood to gain the most from the settlement: attorneys would have collected nice fees, and both Pru Securities and Graham would have escaped from potentially far more expensive consequences. Contrary to Graham's assertions, however, the investors would have been the victims had the $37 million settlement gone through as he and Prudential Securities had proposed. Said a former Graham employee: "It's not hard to see that those guys were trying to get off cheap."

At the time, the properties underlying the limited partnerships were valued at $680 million—or about eighteen times what the sponsors had offered.

A year later, in January 1994, Pru Securities upped the ante and agreed to settle for $90 million. That was seven cents on the dollar, or a nickel per dollar after attorneys' fees. Fortunately for investors, that amount was not the extent of the total recovery. By now, another oil and gas company had stepped in to buy the LP oil and gas assets. Parker & Parsley Petroleum Co. of Midland, Texas, paid $491 million to limited partners, which brought their total recovered amount to $581 million.

That was short of the $780 million settlement that one attorney, Stuart Goldberg, had argued investors should receive. But, combined with the $655 million that investors had received in "distributions" over the preceding decade, Pru Securities clients had fared well, compared to others. All told, they had collected eighty-five cents on the dollar from the asset sale, settlement, and prior distributions. Put another way, investors had lost 15 percent of their savings—or the amount that Pru Securities and Graham had taken at the time of the sale as their partnership "fees"—plus any promised returns that should have accrued from the "safe" investments. According to one U.S. court of appeals writing about a different fraud case, not involving Pru Securities nor Graham, punitive damages equal to three times damages "would be fair, reasonable and well within the public interest."

Yet neither Pru Securities nor Graham nor VMS has so far paid anything approaching that amount in regard to the estimated $2 billion scam. The court in the other case said that "the only sure way of deterring such conduct in the future is to take the profit away from the wrongdoers and slap on an additional amount as punitive damages."

Is that what it takes?

Epilogue

For Jack Graner, the New Year 1994 rang in a new level of despair. He no longer worked for the firm at which he had spent his entire career, and the region that had once been his domain was ridden with regulatory breaches, employee claims, and customer lawsuits.

He slipped downhill slowly, said one of his peers: "After his heart attack, Jack wasn't the same." Paperwork had piled up, basic duties were ignored, and his wife took to filling out his travel and entertainment expense statements to recoup as much as $10,000 a month in reimbursements.

When Sherman departed as president of the retail division in 1988, Richard Sichenzio had become Graner's boss. "That's when Jack's problems started," said Pat Graner. His chain-smoking increased, and the drink and drugs soon ravaged his once handsome face. Shortly after his birthday in 1991, Graner's tenure as Pac South chief ended. In May, when Wick Simmons took over, Graner was demoted from the post he had held for six years. Now he was assigned to manage the office in Beverly Hills, which at one time had been his dream city. There his rockslide accelerated.

"That time was incredibly stressful," his wife later said. "The rules of the game kept changing, only Jack didn't know what the new rules were." Six months later, Sichenzio asked Graner to leave. Jack Graner received a settlement and started a consulting business. "He'd get up in the morning and shower and dress as though he were going into work," said Pat Graner. For a while, he was optimistic about the future. But instead of overseeing an entire region with nearly a thousand employees, he now worked alone in his den, and the change was too dramatic for the gregarious man.

During this time, Graner assisted at least one attorney whose clients sued Pru Securities over their lost investments. In some cases, Graner helped investors win their cases; for a time, he seemed to have found a niche.

Graner had wrestled down the drug addictions that he had acquired while working at the securities firm. He had entered a treatment program and for a time eschewed the expensive habit. But soon his good intentions faltered and he fell back into the misery. His marriage grew troubled, and in 1993, he and his wife separated.

That year, Graner was the subject of an arbitration in which a customer claimed that he had been the victim of unsuitable, unauthorized, and abusive trades. The customer sought $119,000, but, in an unusual decision, the National Association of Securities Dealers awarded $221,000.

Also during this time, Graner met at least twice with regulators from the Securities and Exchange Commission to discuss fraud allegations against the Pru unit and its employees. Those discussions weighed heavily on Graner.

Then, on October 21, 1993, the SEC settled its case against Prudential Securities. When the regulatory agency released its public findings, Graner's handprints were spotted. Of the nine improperly supervised branch offices that the SEC cited, three of them had violated law while under Graner's watch. Yet, as another regional director pointed out, that didn't mean much. "The SEC missed so much that had gone on at Pru, it only picked those infractions it could easily prove." Still, Graner was devastated, and his former friends and colleagues no longer called.

Then Graner abruptly disappeared from sight. He skipped the family's Thanksgiving celebrations that year and the traditional Christmas festivities and even missed his only daughter's wedding. By January 1994, his world had come crashing down, as everything that he had once held dear was slipping away.

He binged for three days on crack cocaine, heroin, and grain alcohol, and at the end died in a cheap hotel in the company of a strange woman. The next morning, two police officers drove up to Pat Graner's sunny house in California. They walked inside her white picket fence and knocked on her front door as the dog barked. Pat Graner knew without even speaking to the officers that her husband had died.

She wept. "I'm angry," she said later. "I'm angry at [management], at Prudential, at the whole damn thing.

"They destroyed Jack."

In New York, at One Seaport Plaza, 1994 dawned with a new advertising campaign for Prudential Securities. In February, the firm inaugurated a $22 million annual advertising budget slated for print and television. The firm—and its salespeople—were eager to forget the limited partnership woes. A new promotion could help. Yet despite the expensive campaign, the company's "Straight Talk" ads rapidly descended into bumbles and feuds.

One TV advertisement featured the firm's CEO, Wick Simmons. Like the other commercials in the series, this one was shot in black-and-white with a hand-held camera, to evoke an old-fashioned, unslick feeling. The focus was soft, sometimes blurred. The lens flickered over Simmons's face in a painfully close shot. Simmons glanced back and forth from his handwritten notes to the camera while reading his lines:

"It's my job to set the tone for this company. To me that means being direct, being truthful. We call that straight talk. . . . I'm straight with people and I expect the same, from our brokers to my kids."

The ad series was derided as "manifestly disingenuous" in *Advertising Age*. "Worst of the bunch is Simmons himself, who comes off as nothing less than shifty." Simmons never quite looked into the camera, and his close-up shot intruded on viewers. Said one broker: "I just wish he'd get his molars off my television set."

Prudential Securities had handpicked other spokespeople besides Simmons to feature in the ads. One television spot focused on broker Jeffery Dagget, a heavyset, dark-haired man with a small mustache and a double chin. Dagget detailed why investors should trust him and the firm. "I try to recommend investments that won't jeopardize my clients' last years on the planet," he said, adding that he had "never been a flashy, slick sales guy."

One of his clients, Monsignor Maximos Mardelli, knew better. The eighty-one-year-old Roman Catholic had told Dagget and other brokers about his special investment needs. The monsignor had inherited money and, during his "last years on the planet," wanted it invested in conservative instruments.

Instead, Dagget sold the elderly cleric $125,000 worth of the VMS Mortgage Investment Fund, which by 1990 was worth a fraction of that. When the priest learned of his loss, Dagget told him the only way he could recover his money was by joining the infamous VMS class action suit. The elderly priest could have filed an arbitration claim for himself, and perhaps recouped all of his lost funds. But, instead, he joined the class action suit, which returned pennies on the dollar.

Before the debut of "Straight Talk," the priest had filed a complaint with regulators. But upon viewing the commercial, the monsignor got fired up again and promptly sued Prudential Securities—and Dagget. The ad was pulled, and the monsignor's lawsuit was later dismissed.

In a second ad designed for print, Pru Securities broker Susan Gooding was pictured and quoted: "From where I sit, preserving integrity is not a lost art. . . . One of my clients is my father." In fact, her father had never been a client and had died two and a half years before the advertisement appeared. Pru-Securities pulled that ad, too, but not before it had run in at least one magazine. A Pru spokesman later explained that the firm had misread her questionnaire, saying her father-in-law was a client. By now, the brokerage firm had stopped many of its multimillion-dollar television spots for fear of more controversy.

"Straight Talk" flopped because it fell short of the truth. The company, which had been plagued with the ten-year-long scandal of deception, could still not play it straight.

"It makes you wonder who's in charge over there," said the chairman of another brokerage house.

By 1994, it seemed evident that Pru Securities' problems extended far beyond any wrongdoing from the go-go eighties. Just as its executives had once allocated expenses to other divisions and so evaded fiscal accountability, the firm now seemed to be allocating blame to other culprits and so dodged any corporate responsibility. Now, however, that practice began to take its toll as customers left the firm and brokers moved to competitors. Even the Pru felt the sting: Individual life insurance policies dropped 20 percent that year.

Shortly after the ill-fated advertising campaign, Simmons in one interview coyly compared himself to his predecessor, George Ball. Said Simmons: "The most important thing for [Chairman Bob] Winters and [Vice Chairman Garnett] Keith was to find somebody whom they could trust to communicate honestly with them," he said in March 1994. "Infer from that what you will."

The obvious implication was, at best, that Ball had not told the board everything. Yet neither Simmons nor his firm was any different when dealing with the public. When Simmons had first joined Pru Securities in April 1991, he believed that the LP mess would cost less than $50 million. Two years later, he estimated $200 million. By October 1993, when the SEC settled its charges and opened Pru Securities' $330 million restitution fund, he and the firm publicly claimed that the amount would cover all investor claims—even though state regulators were telling him and other officers otherwise.

In the winter of 1993, Pru Securities executives tried to reach a settlement with California. (Every state regulator had to negotiate its own terms with the firm as part of the bigger SEC pact.) Gary Mendoza, the state's commissioner of corporations, knew that Pru Securities had agreed with the SEC to pay defrauded investors total compensation. But negotiations stalled when the firm's senior officers refused.

Meanwhile, in January 1994, the other holdout state, Texas, settled its case with Pru. In announcing the record $1.5 million penalty, the Texas securities commissioner said that the agreement had been reached only after Pru Securities' aggressive corporate counsel, Loren Schechter, had left the firm in December. Texas's unusual accord prevented the brokerage firm from opening new business in the state for a week. Now Pru Securities had to mend its ways with California.

In the wake of the Texas pact, Wick Simmons said that "this agreement with Texas means all fifty states are now parties to our global settlement and allows us to move forward."

Mendoza was furious. He immediately called the firm's attorney and said, "Either Prudential is seriously misinformed or they are misleading the public. Either way, we have not settled."

A few weeks later, in February 1994, Pru Securities officers and attorneys met with Mendoza in Los Angeles. The issue boiled down to this: how to fairly repay defrauded investors. LPs were worthless to investors since there was no market for them. However, the LPs had a total residual value of $2 billion; Mendoza wanted California LP investors to receive a portion of that value before he would settle with the firm.

Pru Securities refused, and the meeting broke up.

In March, after weeks of being stonewalled by executives, Mendoza decided to bar the firm from the state. A half-hour away from announcing his decision, Pru Securities relented. Residual values became part of the settlement and applied to all investors. To regulators, that had never been a question, but to the Pru unit a $2 billion refund was not quite real.

Indeed, over that spring and summer, Simmons publicly denied that the LP fund would climb any higher than its current $330 million level. In July, however, he was forced to set aside an extra $305 million to cover LP claims. The humiliating move displeased Pru Insurance officers, who now doubted the veracity of *this* CEO, according to three sources. Said Simmons: "I wasn't lying. I may have been stupid . . . but I genuinely believed" that $330 million would be enough.

At some point, this question arises: where is the board? The Pru's expertise in appraising the price of disaster is world-renowned. Yet where are its actuaries and claims adjustors? This company collects $45 billion *a year* in revenues making smart choices. Why has it fumbled so badly for so long?

Said one former Pru-Bache officer: "I don't think the Rock knew about the sex, drugs, and rock and roll that was going on under its nose, and it's unfortunate, if they didn't know.

"But I do hold them responsible for what they knew once those problems surfaced," he said. "They should have stepped up to the plate, admitted wrongdoing, and written one big beautiful check. That would have been in line with their image."

It also would have closed the case, and garnered an enormous amount of goodwill.

Now, Pru Securities' plague and afflictions may not be so easily solved. In 1994, other serious infractions bubbled to the surface, which simply could not be blamed on the past. In Idaho, the firm paid $1.1 million in fines for improperly selling options and other securities from 1987 until 1993. Under Simmons's nose, Pru brokers inappropriately sold to retail investors derivative mortgage securities—high-risk, extremely complex securities backed by pools of home mortgages. Said one money manager: "Any broker who sells a CMO [collateralized mortgage obligation] to an individual should be tarred and feathered." To its credit, the firm owned up to its mistake and repurchased $70 million from investors, which was, however, a fraction of the amount it had sold clients.

One expert surmised that the company quickly solved the issue "because Prudential has probably been the most aggressive of the major brokers in selling derivatives through its retail network." The sales have increased profits for Pru Securities' mortgage trading operations, but not for its clients. Once again, Pru Securities flunked the "know your customer" test, which its grandfather, Bache, had unwittingly created in 1929.

Then there is the Prudential Insurance Co. of America, owner of 140 subsidiaries, only one of which is Prudential Securities. According to regulators, its insurance agents through 1991 sold limited partnerships and other investments in Oregon without the required securities license. They concealed the improper trades, recording them as sales of mutual funds, which agents were allowed to sell. The Pru agreed to end that practice, but it has spawned litigation that will drag on for years.

Another group of eighty-seven customers sued Pru Insurance, claiming that an agent tricked them into buying policies they didn't need. They settled. Its own employee, Mark Jorgenson, sued the Pru for firing him after he blew the whistle on the company for inflating the values of its real-estate holdings in its institutional fund, PRISA (Property Investment Separate Account). Chairman Winters later apologized to Jorgenson, but only after it became obvious that Jorgenson's case was solid.

And now the Pru's policyholders are suing the corporation for risking their policies by getting into the LP predicament in the first place.

The Pru denies that its emphasis on profits—at the expense of reputation—encourages shady practices. But its record paints a portrait of an aggressive entity intent on dominating every market niche and country it enters.

In the wake of all its scandals and woes, the Pru of late has retrenched and refocused its efforts. For its main market, the Pru has targeted the small vulnerable investor and individual policyholder. "Prudential's emphasis on and the historical strength in the middle-income markets—which are less sophisticated, credit-sensitive, and competitive than the upper-income markets—should help Prudential to maintain its image and reputation in light of the negative publicity developments mentioned above," a Moody's analyst wrote in a credit report. In 1993, Pru cynically reorganized itself around this vulnerable target group—the same unsavvy, middle-class investor who was so easily defrauded.

In October 1994, Prudential Securities finally confessed to fraud in connection with its $8 billion LP sales program. It settled with the U.S. District Attorney's office in Manhattan in order to defer prosecution and, therefore, to avoid a probable bankruptcy. Nevertheless, government attorneys filed criminal charges, which focused on the $1.4 billion Graham Energy LP program. Should the company's ethics falter again, the criminal charges will be prosecuted.

In effect, Pru Securities admitted that it falsely told brokers the Graham LP investments were safe, low-risk, and suitable for all investors; the firm lied when it said the LPs were sheltered from taxes; it misled investors into thinking they were receiving income from LPs when they were only receiving part of their original investment.

Meanwhile, criminal investigations of individuals involved in the securities scandal continue.

Days before Christmas 1994, Prudential was caught violating federal laws. In the largest civil settlement in its history, the Federal Election Commission fined Pru $550,000 for illegally donating money to politicians.

From 1986 until 1993, Pru Securities illegally contributed $250,000 to numerous politicians from two political parties. The payments would have been legal through a political action committee, but not through individuals, and certainly not in the manner practiced by Pru. None of the politicians were found guilty of wrongdoing, although several sat on committees responsible for laws that could have affected Prudential. A few sat on the powerful banking and finance committees.

In its findings, the commission said the company's top officers pressured employees to make political donations. Some employees were later reimbursed for the donations. Others, such as secretaries, were improperly enlisted to help collect money. Pru brushed off the violations, saying they "involved gray areas that were open to different interpretations."

Yet commission chairman Trevor Potter said the violations were particularly serious because the firm knew it was flouting the law. It had paid a penalty in 1987 in a similar case for donating to the 1984 Presidential campaign of Senator John Glenn of Ohio. Potter added that the inquiry exposed "a widespread corporate plan to do something illegal."

Among those who participated in the illegal fund-raising were George Ball and James Tozer, former president of Pru Securities. The commission didn't find a direct link between the political donations and any company favors.

But still, there is a silver lining inside the black cloud following the Pru and its securities unit. After returning, say, about $2 billion to defrauded LP investors, the Prudential family can write off that amount as a deductible business expense on its federal income taxes. That means Pru Securities avoids paying full price for its long-running criminal deeds—at taxpayers' expense.

Following is an update, as of February 1995, of a number of Prudential players:

George Ball is chairman of Sanders Morris Mundy, a venture capital firm, which invested $1.5 million in Investors Financial Group, an Atlanta-based broker dealer; Ball is also a director and consultant of IFG.

Loren Schechter remains executive vice president and corporate counsel at Pru Securities.

Robert Sherman lives in New Jersey, where he runs a heavy machinery company.

James Darr lives in Greenwich, Connecticut.

Richard Sichenzio is a managing director for the securities firm Josephthal & Co.

Paul Proscia is a financial consultant.

Richard Saccullo is a regional director for Alliance Capital, a mutual fund company.

Guy Wyser-Pratte runs his own arbitrage firm on Wall Street.

Christian Wyser-Pratte is starting an investment fund for midsized businesses.

James Crowley runs a corporate meetings firm and an investment boutique.

Ted Fowler is managing director of Private Merchant Banking Co., along with former Pru-Bache broker Rob Hughes, and former Pru-Bache bankers Ralph Carballal and John Marcus.

Michael Kudlik works in Southern California for a real-estate firm.

Carrington Clark runs his own consulting firm.

Jim Trice operates Green & Trice, a headhunting firm specializing in the securities industry.

Former top Pru-Bache broker Gary Zahn was sentenced to two years in jail in 1991 for laundering money that enabled customers to evade taxes. Zahn claimed that a Pru-Bache executive at the time instructed him to handle large cash transactions by depositing less than $10,000 in accounts at one time. He pled guilty to one count, but was found guilty of thirteen counts of tax fraud. He and his wife own a small business in Long Island.

Paul Grattarola is an executive for an energy company.

Kristi Mandt owns her own financial-planning firm while awaiting for her arbitration case to begin.

Susan Clayton still works in the industry.

Hardwick Simmons is CEO of Pru Securities, where, eighteen months into his post at the new Pru, he considered resuming the sales of limited partnerships.

Endnotes

Chapter 1: The Widows' and Orphans' Friendly Society

Pages 1–2: Regarding circumstances of John Graner's death: County of Los Angeles, Department of Coroner, Case Report; Investigator's Report; Report of Toxicological Analyses; and Medical Report. Also, interviews with Police Detective Roger Mason of the City of Burbank; Travelodge manager Mrs. Mike Vaghashia; *Los Angeles Times*, Jan. 20, 1994, page 1; weather report, *Los Angeles Times*, Jan. 28, 1994; stock report: Dave Pettit, "Issues Rally to a Record as Fears About Rising Interest Rates Ease," *The Wall Street Journal*, Jan. 28, 1994.

Page 2: Interviews with Patricia Graner about her husband.

Page 3: Interviews with five of Graner's former coworkers.

Page 3: Michael Siconolfi and Alexandra Peers, "Prudential's 1993 Net Slipped Only 3% Despite Reserves; Salomon Profit Leaped," *The Wall Street Journal*, Jan. 28, 1994, p. C6.

Pages 3–4: Regarding Pru Securities' settlement with the Securities and Exchange Commission, see SEC Administrative Proceeding File No. 3-8209, Oct. 21, 1993.

Page 3, page 7: The story written by Chuck Hawkins and Leah Nathans Spiro, "Pru Securities Isn't Secure Yet," *Business Week*, Sept. 7, 1992, detailed early allegations in the LP tale.

Page 4: By 1993 investors had received little more than $3 billion back in distributions, according to the story written by Greg Steinmetz and Michael Siconolfi, "Partnership Problems at Prudential Embroil Insurance Business, Too," *The Wall Street Journal*, Dec. 1, 1993; Pru defends its energy LPs in story by Kurt Eichenwald, "Prudential's Investments Called Sound," *The New York Times*, Jan. 21, 1994.

Pages 4–5: The law offices of Stuart C. Goldberg produced a video package, "Prudential-Bache's $1.3 Billion Energy Income Limited Partnership Oil Scam," third edition, June 1993, which described his clients, investors, and alleged fraud.

Page 4: Michael Schroeder and Leah Nathans Spiro, "Is Prudential Playing Hardball?" *Business Week*, Nov. 15, 1993.

Page 4: Interview with broker Robert Hughes, regarding success rate of performing LPs.

Page 5: Interview with Jeff Dennis Ferentz, regarding accounting practices used in energy LPs.

Page 5: United States of America v. Prudential Securities Inc., Oct. 27, 1994; *Securities and Exchange Commission v. Prudential Securities*, 93 Civ. 2164; Oct. 13, 1994 letter to U.S. Attorney's office, Southern District of New York from Scott W. Muller and Carey R. Dunne, attorneys for Prudential Securities, all cover Pru Securities settlement of fraud charges.

Page 6: Stephen Labaton, "Drexel Concedes Guilt on Trading; To Pay $650 million," *The New York Times*, Dec. 22, 1988; the newspaper editorial quoted is "Defanging a Vital Watchdog," *Los Angeles Times*, Dec. 19, 1994.

Page 8: A "vocal minority" is blamed for Pru-Bache's problems, according to piece by William Power and Jill Bettner, "Partnership Woes Become Burden for Prudential Unit," *The Wall Street Journal*, Aug. 8, 1990.

Page 8: Pru Securities' $70 million bond buyback explained in story by Andrew Bary, "How Retail Investors Can Get Burned Playing with Derivatives," *Barron's*, Sept, 19, 1994; Michael Siconolfi, "Prudential Unit, U.S. Settle Partnership Case," *The Wall Street Journal*, Oct. 28, 1994, includes facts about Idaho's fine against the firm; Fact Sheet from Prudential Insurance Co. of America, Dec. 31, 1993; "How Prudent," *The Economist*, July 11, 1987; *The Universal Almanac* (1990), edited by John Wright, provides source of developed countries' budgets.

Page 8: Pru Insurance's down business is from story by Siconolfi, "Prudential Plans Cash Infusion for Broker Unit," *The Wall Street Journal*, Dec. 20, 1994.

Page 8: William H. A. Carr, *From Three Cents a Week: The Story of Prudential Insurance Co. of America* (Englewood Cliffs, N.J.: Prentice Hall Inc., 1975), p. 67; many details of Pru's history are provided by this source.

Pages 9–12: Ibid, pp. 15–224.

Pages 11–12; Ibid, pp. 254, 260; interviews with Margaret Shanks Moore, her attorney Dennis G. Merenbach, and documents from American Arbitration Association, Los Angeles Regional Office (Jan. 25, 1993), which detail her case against Pru Securities.

Chapter 2: The Bache Family's Jules

Pages 13, 14: Stephen Birmingham, *Our Crowd: The Great Jewish Families of New York* (New York: Harper & Row, 1967), pp. 9, 236.

Page 14: Interviews with Jules Kurtz, broker at Prudential Securities, formerly the Bache Group.

Pages 14–17: Interviews with Edward I. du Moulin, former vice chairman of J. S. Bache; Sylvia Gellermann, widow of Henry, who kept archives on Bache.

Page 15: Regarding Jules Bache's art collection: The Metropolitan Museum of Art archives; Calvin Tomkins, *Merchants and Masterpieces* (New York: Henry Holt & Co., 1970), p. 316; "Metropolitan to Get Bache Collection as Permanent Gift," *New York Herald Tribune*, Jan. 18, 1944; Interview with Piero Corsini, member of Appraisers Association of America.

Page 17: *Institutional Investor*, March 1991, p. 12, reports Bache's purchase of Wyser-Pratte & Co.

Pages 17–18: Samuel L. Hayes III and Philip M. Hubbard, *Investment Banking* (Cambridge, Mass.: Harvard Business School Press, 1990), pp. 106, 238; Interview with Kurtz; Judith Ramsey Ehrlich and Barry J. Rehfeld, *The New Crowd* (Boston: Little, Brown, 1989), pp. 83, 84; Stephen Fay, *Beyond Greed* (New York: Penguin Books, 1983), p. 180, all provide insight into the changing forces working on Bache and the securities industry in the 1970s.

Pages 18–20: Interviews with six former Bache employees give eyewitness accounts of early DIG days; Kurt Eichenwald, "An Early Warning Haunts Prudential," *The New York Times*, May 2, 1994, provides more data.

Page 20: Ehrlich and Rehfeld, op. cit., p. 181.

Pages 20–22: Fay, op cit., pp. 179–183, provides background on the Hunt silver scandal as do interviews with former Bache professional Fergus Henehan and one former broker.

Page 22: "Bache Group: Serving an Ace," *Banker*, August 1982, p. 108, publishes purchase price.

Chapter 3: A Piece of the Shlock

Page 25: Ibid, p. 282; Fay, op. cit.; *Encyclopaedia Britannica* (1990); St. Regis Hotel archives.

Pages 26–27: 1981 Annual Report of Prudential Insurance Co. of America; Prudential's media relations office; *Who's Who in America* (1989), all give biographical information on officers.

Page 27: Pru's buy of Bache attracted attention stated in "Not So Prudent," *The Economist*, Aug. 31, 1991, p. 59; flurry of similar purchases recited in story by

Miriam Rozen, "Bearing Gifts," *Investment Dealer's Digest*, April 20, 1987.
Pages 27: Phibro's purchase confirmed in Milton Moskowitz, Robert Levering, and Michael Katz, *Everybody's Business* (New York: Doubleday, 1990), p. 677.
Pages 27–28: Details about financial supermarkets taken from Richard L. Stern and Lisa Gubernick, "Financial Services—Who Owns the Future?," *Forbes*, Feb. 24, 1986, pp. 90–94; Lynn Adkins and Leah Nathans, "The Winning Strategies in Financial Services," *Dunn Business Month*, January 1987, pp. 45–53; 1982 Annual Report, Prudential, p. 11.
Pages 29–30: Biographical data in *Who's Who in America* (1989); Prudential Insurance Co.'s media relations office.
Pages 28–31: Interviews with former Pru-Bache Securities executives.

Chapter 4: Ball and the Blue Sky Years

Page 34: VMS Realty Partners' early years described in Marcia Berss, "Tale of Two Syndicators," *Forbes 400*, Oct. 22, 1990, p. 352.
Page 35: VMS history from Andrew Patner, "Real Estate Syndicator Spins an Intricate Web and Gets Tangled in It," *The Wall Street Journal*, Feb. 1, 1990, p. 1.
Pages 35–36: Van Kampen profile in story by Marcia Berss, "Let Not the Rich Man Boast of His Riches," *Forbes 400*, Oct. 23, 1989, pp. 44–46; hotel's history from Donald W. Curl and John P. Johnson, *Boca Raton* (Virginia Beach, Vir.: The Donning Co., 1990) and Stanley Johnson and Phyllis Shapiro, *Once Upon a Time* (Boca Raton, Fla.: Arvida Co., 1987).
Pages 36–37: "Confidential Private Placement Memorandum, Boca Raton Hotel and Club Limited Partnership," Sept. 12, 1983, provides facts, as does Howard Rudnitsky and John Heins, "Cover Story," *Forbes*, Dec. 19, 1983.
Page 37–39: Thomas Moore, "Ball Takes Bache and Runs with It," *Fortune*, Jan. 24, 1983, p. 97, and Gregory Miller, "Can George Do It?," *Institutional Investor*, July 1984, p. 101, detail Ball's challenge and stated plans.
Page 38: Ball's time at E. F. Hutton detailed in book by Mark Stevens, *Sudden Death* (New York: Penguin Books, 1989), pp. 76–86.
Pages 39–40: Ibid, pp. 125–143. Interviews with brokers; interview with George Ball.
Page 40: Ball's offer from Pru in Donna Sammons Carpenter and John Feloni, *The Fall of the House of Hutton* (New York: Henry Holt, 1989), p. 36.
Page 41: "Pru-Bache: An Imported Team Has to Play Catch-Up," *Business Week*, Dec. 20, 1982; *Who's Who in America* (1989); Carpenter, op. cit., pp. 34–36; "Not So Prudent," *The Economist*, p. 59.
Page 42: Interviews with Ball.
Pages 42–43: Interviews with three former employees.
Page 44: Miller, op. cit., *Institutional Investor*, July 1984.

Chapter 5: Bull Markets and Phantom Expenses

Page 48: Market quote from Raymond F. DeVoe, Jr., a market analyst for Legg Mason Wood Walker Inc. "Bull In the Afternoon"; Arthur Howe, "Taking Stock— A New Wave of Investments Hits Wall Street," *Philadelphia Inquirer*, May 22, 1983, details heady mood in stock exchange at the time.
Pages 48–51: David F. Windish, *Investor's Guide to Limited Partnerships* (New York: New York Institute of Finance, 1988), pp. 7–28; numbers and facts collected from interviews with (and materials checked by) unnamed accountant; data from Research Institute of America.
Page 49: Real-estate prices cited in piece by Kathleen Sharp, "The California Resale Housing Market Is Cooling Off," *The New York Times*, March 11, 1990, and "A Yen for Real Estate," *Islands* magazine, October 1988.
Page 51: Federal securities rules from spokesman for Securities and Exchange Commission; formal tax laws from John Downes and Jordan Elliot Goodman, *Dictionary of Finance and Investment Terms* (Woodbury, N.Y.: Barron's Educational Series, 1985).

Page 50: Details of Graham's and Pru-Bache's association taken from feature story written by Scot Paltrow, "Partners in a Troubled Venture," *Los Angeles Times,* June 22, 1993.

Pages 50–52: Limited partnership sales figures and data provided by *The Stranger Report.*

Page 53: Interviews with two employees of the New York Restaurant Group (owners of Smith & Wollensky) and five sources who attended DIG parties.

Chapter 6: Marketeers and Buccaneers on the Thirty-Third Floor

Page 55: Darr's background taken from a Darr interview (through his attorneys); Chuck Hawkins and Leah Nathans Spiro, "The Mess at Pru-Bache," *Business Week,* March 4, 1991; alumni directory, College of The Holy Cross; Verification and Middle East Studies departments, University of Utah; Military Personnel Records Center.

Page 56: Darr's resumé taken from Prudential-Bache Securities Litigation, U.S. District Court, Eastern District of Louisiana, James J. Darr, Vol. 1, pp. 1–30; records of National Association of Securities Dealers; details of Darr's early unusual payments from Eichenwald, op. cit., May 2, 1994.

Pages 57–59: Interviews with seven former DIG employees regarding office environment.

Page 61: Securities Act of 1933, Sec. 11.

Page 61: Allegations about Clifton Harrison from Hawkins and Spiro, op. cit., March 4, 1991.

Page 62: Details of Pru-Bache's internal investigation taken from report by Locke Purnell and Rain Harrell, "Final Report on James Darr Transactions," and attachments, Feb. 23, 1988.

Page 63: Other DIG employees who allegedly invested in side deals from Pru-Bache Securities Litigation, Darr, Vol. 1, pp. 124, 125.

Page 63: Darr's quote from ibid, vol. 2, p. 405; Darr's response to the Locke Purnell Report, July 14, 1993.

Page 64: Move to Seaport Plaza taken from 1984 Annual Report, Pru Insurance, p. 8.

Page 64: Historical data of area from the South Street Seaport Museum.

Chapter 7: Laissez les Bons Temps Rouler

Pages 66–68: Graham data from Pru-Bache's marketing materials; piece by Leslie Haines, "Deep Pockets," *Oil and Gas Investor,* August 1988; Paltrow, op. cit., June 22 and 23, 1993.

Page 69: Oil prices taken from U.S. Bureau of Labor Statistics, U.S. Wellhead Crude Oil Price Index, from 1980 to 1992; also Stephen Koepp's "Poor Little Energy-Rich Kids" and "Cheap Oil," *Time,* April 14, 1986.

Pages 69–70: Description of Cancún from *The Penguin Guide to Mexico* (New York: Penguin Books, 1990), pp. 503–505.

Page 70: Sherman's biographical details from his record with the National Association of Securities Dealers; interviews with former employees.

Page 73: Figures from Pru-Bache's internal marketing material.

Page 74: Regarding Shanks's purchase of LPs, details taken from documents from the American Arbitration Association, Los Angeles Regional Office (Jan. 25, 1993).

Page 74: Pru-Bache dissuaded people from reading prospectuses, according to some brokers' affidavits filed with the U.S. District Court, Eastern District of Louisiana, in multidistrict litigation Docket No. 888; also Siconolfi, "Investigators Query Former Prudential Brokers," *The Wall Street Journal,* Jan. 5, 1994; promises detailed in Goldberg, op. cit., pp. 35, 38; also in federal criminal complaint, Oct. 27, 1994.

Pages 75–76: Ball memo, Nov. 26, 1984; 1984 Annual Report, Pru Insurance, pp. 2, 5.

Chapter 8: *Going Global*
Page 77: Financial figures from 1984 Annual Report, Pru Insurance; also from company's Annual Audited Report Form X 17A-5 reported to SEC for the periods ending December 1981, December 1983, and December 1986; poor conditions in stock market cited in 1984 Annual Report, p. 4.
Pages 77–78: Miller, op. cit., July 1984.
Pages 78–80: Details of Hutton's check-kiting from Carpenter and Feloni, op. cit., pp. 21, 90, 141, 142; David Warsh, "It's a Wonder Anyone Goes to Jail," *Boston Globe*, July 7, 1985; Robert L. Jackson and Ronald J. Ostrow, "Hutton Head Approved Overdrafting, Papers Show," *Los Angeles Times*, July 9, 1985; Nicholas Varchaver, "Loren Schechter's Toughest Battle," *The American Lawyer*, April 1994.
Pages 80–81: About firm's early efforts at investment banking, see Glenn A. Kessler, "George Ball's Project '89," *Investment Dealer's Digest*, Oct. 13, 1986, p. 27.
Page 81: Boesky's book, *Merger Mania*, "owed a great debt" to Guy Wyser-Pratte's monogram, said Ehrlich and Rehfeld, op. cit., p. 326.
Page 81: Pru-Bache underwriting figures provided by Securities Data Co., all domestic new issues, manager ranking, 1985; also figures from collaterized debt securities underwritings and domestic straight debt.
Page 84: Pru-Bache summary material of Sillerman-Magee Communications Partners LP offering of $25 million; prospectus from First Carolina Communications $45 million offering by Morgan Stanley & Co., Nov. 25, 1986.
Page 87: Quote taken from memo to Chip Barnes from George Ball, May 31, 1985.
Page 87: Financial results from 1985 Annual Report; Ball's testimony before Congress as reported by Carpenter and Feloni, op. cit., p. 142.
Page 88: 1985 Annual Report, pp. 4, 16, 17.

Chapter 9: *"Camouflage, to the Extent We Can . . ."*
Page 89: Pru-Bache's 1986 LP sales figures from *The Stanger Report*.
Page 90: List of Pru-Bache's LP sponsors from U.S. District Court, Southern District of New York, re: Pru Securities Inc. LP ligitation, MDL Docket No. 1005, M-21-67, consolidated complaint, table of contents for Volume II; details regarding LPs from Windish, op. cit., pp. 69, 70.
Pages 91–93: Tax information gleaned from accounting source; the Research Institute of America; Downes and Goodman, op. cit., pp. 211, 425–429.
Page 93: *The Stanger Report* on LP sales figures; on DIG's profit contributions, Hawkins and Spiro, op. cit., p. 70.
Page 94: Quotes from 1986 Annual Report, pp. 5, 13; "tax-sheltered" quotes from Pru-Bache material, "What Type of Client Should Genesis Income Partners Appeal To?" 1987; Pru-Bache's Fact Sheet Series III, May 1986.
Pages 97–98: Oil prices were down, according to Aug. 20, 1985, memo to all Pru-Bache sales offices from Joe DeFur, an executive with direct investment group; accounting technique outlined in Jan. 9, 1985, memo to Anton H. Rice III from Mark W. Files; also in story by Chuck Hawkins, "Fresh Rue for the Pru?," *Business Week*, Nov. 30, 1992; loans described in Paltrow, op. cit., June 23, 1993; Pittman's concern about LPs borrowing money from Darr's deposition, pp. 425–430.
Page 98: SEC rules explained by spokesman; NYSE contained in piece, "Compensation Values Increase for NYSE Members, Employees," *Wall Street Letter*, July 13, 1992; descriptions from Longleaf Plantation Inc.'s brochures and employees; discussion of Longleaf from Darr's deposition, pp. 795–606.
Page 98: Darr's quote from ibid, p. 605; Childs listed also, p. 462.
Page 99: Memo to Joe DeFur, William Pittman and Paul Proscia from James C. Sweeney, Jan. 23, 1986, in which Chanin puts Pru's Graham Energy investments "on ice"; also Siconolfi and Greg Steinmetz, "Prosecutors Are Examining Involvement by Prudential Insurance on Partnerships," *The Wall Street Journal*, Nov. 15, 1993.

Page 99: Back-dating of oil properties' purchase from Associated Press report, "$1.1 Billion Suit Hits Prudential's Accounting Firms," *The Orange County Register,* Jan. 11, 1994; Paltrow, "Account Firm Accused of Fraud in O.C. Suit," *Los Angeles Times,* Jan. 10, 1994; quotes of Pru executives defending the practice from report by Eichenwald, "Prudential Settlement Complicated," *The New York Times,* Jan. 11, 1994.

Chapter 10: The Year of the Deal
Page 102: Investment Dealer's Digest, Oct. 13, 1986.
Page 103: "1986 Deal Awards," *Investment Dealer's Digest,* Dec. 8, 1986; industry total of investment banking deals by year from Securities Data Co.; Adam Smith, "But What Do Investment Bankers Do?," *Esquire,* November 1986, p. 97; on the changing roles of bankers, see Antony Michels, "Building the New Smith Barney," *Investment Dealer's Digest,* March 20, 1989.
Page 103: Quote from Hayes and Hubbard, op. cit., p. 109; effect of shelf registration on banking, p. 111.
Page 104: Ranking of bankers in 1986 from Securities Data Co. (lead managed deals); about Lehman Brothers, see Ken Auletta, *Greed and Glory on Wall Street* (New York: Warner Books, 1986), p. 233.
Page 105: Steven Solomon, "How Lewie Raised the Roof on Wall Street," *Esquire,* December 1985, p. 109; Statford P. Sherman, "Why the Youngsters' Party May Be Ending," *Fortune,* Nov. 24, 1986, p. 29.
Page 105: Figures from Pru-Bache's growth of mutual funds from interview with Ball; expenditures from Pru-Bache's Annual Audited Report form X-17A-5, Part III, for year ending December 1986.
Pages 108–109: Kessler, op. cit., p. 29; Nicholas D. Kristof, "Los Angeles: Money Center Series," *The New York Times,* March 25, 1986.
Page 110: Report is called "Pru-Bache Securities' Global Investment Banking Research, Capital Markets, A Coordinated Strategy," Executive Committee Planning Session, March 26, 1986.
Page 111: Details of CS First Boston's internal affairs taken from Hayes and Hubbard, op. cit., pp. 302–306.
Page 112: Project '89's goals taken from Pru-Bache's executive committee report, op. cit., pp. 4, 5, 57.
Page 113: Gahan's profile from piece by Glenn Kessler, "Gahan Is Big Winner in Pru-Bache Shake-Up," *Investment Dealer's Digest,* May 26, 1986; Kessler, "George Ball's Project '89," op. cit., pp. 28, 31.

Chapter 11: The Rattlesnake Theory
Page 115: Data on Richard Keith Saccullo from National Association of Securities Dealers records; Securities and Exchange Act 1934, Administrative Proceedings (Dec. 31, 1985), Release No. 22754; Files Nos. 3-6600 and 3-6601, In the Matter of Prudential-Bache Securities Inc., p. 1457; also SEC Litigation Release 13840, p. 13.
Pages 115–117: SEC Act 1934 in the matter of Pru-Bache, File No. 36602, pp. 1497–1503; also Hawkins and Spiro, op. cit., Sept. 7, 1992, p. 83.
Page 117: Schechter assuring the SEC taken from piece by Michael Schroeder and Leah Nathans Spiro, "Is George Ball's Luck Running Out?," *Business Week,* Nov. 8, 1993, pp. 74–75; titles from Pru-Bache Corporate Telephone Directory, 1987.
Pages 118–121: SEC Release No. 22754; SEC Litigation Release 13840; also Kurt Eichenwald, "New Cloud Over Prudential Branches," *The New York Times,* Dec. 17, 1993.
Page 122: Data from piece written by Benjamin Mark Cole, "Pru-Bache Comes Under Fire for Alleged Improprieties," *The Los Angeles Business Journal,* Aug. 1–7, 1988.

Chapter 12: The Men Behind the Corporate Veil

Page 125: New Jersey's data from "New Jersey, the Garden State," *World Book Encyclopedia* (1994 edition); media relations offices of New Jersey's Secretary of State, Insurance Department, and Administrative Office of The Courts, which provided a summary of The Hillery Committee's Report (1907); Carr, op. cit., pp. 101–103.

Page 126: List of Pru's directors taken from 1986 and 1993 company's annual reports; *Who's Who in America* 1990–1991, 1992–1993, and 1995; Standard and Poor's Register (1993); Thomson's Bank Directory (1991); Martindale-Hubbell Law Directory; internal papers prepared by the Administrative Office about Pru; Burke description from Moskowitz, Levering, and Katz, op. cit., p. 190; also pp. 317, 453; Schneberle mention from work by Bryan Burrough and John Helyar, *Barbarians at the Gate* (New York: Harper Perennial, 1990), p. 72.

Page 127: Beck's retirement from wire story, "Prudential Chairman to Retire in '87," *San Jose Mercury News*, Sept. 16, 1986; 1986 Annual Report.

Page 127: Financial comparisons made by comparing Pru's financial figures from 1980 with those from 1986, as provided in the annual reports; salaries from story by Jennifer Lin, "Wall Street Pay Raising Eyebrows—And Concern," *Philadelphia Inquirer*, June 21, 1987.

Page 128: Merger problems discussed by William H. Miller, "Why Mergers Fizzle," *Industry Week*, Aug. 5, 1985, p. 46.

Pages 128–129: Advertisement in *Investment Dealer's Digest*, Dec. 6, 1986, p. 36; Pru's viewpoint expressed in "How Prudent?," *The Economist*, July 11, 1987.

Page 129: Keith's salary from 1986 Annual Report, p. 32.

Pages 132–133: DIG's sales figures from *The Stanger Report*, 1987 tallies; Ball asks Darr for more data on the Pru withdrawing from Graham, Darr's deposition, Vol. II, pp. 442–446; memo to DeFur et al. from Sweeney, op. cit.; Paltrow, op. cit., June 23, 1993; Hawkins, op. cit., Nov. 30, 1992; Darr's deposition, Vol. II, 462–463.

Page 134: Hawkins, op. cit., March 4, 1991; Darr's deposition, Vol. 1, p. 58.

Pages 135–136: Darr is not listed in the investment banking department in the 1988 Pru-Bache Corporate Telephone Directory, but rather in direct investments department; same for 1987; in his deposition, Vol. 1, p. 27, Darr says he was placed in the investment banking department from about 1987 until he left in 1988; First Australia reference in "Best Deal in a Foreign Language," *Investment Dealer's Digest*, Dec. 8, 1986, p. 35; deals taken from list in *Dealer's Digest*, Directory of Corporate Finance, Second Half of 1986, 1987; Reliance Electric data from internal documents from Pru-Bache Interfunding Inc., Summary Results, from 1987 through 1993.

Chapter 13: A Ton of Positions, a Load of Laundry

Page 140: Saccullo data from NASD records; SEC administrative proceedings, op. cit., and litigation release, op. cit.

Page 141: Internal sales ideas sent to all account executives, Jan. 26, 1988, p. 2.

Page 142: Kett testifying for ex-employee, Cole, op. cit.

Pages 144–145: Money laundering supplemented with stories by Joe Nabbefeld, "Prudential-Bache Under Investigation for Laundering," *San Diego Daily Transcript*, May 29, 1987; Jim Schachter, "Customs Man Charged with Letting Pot Cross Border," *Los Angeles Times*, May 6, 1987; J. Stryker Meyer, "Customs Inspector Arraigned," *San Diego Transcript*, May 6, 1987; "Brokerage Firm Cooperates with Customs Probe," *Los Angeles Times*, May 29, 1987; Schachter, "Stockbroker Linked to Laundering of Drug Cash," *Los Angeles Times*, June 13, 1987; Benjamin Mark Cole, "Drug Money, Account Churning Reported," *Los Angeles Business Journal*, Aug. 1–7, 1988; latter story contained allegations of flipping funds.

Pages 145–148: Portions of Mandt's allegations are contained in the New York Supreme Court's Appellate Division, First Division, in the matter of Prudential Securities and Kristi Mandt (Index No. 17354/92).

Chapter 14: A New Culture Takes Root

Page 149: Small portions of Andrew K. Simpson, "Subversive Corporate Finance," are quoted with permission.

Page 150: Quotes from "Investment and Merchant Banking Group (IMB), Mission and Strategy Statements" (March 1986).

Page 151: Pru's commitment contained in "Pru-Bache Capital Funding Successfully Recruits Four," *The Market Chronicle,* June 16, 1987; Sarah Bartlett, "It's Deadline Time for George Ball," *The New York Times,* Jan. 14, 1990.

Page 152: Deals from internal documents listing all IMB activities for 1987; 1987 Annual Report, pp. 17, 24–30; *Dealer's Digest,* deals for 1987.

Pages 152–153: Deals also contained in internal documents from PBCF.

Pages 153–154: High salaries quoted in "Pru-Bache Hires Two More, But Some on Street Remain Unimpressed," *Corporate Financing Week,* June 15, 1987; hiring binge mentioned in "Pru-Bache Nabs Citi Exec for LBO Unit," *Investment Dealer's Digest,* June 1, 1987; twelve-page memo from "Pru-Bache's Ball Sends Memo Encouraging Teamwork for Project '89," *Securities Week,* July 27, 1987; personnel numbers from "Business Review and Strategic Overview of the Investment and Merchant Banking Division of Prudential-Bache Securities," Nov. 1989, p. 12.

Page 154–155: William Power and Michael Siconolfi, "Memo To: Mr. Ball, Re: Your Messages. Sir: They're Weird," *The Wall Street Journal,* Nov. 30, 1990; Ball interviews; Vivian Gornick, "Letters Are Acts of Faith," *The New York Times Book Review,* July 31, 1994, p. 3.

Page 155: Financial figures from Pru's annual reports; "Business Review and Strategic Overview," op. cit., p. 11.

Pages 155–157: Details from brochure from Rye Town Hilton; Jessica Sommar, "Rock Slide," *Investment Dealer's Digest,* April 1, 1991.

Page 157: "Stocks Plummet 508 Amid Panicky Selling," *The Wall Street Journal,* Oct. 20, 1987, p. 1; editorial quoted.

Pages 157–158: Definition from book by Alberto Tedeschi and Carolo Rossi Fantonetti, Mondadori's *Italiano-Inglese Dizionario* (New York: Pocket Books, 1959); Ehrlich and Rehfeld, op. cit., p. 31.; Stephen Taub, "Arbs Are Still Alive and Well," *Financial World,* May 28, 1991.

Page 158: Numbers based on Pru-Bache internal records; "Relationship Between Results, of Pru-Bache and Arbitrage," March, 8, 1991; and "Wyser-Pratte Performance Record."

Page 158: 80 percent drop in arbitrage from Laurence Zuckerman, "For Arbitragers, The Game Is Afoot Once Again," *The New York Times,* Dec. 4, 1994; other market conditions, Evan Guillemin, "Who Survived the Crash?," *Investment Dealer's Digest,* Jan. 11, 1988, pp. 19–23; DIG sales from the Stranger Report; Mark Fadiman, "Pru-Bache Freezes Salaries for New Year," *Investment Dealer's Digest,* Dec. 21, 1987, p. 6.

Pages 159: IMB results from "Business Review and Strategic Overview," op. cit., p. 9; 1987 annual report for firm's financial results.

Chapter 15: RISERS and Departures

Pages 166–167: Darr's deposition, Vol. I, pp. 150–161; Hawkins, op. cit., March 4, 1991.

Pages 167–168: Locke Purnell report, op. cit., and attachments; Darr's deposition, pp. 91–128.

Page 168: Darr's NASD records; Sherman's NASD records; Nathan's Famous Hot Dog public relations department; salaries from Darr's deposition, Vol. II, pp. 401–408; Sherman's from an arbitration case; Mark Fadiman, "Pru-Bache Housecleaning Continues," *Investment Dealer's Digest,* Jan. 16, 1989.

Page 169: Some data about RISERs contained in Chuck Hawkins, Jon Friedman, and David Greising, "How Pushing Real Estate Backfired on Pru-Bache," *Business Week,* Feb. 26, 1990.

Page 172: "Censure for ex-Hutton Chief," *Chicago Tribune*, March 1, 1988, Sec. 3, p. 6; Associated Press, "E. F. Hutton Will Be Fined $400,000," *Chicago Tribune*, Dec. 16, 1987; Pru spokesman quote from piece by James Sterngold, "Censures in Hutton Case Reported," *The New York Times*, Feb. 29, 1988.

Page 172: Stephen Labaton, "Drexel Concedes Guilt on Trading; To Pay $650 Million," *The New York Times*, Dec. 22, 1988.

Chapter 16: "Perception vs. Reality"

Pages 173–174: "Xerox Unit Buys Stake," *The New York Times*, Feb. 6, 1987; Berss, op. cit., Oct. 22, 1990; Laurence Hooper and Andrew Patner, "Xerox to Take Pretax Charge of $400 Million," *The Wall Street Journal*, April 4, 1990.

Page 174: Some allegations from U.S. District Court, Southern District of Florida, *Michael Dubelko et al. v. VMS Realty Investment, et al.* Case No. 92-8604-CIV; also "Boca Raton Hotel & Club, LP, Fall 1992, Proxy Contest," p. A 5–9.

Page 174: Pru-Bache fees taken from 1983 offering of Boca Raton LP, op. cit., financial statements, pp. 28, 29; Kelso statements from piece by Siconolfi, "Prudential Official Concedes VMS Risks," *The Wall Street Journal*, June 18, 1991.

Pages 174–175: Footnotes to audited financial statements on Boca LP from 1987 to 1994, inclusive; and March 14, 1994, letter on LP status from the Boca Raton Managment Co.; quotes from VMS letter to LPs, Sept. 10, 1992; Eric N. Berg, "How Syndicators Have Shifted," *The New York Times*, Aug. 17, 1988.

Page 175: Benjamin Mark Cole, "Investors Reeling After Pru-Bache 'Guaranteed' Investment Goes Bust," *Los Angeles Business Journal*, May 13–19, 1991; Hawkins, Friedman, and Greising, op. cit., *Business Week*, Feb. 26, 1990, about Fogelman; letter from Pru-Bache manager David Wrubel to broker Gary Zahn, Oct. 4, 1988.

Page 176: In-house sales materials, including trips to Land o' Castles.

Page 177: Data from March 31, 1988, internal memo to Investment Banking Group.

Page 177: Cole, op. cit., May 13–19, 1991; trading prices of VMS funds listed in piece by Andrew Patner, "VMS Suspends Payments to Lenders, Funds," *The Wall Street Journal*, Feb. 13, 1990.

Pages 178–179: Deals from *Dealers' Digest*, Fall 1988; internal documents listing merger and acquisitions; Phyllis Feinberg, "Pru-Bache Proves Quick Flip LBO Profits Still Possible," *Investment Dealer's Digest*, April 18, 1988.

Pages 179–182: "Prudential-Bache Capital Funding, Investment/Merchant Banking Group, Marginal Economic Analysis—Enterprise Consequences" used as a model.

Page 182: Quote from "Business Review and Strategic Overview," op. cit., p. 20.

Pages 182–184: Antony Michels, "Waiting for the Equity Ship to Come In," *Investment Dealer's Digest*, Oct. 10, 1988, pp. 17–39; financial figures and rankings from Securities Data Co.; internal gross revenues from "Business Review and Strategic Overview," op. cit., pp. 9–10; salary rankings in memo to Ball and Gahan from Crowley and Fowler, July 27, 1989, p. 2.

Page 186: Some bankers later recalled a party from Sommar, op. cit., April 1, 1991.

Chapter 17: Murders and Inquisitions

Page 187: 1988 Annual Report; figures compiled from Pru's annual reports; Labaton, op. cit., Dec. 22, 1988; "Morality Among the Supply-Siders," *Time*, May 25, 1987.

Pages 188–189: Pru's ambitions outlined in piece by Robert W. Casey, "Prudential Muscles In," *United States Banker*, April 1989; Volcker's role in Bache detailed in Fay, op. cit., pp. 228–230; quotes from 1988 Annual Report, pp. 16, 31.

Page 189: Item about Tozer from *MuniWeek*, Feb. 21, 1989, p. 3.

Page 189: Quotes from Keith's speech at Wharton, January 1989; rankings from Securities Data Co.; return rates from internal documents, "Prudential-Bache Interfunding," Summary Results; first nine-month figures from "Business Review and Strategic Overview," op. cit., p. 8.; Strategic Planning Associates mentioned in Bartlett, op. cit., Jan. 14, 1990.

Page 190: Project '89 declared a success in Ball's June 8, 1989, memo to officers, managers, and department heads; also in Gahan's June 9, 1989, memo to all Prudential-Bache Capital Funding staff, in which he wrote, "Apart from more than doubling revenue, making a profit and building a healthy residual value in PBIF for our shareholder, in a three-year period we have done considerably more." This memo reflects the new plan to split PBCF into the capital markets group and the IMB group.

Page 190: Cited piece is by Matthew Winkler, "Prudential-Bache to Reorganize in Effort to Boost Performance," *The Wall Street Journal*, June 9, 1989: "Disappointed by its lackluster performance in investment banking, Prudential-Bache Securities Inc. is launching a major reorganization today."

Page 191: Quotes from taped speech at IMB conference, Asia Society, June 15, 1989, pp. 1–4, 14.

Page 191: That the firm hopes to "elbow its way into the ranks of the top six firms" by 1991 was stated in piece by James Sterngold, "Bache Braves a New World," *The New York Times*, July 3, 1987; also piece by Leah Nathans Spiro, Larry Light, and Chuck Hawkins, "George Ball Finally Falls off the Rock," *Business Week*, Feb. 25, 1991: "Pru-Bache never came close to taking on the pros in dealmaking or underwriting, and those ambitions came to an abrupt end. . . . The immediate cost: a charge of $370 million, which sent the firm's results plunging to their lowest point ever"; also "Not So Prudent," *The Economist*, Aug. 31, 1991: "Pru-Bache foundered by trying to become an investment bank"; also Kurt Eichenwald, "Prudential-Bache Chairman Resigns," *The New York Times*, Feb. 14, 1991: "In 1986, Mr. Ball began the ill-fated Project '89 to create an investment bank that could elbow its way in the big takeover deals of the 1980s. But the project, named for the year it was to be completed, never made Pru-Bache into a force. . . ."

Page 191: "Pru-Bache to Buy Thomson McKinnon," *San Francisco Chronicle*, June 14, 1989; "Pru-Bache Strikes Deal with Thomson," *Newsday*, July 18, 1989.

Page 192: "Beyond Friday the 13th," *Investment Dealer's Digest*, Oct. 23, 1989.

Page 195: Bartlett, op. cit., Jan. 14, 1990.

Page 196: 1989 Annual Report; IMB from internal figures.

Page 196: Quotes taken from Crowley speech, "The Year That Was."

Page 197: Bloomsberg Business News, "Some Key Units Revamped by Prudential Securities," *Los Angeles Times*, June 25, 1994; Anita Raghavan, "Prudential Sets New Division for Equities," *The Wall Street Journal*, June 24, 1994.

Chapter 18: In the Mouth of the Rat

Page 200: James Walsh, "Independent Productions," *California Business*, May 1990, p. 147.

Pages 200–201: Fees and projections from "Boca Raton Hotel & Club LP," private memorandum, op. cit., financial statements, pp. 3–4, 27–28.

Pages 201–202: Allegations also from information in Boca Raton Hotel & Club LP Proxy Contest, Fall 1992, op. cit.; also in first matter, Consolidated Pretrial Proceeding, Case No. 90 C2412, "Opposition of Plaintiff Michael Dubelko to Defendants' Emergency Motion to Enjoin State Court Proceeding."

Page 203: "Xerox Unit Buys Stake," op. cit., Feb. 6, 1987; Berss, op. cit., Oct. 22, 1990; Hooper and Patner, op. cit., April 4, 1990; Eric N. Berg, "VMS Short on Cash, Shifts Officers," *The New York Times*, Nov. 15, 1989; Andrew Patner, "VMS Realty's President, Chief Resigns Just Three Months After Being Installed," *The Wall Street Journal*, Feb. 22, 1990.

Pages 203–204: Regarding VMS suits, data taken from interviews with Norman Rifkind of Beigel Schy Lasky Rifkind Goldberg & Fertik; Jeff Leonard of Sonnerschin & Rosenthal; lawsuits such as *Albert* v. *VMS-Pru-Bache* and *Intuono* v. *Cigna & VMS*; also 11 Broadway Associations class-action litigation, U.S. District Court, for the Northern District of Illinois, Eastern Division, No. 90 C2041; the Mieles case detailed by Eric Staats, "Naples Pair Wins Investment Case," *Naples*

Daily News, June 20, 1991, as well as interviews with their attorney, Thomas R. Grady.

Page 203: Pru-Bache's tactics described by Michael Schroeder and Leah Nathans Spiro, "Is Prudential Playing Hardball?," *Business Week,* Nov. 15, 1993; Scott Paltrow, "Prudential Faces More Accusations," *Los Angeles Times,* Nov. 8, 1993; gangster ploy from Hawkins and Spiro, op. cit., Sept. 7, 1992.

Page 204: Andrew Patner, "VMS Partners Settlement Plan Is Sent to Judge," *The Wall Street Journal,* July 3, 1990; James P. Miller, "Real Estate Funds, VMS Plan to Settle Suit for $66 Million," *The Wall Street Journal,* Sept. 26, 1991.

Page 204: Michael Siconolfi, "Investors Say NASD Ignored Them in Prudential Case," *The Wall Street Journal,* Sept. 8, 1994; Siconolfi, "Securities Unit of Prudential Is Dealt Blow," *The Wall Street Journal,* July 6, 1994.

Pages 205–207: Details from Boca Raton LP Proxy Contest, op. cit.; letter to the Collaborating Limited Partners from Rob Hughes, March 31, 1992; letter to limited partners from the Boca Raton Management Co., March 14, 1994; advertisement "RTC Sales Centers, Notice of Intent to Sell," *The Wall Street Journal,* March 26, 1992; Christopher Barton, "Boca Resort Faces Future," *Boca Raton News,* Sept. 7, 1991; financial statements for 1994.

Chapter 19: "Rock Solid, Stone Broke"

Page 208: Letter from Bob Jackson, executive vice president, Graham Securities, to Pete Theo, president, Aug. 23, 1989.

Pages 208–209: Burton news and quotes from Leah Nathans Spiro, "Exit Pru-Bache, Licking Its Wounds," *Business Week,* Nov. 19, 1990; William Power, "Prudential's Ball Gets Parent Firm's Vote of Confidence," *The Wall Street Journal,* March 15, 1990.

Page 209: Martini quote from piece by Jennifer Linn, "Brokers Told Frenzy of Market Won't Last," *Philadelphia Inquirer,* Jan. 22, 1987; "Business stinks" from Associated Press story, "Prudential-Bache Will Lay Off Most of Investment Division," *Charlotte Observer,* Nov. 7, 1990; financial figures from annual reports.

Page 209: Ball quotes from Spiro, op. cit., Nov. 19, 1990; arbitragers hurt from Zuerckan piece, op. cit., Dec. 4, 1994.

Pages 210–212: Some details taken from National Association of Securities Dealers Award (Case 91-03453); numbers supplemented by Wyser-Pratte Performance Record, based on internal Pru-Bache figures and Wyser-Pratte interviews.

Page 212: 1990 Annual Report, pp. 4, 5; losing ratings from Spiro, Light, and Hawkins, op. cit., Feb. 25, 1991; "lost a notch" from piece by Larry Light, "How Much Prudence Is Good for Prudential?," *Business Week,* July 13, 1992.

Pages 212–213: NASD (Case 91-03453); also, Siconolfi, "NASD Panel Levies Sanction on Prudential," *The Wall Street Journal,* Feb. 18, 1994.

Page 214: Memo from Paul Proscia to Mike Kudlik, April 29, 1986.

Pages 214–215: The New York Supreme Court's Appellate Division, op. cit., No. 17354/92; Trice letter to Winters, March 19, 1990.

Page 215: Hawkins and Spiro, op. cit., March 4, 1991; the magazine appeared on newsstands the last week of February, according to story by Beth Belton, "Magazine Alleges Prudential Conflicts," *USA Today,* Feb. 22, 1991.

Pages 215–217: Ball's accomplishments from Ball interview; "Pru-Bache's Ball Sets Out State of Firm in Latest Internal Memorandum," *Securities Week,* Oct. 29, 1990, details memo; Eichenwald, op. cit., Feb. 14, 1991; balance from Ball interviews.

Pages 216–217: 1 Annual Report, p. 2; "Prudential Chief Exits Admit Losses," *Chicago Tribune,* Feb. 14, 1991, details Beck's new position; name change in Associated Press piece, "What's in a Name? Not Bache (Not Anymore)," *St. Louis Dispatch,* Feb. 21, 1991; "Simmons the CEO of Pru Securities," *Financial Services Week,* May 13, 1991; Ellyn E. Spragins, "Fixing a Piece of the Rock," *Newsweek,* Aug. 8, 1994; quotes from 1991 Annual Report, p. 5.

Page 217: Hawkins and Spiro, op. cit., Sept. 7, 1992, report regulatory investigations; rogue brokers blamed as cited by Siconolfi, "Prudential Unit, U.S. Settle Partnership Case," *The Wall Street Journal*, Oct. 28, 1994; ethics hotline cited in Hawkins and Spiro, op. cit., Sept. 7, 1992.

Chapter 20: History Repeats Itself

Page 219: Memo from Winters to all Prudential employees, Oct. 17, 1991; "Policy Statement on Sexual Harassment," Prudential internal paper, October 1991.

Pages 220–222: Portions of this story are contained in a claim filed with the Equal Employment Opportunity Commission (370920392); from a letter to Schechter from Richard K. Ellingboe, Clayton's attorney, dated Jan. 31, 1992.

Page 222: Clark's address reported in "Clark Apologizes to Branch Managers, Denies Wrongdoing," *The Wall Street Letter*, May 25, 1992; also alleged loss of $40,000 bonus for his misconduct.

Page 222: EEOC claim; "Pru Securities Former Retail Head Named In Sexual Assault Suit," *Wall Street Letter*, June 22, 1992; "More Allegations of Harassment to Surface in Possible Suit vs. Prudential," *Securities Week*, June 8, 1992; "Tankersly Gets New Pru Post; Clark Resigns," *Wall Street Letter*, June 8, 1992; "Pru Securities Regional Director Departs Amid Sexual Harassment Allegations," *Wall Street Letter*, Jan. 30, 1995.

Page 222: SEC litigation release, op. cit., Oct. 21, 1993; number of attorneys contained in Pru-Bache's response to U.S. District Attorney, Oct. 13, 1994; Phoenix suit reported by Paltrow, op. cit., Nov. 18, 1993.

Page 223: Barry Vinocur, "In or Out?," *Barron's*, Jan. 18, 1993; Siconolfi, "Prudential to Pass Some Severance Costs to Investors in Energy Parnterships," *The Wall Street Journal*, June 1, 1993.

Page 224: Scot Paltrow, "Judge Stalls Prudential Settlement," *Los Angeles Times*, Feb. 22, 1993; cruel joke from Vinocur, op. cit., Jan. 18, 1993; Mary Judice, "Running on Empty," *New Orleans Times-Picayune*, May 2, 1993; Paltrow, "Lawyers to Get 25% of Prudential Class-Action Settlement," *Los Angeles Times*, May 20, 1994.

Pages 224–225: Kurt Eichenwald, "Settlement Approved," *The New York Times*, Jan. 22, 1994; U.S. Court of Appeals for the Fifth Circuit cited is *Miley* v. *Oppenheimer & Co.*, as quoted from Goldberg, "Fraudulent Dealer Practices" (1978).

Epilogue

Page 226: Graner's resumé is source for some details.

Page 227: Graner's NASD record.

Page 227: Interview with police detective Roger Mason of the City of Burbank.

Pages 227–229: Bob Garfield, "Prudential's Sincerity Effort Sinks Like a Rock," *Advertising Age*, Feb. 21, 1994; Eichenwald, "Prudential Image-Mending Stumbles," *The New York Times*, Feb. 17, 1994; Siconolfi, op. cit., July 6, 1994; E. Scott Reckard, "Prudential Pulls an Ad with Mistake," *Santa Barbara News-Press*, March 21, 1994; advertisements, *Architectural Review*, April 1994.

Page 229: Simmons quote reported by Terence P. Pare, "Scandal Isn't All That Ails the Pru," *Fortune*, March 21, 1994; Leah Nathans Spiro, "Trying to Heal Pru's Black Eye," *Business Week*, Nov. 8, 1993; Michael Siconolfi, "Prudential Securities Escapes an Indictment, But Firm is Still Shaky," *The Wall Street Journal*, Oct. 12, 1994.

Pages 229–230: From interviews with Commissioner Mendoza; Michael Siconolfi, "Prudential to Suspend New Accounts in Texas Under Accord on Partnerships," *The Wall Street Journal*, Jan. 18, 1994; "California Finalizes Settlement with Pru Securities," news release, California, Department of Corporations, April 22, 1994.

Page 230: Simmons estimates in Hawkins and Spiro piece, "Pru Securities: What the Scandal May Cost," *Business Week*, July 5, 1993, quote from Siconolfi, op. cit., Oct. 12, 1994; Pru's collections from 1993 Annual Report.

Page 231: Andrew Bary, "How Retail Investors Can Get Burned Playing with Derivatives," *Barron's,* Sept. 19, 1994. Kurt Eichenwald, "Prudential Securities Settles Sales Charges in Idaho Case," *The New York Times,* Sept. 20, 1994.

Page 231: The Pru's problems detailed in Michael Siconolfi, "Partnership Problems at Prudential Embroil Insurance Business, Too," *The Wall Street Journal,* Dec. 1, 1993; "Prudential Insurance Co. of America," *Moody's Investors Service* report, February 1994.

Page 232: United States of America v. *Prudential Securities Inc.,* Oct. 27, 1994.

Pages 232–233: "Prudential Agrees to Pay Record Penalty," *Los Angeles Times,* Dec. 22, 1994; Richard L. Berke, "Prudential Accord on Donations," *The New York Times,* Dec. 22, 1994.

Page 233: Tax deductions from John Greenwald, "Socking the Rock," *Time,* Nov. 1, 1993.

Index

Wyser-Pratte, Eugene, 17
Wyser-Pratte, Guy P., 17, 44, 81, 158
  bio of, xiii
  update, 233
Wyser-Pratte & Co., 17

Xerox
  and VMS Realty, 174, 203

York International, 189

Zahn, Gary, 43–44, 91–92, 175, 176
  bio of, xiv
  DIG annual meeting, 198
  money laundering charge, 234
  update, 234
  and VMS, 202–203
Zinbarg, Edward, 179